WRITING AS A WAY OF BEING

WRITING INSTRUCTION, NONDUALITY, AND THE CRISIS OF SUSTAINABILITY

Dualistic

Epistemology

Ontology

Cartesian

Al Gore

Sustainability

Research and Teaching in Rhetoric and Composition
Michael M. Williamson, series editor

WRITING AS A WAY OF BEING

WRITING INSTRUCTION, NONDUALITY, AND THE CRISIS OF SUSTAINABILITY

Robert P. Yagelski

State University of New York-Albany

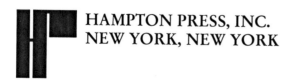

HAMPTON PRESS, INC.
NEW YORK, NEW YORK

Printed in the United States of America

Library of Congress Cataloging-in-Publication Data

Yagelski, Robert.
  Writing as a way of being : writing instruction, nonduality, and the crisis of sustainability / Robert P. Yagelski.
      p. cm.
  Includes bibliographical references and index.
  ISBN 978-1-61289-056-2 -- ISBN 978-1-61289-057-9 (pbk.)
  1. English language--Rhetoric--Study and teaching.
  PE1404.Y35 2011
  808'.042--dc23
                              2011034765

Hampton Press, Inc.
307 Seventh Avenue
New York, NY 10001

For Mary, Gary, and Dianne
and our beloved sister Cindy (1965–2010)

CONTENTS

PREFACE

The main idea for this book—that writing is an ontological act—evolved over more than a decade as I explored connections between writing instruction and the broad set of economic, political, and environmental developments that education scholar David Orr has called "the crisis of sustainability" (4). As a writer for more than thirty years and a teacher of writing for nearly that long, I have always believed that, to quote the National Commission on Writing, "At its best, writing has helped transform the world" (10). Such a statement sounds a positive and hopeful note, but it cuts both ways: Transformation isn't necessarily for the best. It has long seemed to me that the transformation of the earth that we have been witnessing in recent decades—a transformation now popularly referred to as "global warming"—might have something to do with schooling. In this regard, the analyses of Orr and a few other theorists, especially C. A. Bowers, illuminated for me "the connections between the Western ideas and values [students are] inculcated with in schools and universities, their consumer-oriented life style, and the depletion of fish stocks, aquifers, old growth forests, petroleum reserves, and the accumulation of toxic wastes at all levels of the biosphere" (Bowers 1). In these analyses, schooling is implicated directly in the crisis of sustainability. And if schooling is implicated in this crisis, then writing, which is so central to schooling, also must be implicated. But how, exactly? This book is an effort to answer that question.

The main arguments in this book began to come together in the late 1990s in a remote camp in the Wind River Range in Wyoming. I was on a climbing trip with several friends, including Irwin "Bud" Weiser, who was then the director of composition at Purdue University, where I had been a faculty member a few years earlier. One evening as we sat watching the last rays of the sun illuminate the spectacular mountain peaks surrounding our base camp in Titcomb Basin in the northern part of that mountain range, Bud and I resurrected the old debate in Composition Studies about whether or not first-year composition courses should be required of all college students. By then Bud was a so-called abolitionist, who believed that first-year composition should be "abolished" as a universal requirement for undergraduate students. His position on this issue grew out of his experiences with the difficulties of ensuring effective writing instruction in large first-year composition programs such as the one he oversaw at Purdue, in which thousands of students were enrolled in hundreds of sections of composition classes. Typically, such programs are staffed primarily with graduate teaching assistants (TAs) and adjunct instructors rather than full-time faculty, and Bud argued that no matter how well designed the training and mentoring programs for TAs might be, most of the teaching of writing in colleges and universities is done by inexperienced instructors, many of whom are not interested in writing instruction but are teaching composition as a way to fund their graduate education in unrelated areas such as Elizabethan literature or modern poetry. If colleges and universities genuinely valued writing, he argued, they would provide adequate resources to hire experienced instructors with formal graduate training in appropriate disciplines like rhetoric and composition. If institutions are unwilling to make such a commitment, then they should abolish the first-year writing requirement.

I had heard this argument often, not only because it is well established in the scholarly literature, but also because my colleague at the State University of New York (SUNY)-Albany, Steve North, had long been making a similar one. In the 1980s, North was instrumental in replacing the conventional composition program at SUNY-Albany with a writing-intensive program that is part of the university's general education curriculum. In effect, SUNY-Albany abolished first-year composition, which was offered by the English Department (as is the case in so many postsecondary institutions), and required its students to take two writing-intensive courses that could be in any academic discipline. Composition scholars will be familiar with the well-worn justification for teaching writing in the disciplines, part of which is that because writing always occurs in context, students should practice writing within the academic subjects that make up the college curriculum; moreover, when writing instruction is located within academic disciplines, students will not only learn to write more effectively in academic contexts but they will also better learn the subject matter about which they are writing. Accordingly, SUNY-Albany's writing-intensive program was intended to bring "diverse, continuous, and supported practice in writing to the service of learning the concepts and modes of inquiry characteristic of a particular academic discipline" (qtd. in "Report of the UAlbany Task Force" 1). In North's view, conventional first-year composition courses did not accomplish these goals.

North shared Weiser's concerns about how writing instruction typically is configured in postsecondary institutions. In "Revisiting the Idea of the Writing Center," North complains that he "never had much faith in [composition courses] as they were institutionalized at Albany (and, to be candid, elsewhere), i.e. understood as pre-college, or pre-disciplinary, literally extracurricular, some sort of literacy inoculation program" (15). What's more, he continues, "at least in the history of my institution (and from what I know of lots of others), nobody ever wants to pay for [composition courses], so that they have been and still are nearly always taught by the underpaid, the overworked, the undertrained" (15). Like Weiser, North argued that institutions should not force students to take composition courses if those institutions are unwilling to make those courses worthwhile and effective.

These are valid concerns, but my response to these arguments was Freirean. Because humans constitute the world through language, I argued, writing—as a technology for language—is a powerful and essential means for individuals to claim agency and thus gain greater control over their lives. Moreover, writing, as a means to agency, also is a potentially powerful vehicle for individuals to participate in broader social change of the kind Paulo Freire envisioned; writing, in other words, can be a vehicle for creating more just and equitable societies. (My book *Literacy Matters* rests in part on this premise.) From this point of view, first-year college composition courses— and secondary and postsecondary writing instruction in general—because they touch virtually every American student, represent perhaps the most potent site of social change available to us. Abolishing first-year composition as a universal requirement, I argued, would be tantamount to throwing away perhaps our best opportunity to harness writing as a means to creating a better future.

Leaving aside the idealism in my argument, I remain committed to the view that writing represents a unique and potentially powerful force for progressive change, individual and collective—perhaps even more so in this new digital age. Writing can be a means by which we imagine and create a better future together. This book will make a version of that argument. But I no longer believe that mainstream writing instruction as it currently exists can harness the transformative power of writing, and so I no longer embrace the view that first-year composition courses should be required of all students. In this regard, my good friends Irwin Weiser and Steve North have won me over, but for different reasons than perhaps they might have expected.

It was both serendipitous and appropriate that Bud and I were having our debate in that spectacular mountain setting in western Wyoming, for it was there that we saw firsthand what seemed to be concrete evidence of the deeply troubling impact of climate change. Just a few miles from our base camp we could see the snow fields that rise up toward the surrounding peaks. Above 10,000 feet in elevation in that part of the Wind River Range those "permanent" snow fields never melted, even in the intense sunshine of the short alpine summers or in years of extended drought. Until recently, that is. For the past few decades, those snowfields have been shrinking, and many now disappear completely each summer. Additionally, the glaciers on Gannett Peak, Wyoming's highest mountain, which rises to the north of Titcomb Basin, have been rapidly shrinking. For years I had been reading about the dramatic retreat of glaciers around the world (a problem that only recently seems to have captured the attention of the mainstream media), but it wasn't until a subsequent climbing trip in 2002 that I saw those shrinking glaciers for myself.

On that trip, our small climbing party hiked from our base camp to the head of Titcomb Basin, where we ascended a steep mountainside to a pass that would give us access to Gannett Peak, which we intended to climb. In 1999, when Bud and I had our debate about first-year composition, that mountainside was covered by what had always been a permanent snow field. In 2002, however, we scrambled up a bare, rocky slope; the snow was gone. Another climber we encountered who lived nearby told us that the snow field also had completely melted out during the previous two summers. When we reached the top of the pass, the view before us was strikingly different from the photographs we had reviewed as we planned our climbing route in the months before our trip. In those photos, many of which were taken in the 1970s, when the climbing guidebooks we were consulting were first published, the glaciers that swept down Gannett's flanks extended much farther into the valley than what we were seeing on that brilliant July morning in 2002. Where glacial ice had once been we saw huge, dry troughs of rock and dirt; the glaciers now began several hundred yards farther up the mountain than they did in the photos. To compare the glaciers in front of us to those in the old photos was to see a transformed landscape—and not for the better.

As I write these words late in summer 2010, the American public seems finally to have accepted the reality of global climate change. One poll released in 2010 indicated that 74% of Americans believe global warming to be "real," and 76% supported government limits on the release of the greenhouse gases now widely believed to be contributing to climate change (Teixeira). After three decades of warnings from scientists, people were finally acknowledging the connection between the degradation of the planet and our consumer-driven lifestyle, with its SUVs, ever-larger homes, and plastic throw-away everything. The apparent suddenness of this change in public opinion is almost as shocking as what many scientists believe climate change might bring about: deeper and longer droughts, more frequent severe weather, failed ocean fisheries, shrinking northern forests, massive dislocations caused by food and water shortages, armed conflict over diminishing resources, widespread famine (see International Panel on Climate Change; Kolbert; National Intelligence Council). Such predictions of what global climate change could mean for us are terrifying. No wonder we were finally paying attention. The real question is, What took us so long?

As I noted previously, according to scholars like Orr and Bowers, part of the answer to that question is schooling. In simple terms, these scholars argue that schooling teaches students powerful lessons that go beyond the subject matter of the conventional curriculum in mainstream Western education—fundamental lessons about who we are and how we relate to the world around us. As Bowers puts it, traditional education has understood "the well-being and self-determined interests of the individual as the basic social unit for determining the moral tenor of social life" (6). Moreover, this individual is understood as an autonomous being that exists separately from the earth—the classic Cartesian self. Orr argues provocatively that "formal education happens mostly as a monologue of human interest, desires, and accomplishments that drowns out all other sounds. It is the logical outcome of the belief that we are alone in a dead world of inanimate matter, energy flows, and biogeochemical cycles" (90). That belief, Orr asserts, informs the mainstream curriculum at all levels of schooling. Schooling thus fosters a way of being in the world that is characterized by disconnection: We exist individually in the world, not of it; therefore, we see the earth as something for us to use—and to transform according to our desires—rather than conceiving of ourselves as fundamentally part of the living earth.

whose?

The closer I looked at mainstream education, the more compelling these arguments became. Moreover, some scholars—notably Marshall McLuhan and Walter Ong—theorize that writing itself fosters the disconnection that Orr and others associate with Western education. In McLuhan's well-known analysis, writing separates communication from the body and thus frees human speech from the constraints of time and space. Ong extends this analysis, arguing that alphabetic literacy fosters a kind of analytical thinking that helps give rise to introspection, "opening the psyche as never before not only to the external objective world quite distinct from itself but also to the interior self against whom the objective world is set" (105). Writing, in other words, fosters a sense of the self as fundamentally intellectual and separate from the physical world. These analyses have been controversial, but they nevertheless seem to suggest that writing itself is implicated in the disconnection that Orr believes characterizes Western education and contributes to the crisis of sustainability. Such a conclusion called into question my embrace of a Freirean conception of literacy as a tool for progressive social change, and eventually my inquiry led me to an impasse: Was writing itself an obstacle to the vision of a more just and sustainable future that I believed we should pursue?

Paradoxically, it was through writing—the *act* of writing—that I began to find a way out of that impasse. As I explored these questions, I began to do something that Donald Murray, one of my first mentors, advocated many years before: Pay attention to the writing. I did. And just as Murray said it would, the writing began to teach me. I began to write more mindfully, to notice what happens as I write. I began to study myself *writing*. I was no longer writing exclusively to produce a text but also to see what happened as I wrote, to follow where writing might take me. Not coincidentally, during this time I was also helping to re-establish a National Writing Project (NWP) site in Albany, New York. In the course of that work, I participated in countless meetings, large and small, in which I wrote together with my Writing Project colleagues. The writing we did in those meetings was almost never intended to be revised or published or even read by anyone other than the writer; the audience was usually ourselves at that moment. Sometimes we shared that writing, sometimes not. And once the meetings ended, the writing was usually disregarded. In other words, at those many meetings, we wrote for many purposes: to reflect, to explore, to focus, to question, to understand, to share, to connect, to dream. But we rarely wrote to produce a text. Our acts of *writing*, that is, were not acts of textual production. We simply wrote.

Those experiences were revelatory for me. In the context of my inquiry into writing instruction and into writing itself (which led me to Phenomenology and Zen, as is seen in the following pages), they opened up a window on the nature of writing that had previously been closed to me. They taught me that writing can be more than textual production, which is how it tends to be understood and taught in school. They taught me that the act of writing can be glorious, as one of my graduate students recently described it. Slowly, I began to recognize that so much of the power of writing—the power that I witnessed and felt time and again as I wrote together with my NWP colleagues—was missing from the experience of writing that students tend to have in school, where the focus is on the production of a narrow range of texts constrained by rigid conventions, where the purpose of writing is almost always to demonstrate mastery and to be judged. No matter how successful a student writer is in school, rarely if ever does that student truly experience the transformative power of writing.

This book is about what I now believe to be the source of that power: the experience of writing itself. That power lies primarily in the writer *writing*, not in the writer's writing. But mainstream writing instruction largely ignores the act of writing, focusing almost exclusively on the text that is produced as a result of that act. The problem, I came to see, is not writing; the problem is how we understand it and teach it.

I now believe that the implications of mainstream writing instruction are more troubling than Weiser, North, and other abolitionists have asserted. It is true that we teach writing ineffectively, as they have argued; moreover, for the most part mainstream writing instruction does not seem to accomplish the widely embraced goals of preparing students to write effectively in school or the workplace. But the real problem has to do with the lessons students learn as a result of writing instruction—lessons about what writing is, what it is for, and how it should be practiced. We teach students that writing is a procedure rather than a way of experiencing themselves as beings in an inherently interconnected world. And in teaching writing in this way, we reinforce the problematic conception of the human self that leads to our fundamental disconnection from the earth—a conception of the self that shapes our ways of being on the earth, which in turn lead to the crisis of sustainability.

In the following pages, I explore this connection between writing instruction and the crisis of sustainability. I also explore the experience of writing and what it can teach us about the transformative power of writing. In the process, I propose a new theory, which I call an ontological theory of writing, that I hope reveals genuine possibilities for harnessing that power. For I continue to embrace Freire's view of hope as "an ontological need" (*Pedagogy of Hope* 8): "I do not understand human existence, or the struggle needed to improve it, apart from hope and dream" (8). At some level, every act of writing is an expression of hope—hope that our words will matter, that they can matter, and that they might make some discernible difference to ourselves and to others, in the moment and in the future. This book is an expression of such hope: that we will imagine and create a more just and sustainable future together, and that writing will be part of the process by which we do so.

ACKNOWLEDGEMENTS

For a book that has been more than a decade in the making, any effort to acknowledge those who in some way have contributed to its development will be inadequate.

Many of the ideas presented here grew out of numerous conversations with colleagues and friends, including Steve North, Irwin Weiser, Derek Owens, Dan Collins, Nedra Reynolds, Rich Haswell, Bob Tremmel, Bruce Ballenger, Scott Leonard, Jerry Nelms, Carole Clark Papper, and Becky Rickley. I am grateful to them for the opportunities they provided to explore my ideas and arguments and for the interest they showed in this work.

I presented versions of the main arguments of this book in talks I gave at Saint Joseph's University, SUNY-Cortland, and the University of Akron; I wish to thank Ann Green and Melissa Goldthwaite of Saint Joseph's, David Franke and Karen Stearns of SUNY-Cortland, and Bill Thelin of the University of Akron for giving me the opportunity to share my ideas with audiences at their institutions.

Andrea Lunsford and Beverly Moss, mentors and friends, offered advice that helped me find the right home for this project. I am deeply grateful to them for their help and support over the years.

Cathy Fleischer and Dana Fox invited me to explore some of the ideas developed in this book in an article for *English Education*, which they edited at the time. Michael Moore, their successor as editor of *English Education*, encouraged me to pursue these ideas further in a subsequent article that became the basis for Chapter 5. I am indebted to them for their encouragement and their confidence in me.

I would be remiss if I did not acknowledge the profound influence that the late Donald Murray has had on my thinking and writing through the years. His implicit respect for my work gave me confidence to continue, and his example as writer and teacher gave me direction and inspiration. This book is in many ways the result of his guidance.

I must also acknowledge the important influence of Janet Emig on my thinking and my work. As these pages demonstrate, her scholarship has deeply shaped my ideas about the experience of writing, and her support for my work has helped energize the inquiry into writing that resulted in this book.

My colleagues in the NWP have increasingly provided a community where I have found rich opportunities for shared inquiry into writing and writing instruction. My close friend and colleague Carol Forman-Pemberton, who also is my co-director at the Capital District Writing Project (CDWP), always offers encouragement at the right time and is a tireless cheerleader for my ideas; I owe her a debt of great gratitude. My colleagues on the leadership team at CDWP, especially Alicia Wein, Molly Fanning, Liza Schofield, Aaron Thiell, Chris Mazura, Agnes Zellin, Leah Claron, and Amy Salamone, have become my teachers as well as close friends who have helped me understand writing and teaching in more ways than they know. Pat Fox and Rick Vandeweghe of the NWP have graciously invited me to participate in the organization's work at the national level and opened doors for me to pursue new avenues of inquiry into writing. The insights I have gained about writing and teaching through my work with these NWP and CDWP colleagues thoroughly inform this book.

I am deeply grateful to Arthur N. Applebee, chair of my department at SUNY-Albany, and Robert Bangert-Drowns, dean of the School of Education there, for their sustained support, without which I could not have completed this project. Thanks also to Susan Phillips, provost and vice president for Academic Affairs at SUNY–Albany, for her ongoing support for my work on writing instruction at the university.

Mike Williamson, editor of the Research and Teaching in Rhetoric and Composition series at Hampton Press, provided thoughtful comments on the manuscript and generous support for this project throughout. I am grateful to him not only for his confidence in this project but also for his willingness to discuss at length many of the issues I address in these pages, especially issues related to the evolution of Composition Studies as an academic discipline.

My family has become a de facto writing support group without ever really seeing my writing-in-progress. My siblings (Mary, Gary, and Dianne) and my parents (Ron and Joan Yagelski) sustain me with their pride in my work. My sons, Adam and Aaron, have given me countless opportunities to talk about many of the issues I take up in this book, and their questions and challenges have helped me think through my arguments and sustain my efforts to answer questions that seem important to me and to them. I cannot imagine being the writer I am without their presence in my life.

Most important, Cheryl, my wife, best friend, and lifelong companion, always is there with love, patience, and undying encouragement, no matter the project. Her willingness to listen and her complete confidence in me are precious gifts that enrich my life and enable me to pursue this work. I have no words to adequately express my gratitude and love for her.

INTRODUCTION

The Writer Writing

As the effects of global warming become more and more difficult to ignore, will we react by finally fashioning a global response? Or will we retreat into ever narrower and more destructive forms of self-interest? It may seem impossible to imagine that a technologically advanced society could choose, in essence, to destroy itself, but that is what we are now in the process of doing.
—Elizabeth Kolbert, *Field Notes From a Catastrophe*

At its best, writing has helped transform the world.
—National Commission on Writing, *The Neglected 'R'*

If you pay any attention to the public discourse about education reform and the latest literacy crisis, you will hear a lot about the importance of writing. The same is true of the professional literature in academic fields like rhetoric and composition, literacy, education, and English education in particular. It has become a truism that writing is not only important but an essential skill in contemporary society. But just what is writing?

If that question seems self-evident, purely academic, or even silly, it also is a question that rarely seems to be addressed in a serious way in the ongoing debates about writing instruction—which is surprising, given how much

emphasis is placed on writing at all levels of education. Just about every college student in the United States is required to take written composition, no
matter the student's major. Each year some two million college students take
a course in first-year composition. No other academic discipline can claim
as large an annual enrollment in its introductory course. Nor is any other
academic subject as important in secondary education, at least if state man-
dates are any indication. Every state in the country requires its middle and
high school students to take English, usually for all three years of middle
school and all four years of high school, and state standards for the English
language arts always include some form of writing competency.
Additionally, business leaders regularly expound on the importance of good
written communication skills in the emerging globalized workplace, and
blue ribbon panels, such as the National Commission on Writing (NCW),
warn about the dangers of inadequate writing instruction for the nation's
economic and political health. Yet efforts to define writing in these contexts
are usually superficial, cliché, sometimes platitudinous, or missing altogether. For example, in its somewhat alarmist report about the state of writing
instruction in the United States, the NCW described writing as learning, a
"way of knowing," and "an act of discovery" (13–14)—all very common if
somewhat hackneyed ways of describing writing. The NCW also defined
writing as "a complex intellectual activity that requires students to stretch
their minds, sharpen their analytical capabilities, and make valid and accurate distinctions" (13). Fair enough. Few writing teachers (and perhaps
fewer policymakers) would object to such a definition. But what does it really tell us about what writing is? What does it mean to say that writing is "a
complex intellectual activity"?

Each year in a graduate seminar that I teach on the teaching of composition, I pose a version of this question in three parts to my students, most
of whom are secondary school teachers in addition to a few aspiring or practicing college composition instructors:

1. What is writing?
2. Why should we teach writing?
3. How should we teach writing?

They usually have familiar answers to the second question (writing is essential for success in school and the workplace; writing is an important vehicle
for learning; writing is a powerful means of self-expression), but, not surprisingly, it is the third question that most engages them. They are preoccupied with method and often assume that my course will provide them with
the secret of how to teach writing effectively. I do my best to disabuse them
of this notion, and I forestall our inevitable examination of pedagogy, insist-
ing that such an examination is premature, because we must first try to

understand what writing is before we can work out why and how we should teach it. In other words, understanding the nature of writing and, more important, the *experience* of writing is essential for formulating a workable and ethical writing pedagogy. So it is the first question—What is Writing?— a question that usually stumps them, that becomes the focus of my course. In large part, this question—What is writing?—also is the focus of this book.

Simply put, my answer to this question is that writing is a way of being in the world. Whatever else it may be (and it is many other things, too), writing is an ontological act. When we write, we enact a sense of ourselves as beings in the world. In this regard, writing both shapes and reflects our sense of who we are in relation to the world around us. Therein lies the true transformative power of writing.

We don't tend to think of writing in these terms. Indeed, I argue in this book that despite half a century of research and theoretical scholarship illuminating and complicating the connections among writing, knowing, and being, writing continues to be understood by most people, including most educators, in relatively simple terms as a technology for communication and a straightforward, rule-governed process of encoding a more-or-less stable meaning in a text. This conception of writing, which I call the Cartesian view of writing, informs mainstream writing instruction at all levels of schooling. It is the foundation for the conventional answers to the questions of why we should teach writing (effective communication skills are essential in both the classroom and the workplace; writing supports learning; effective participation as a citizen and consumer in our society requires mastery of specific textual forms and discourse conventions) and how we should teach it (largely as a matter of learning and applying the conventions of academic writing and producing conventional textual forms). I argue that these widespread and seemingly reasonable beliefs about writing are actually deeply problematic, because they reflect a dualistic worldview in which the writer is understood as a version of the classic Cartesian subject: an autonomous, thinking being so perfectly captured in Descartes' famous line, "I think; therefore, I am." As a result, when we teach writing, we are teaching problematic lessons about the self, its relation to other selves and to the wider world, and how we know ourselves and the world around us; in short, we are really teaching a dualistic way of being in the world.

I have come to believe that these lessons are at best troubling and, at worst, damaging—to ourselves and the planet we share. That belief is the impetus for this book, which proposes that mainstream writing instruction is implicated in the looming social, economic, political, and environmental crises for which the terms *global warming* and *climate change* have become shorthand; writing instruction, that is, contributes to what I refer to as the crisis of sustainability, a term I borrow from David Orr. A decade and a half ago, Orr pointed to the intimate connections between conventional education and our unsustainable contemporary Western lifestyle. According to Orr, sustainability, "which refers to the fit between humanity and its habitat, is manifest in varying ways and degrees everywhere on earth. It is not only a feature on the public agenda; for all practice purposes it is *the* agenda. Sustainability is about the terms and conditions of human survival, and yet we still educate at all levels as if no such crisis existed" (83). That remains true even as I write these words in 2010, when government and the public finally seem to have acknowledged the destruction we are collectively doing to the earth. "Living green" has now become trendy, displacing (perhaps only temporarily) the outlandish conspicuous consumption that characterized the wild economic growth and the related expansion of Western consumer culture of the last two decades before the collapse of the financial markets in 2008 led to the current global recession. These developments may be positive signs that a larger percentage of the public is beginning to understand the depth of the crisis of sustainability that Orr began to describe in the early 1990s and that other thinkers were warning about even before the first Earth Day in 1970. But for the most part the recent emergence of a widespread green consciousness seems to reflect relatively superficial changes in lifestyle rather than a fundamental reconsideration of our values with respect to our relationships to one another and to the earth we are part of. More to the point, Orr's charge from 1993 that we still educate as if no crisis of sustainability existed remains true today. And writing instruction is a central part of that equation.

As I demonstrate in this book, the basic lesson of mainstream writing instruction (and of formal schooling in general) is disconnection, and it is this sense of disconnection that is at the root of the crisis of sustainability. In other words, when we teach writing in conventional ways, we are teaching fundamental lessons about the self and its relation to the world around us that in turn lead to problematic ways of being in the world; we teach lessons that become the foundation for the destructive, self-centered, consumer-oriented lifestyle that has been embraced throughout the world as globalization reshapes regional economies and influences local cultures (think here of China and India, for example). This dynamic between writing instruction and the crisis of sustainability is the basis for my answer to the question of why we should teach writing: Writing has the potential to shape our ways of being together on the earth. That's why we teach it—or why we should.

In order to understand this dynamic, however, we must first understand writing as an act of being, which in turn will enable us to identify the implications of mainstream writing instruction for our sense of ourselves as beings in the world. An ontological understanding can also help us find a way to a better alternative to mainstream pedagogies. That project is the focus of the first three chapters of this book.

In Chapter 1, I examine the crisis of sustainability and argue that it is inherently a social crisis rather than an exclusively environmental or technological problem, as it is often portrayed. The root of the crisis lies in our sense of ourselves as autonomous thinking beings—the classic Cartesian self—existing separately from the earth we inhabit. Ultimately, then, this crisis is a function of how we conceive of ourselves in relation to the world around us. As I noted earlier, formal education and mainstream writing instruction are implicated in this crisis because they continue to promote a dualistic worldview that rests on the traditional Cartesian hierarchies of mind over body and the intellectual over the physical. Despite the prominence of critical or progressive pedagogies within the academic discipline of Composition Studies and despite the emergence of "eco-composition," which focuses on the connections between writing and broader environmental concerns, the prevailing Cartesian view of writing has made it difficult for compositionists to reconcile their work as teachers of writing with the seemingly "external" matters of living together on the earth in the context of the looming crises that are commonly referred to as global warming or climate change. This Cartesian view of writing thus prevents Composition Studies from realizing its potential as a site of progressive change.

In Chapter 2, I look more closely at the Cartesian view of writing to uncover its fundamental tenets and reveal how they manifest themselves in mainstream instruction. I begin with a critique of how Composition Studies has understood its mission within institutionalized education and as a broader social project. Then, reviewing contemporary writing theory, I trace the emergence of "post-process" composition theory and argue that the field has in fact not moved beyond the writing process paradigm, which remains the overarching framework for both secondary and postsecondary writing pedagogy. Failing to grasp the radical anti-Cartesian perspective of Thomas Kent's paralogic rhetoric, which is a theoretical starting point for much post-process theory, post-process theorists, I argue, continue to conceptualize writing instruction within a Cartesian worldview, which ultimately reinforces the problematic conception of the writer as fundamentally separate from the physical world; in other words, post-process theorists attempt to move "beyond process" but without abandoning the Cartesian framework that informs mainstream writing instruction. Thus, even progressive theories of writing remain implicated in the crisis of sustainability. Building on Kent's anti-Cartesian perspective, this chapter underscores the need for an alternative to the mainstream Cartesian view of writing.

Chapter 3 moves toward such an alternative by laying a theoretical foundation for an ontological perspective on writing. First, I revisit the old philosophical problem of the role of language in our sense of ourselves as beings in the world. Taking up the challenge Derrida presented in his critiques of Husserl and related philosophers, in which Derrida argues that writing is essential for our sense of being, I examine the relationship of language (and writing) to our sense of being in the world and address the question of whether language can be the (or *a*) means to truth. In confronting these questions, I argue that although language is crucial to our efforts to make sense of our experience of our selves in the world, these two things—our experience and our use of language to represent it—are ultimately separate. This position becomes the key for confronting the problem of relativism that emerges from Derrida's analyses and from postmodern theory in general—a problem that has befuddled composition theorists and, appropriately, has become a focus of much contemporary theory, especially the neo-sophistic rhetoric of Jasper Neel and Susan Jarratt as well as Barbara Couture's phenomenological rhetoric. My analysis reveals that the poststructuralist embrace of language (or discourse) as the locus of truth rests on the same dualistic Cartesian worldview that remains the foundation not only for Derrida's critiques but also for the view of writing that emerges from his work as it has been interpreted by composition scholars. As a result, I join Couture in abandoning the poststructuralist view that truth is located in language.

This analysis leads to a consideration of nonduality as an alternative to the Cartesian worldview. Drawing on Eastern philosophical traditions, especially the work of thirteenth-century Zen philosopher Eihei Dogen, on more recent philosophical analyses of poststructuralism, and on phenomenology, I examine the possibilities for a nondualistic worldview, using Dogen as the primary basis for a radical conception of nonduality and Maurice Merleau-Ponty's phenomenology as a vehicle for reconceptualizing the role of language within a framework of nonduality. On that basis, this chapter presents the main features of a nondualistic conception of writing as a way of being in the world and demonstrates how such a theory enables us to address the problem of relativism that has plagued contemporary writing theory. It also shows how nonduality informs the work of key theorists, especially Paulo Freire and Couture, and argues that their work represents a crucial step toward a theory of writing as a way of being and toward a nondualistic writing practice.

My analysis of the connections among language, knowing, and being in Chapter 3 also raises fundamental questions about the role of the text in our efforts to use writing as a vehicle for truth-seeking, as Couture understands it. Drawing on Crispin Sartwell and again on Dogen, I argue that there is an "extra-linguistic" component to our experience of the world, which can never be fully captured in a text. This analysis exposes the limitations of the text as a vehicle for meaning-making and truth-seeking. These limitations, which are acknowledged in contemporary writing theory but ignored in mainstream writing instruction, highlight serious shortcomings in conventional approaches to teaching writing. As both Kent and Couture have argued, we teach writing as if it is a relatively unproblematic vehicle for meaning-making and truth-seeking while embracing theories of language that suggest otherwise. Such an untenable situation requires that we re-examine writing as an act of meaning-making and reconsider the teaching of writing as a process of textual production. In other words, if the text cannot fully represent our experience, then we must attend more carefully to the *act* of writing rather than just focusing on the production of text as the exclusive end of writing, as mainstream writing instruction does. I take up this task in Chapters 4 and 5.

Chapter 4 presents a phenomenological exploration of the act of writing. My purpose is to describe writing as a way of being. Drawing on my own experience as a writer and on descriptions of writing from other writers, I examine the *experience* of writing and tease out implications of that experience, both in the moment and over time. This examination becomes the foundation for my argument that writing encompasses much more than the text and should therefore be understood as much more than textual production. Building on the analysis of Chapter 3, in which I illuminated the limitations of the text, I demonstrate that mainstream writing instruction, because of its obsession with the text (especially the *form* of the text), not only ignores much of what is important about an act of writing but also fails to harness the truly transformative power of writing, which lies in the experience of writing rather than the text produced as a result of that experience. Mainstream writing theory, in other words, because it neglects the effects of the *act* of writing on the writer's sense of being, offers an inadequate account of what happens *as a writer writes*. Whatever happens to a text *after* it is written does not affect what is happening to (or *in*) the writer *as she or he is writing that text*. The text, no matter how important it might eventually become to the writer or to a reader, ultimately is separate from the experience of writing it. It is this *experience*, which current theory fails to explain, that is the focus of this chapter and the basis for the pedagogy I advocate in Chapter 5.

If writing is more than textual production and if the experience of writing truly does matter in terms of its potential impact on the writer's sense of self as a being in the world, then how should we teach writing? This question, the third of the three questions I pose to the students in my seminar on teaching writing, is the focus of Chapter 5. In the pedagogy I describe in this chapter, the experience of writing, rather than the production of a text, moves to the center of writing instruction. In other words, I advocate a pedagogy that focuses on the *writer writing* rather than the writer's writing. The text does not disappear in this pedagogy, but rather than being the focus of writing instruction, it becomes a component of the process of inquiry into self and world that the act of writing can be. In this way, the text becomes part of a larger act of inquiry through writing, which in turn becomes a vehicle for truth-seeking, in Couture's sense of that term. In other words, we write as a way of being together in the world—as a way to understand our-selves and our connection to what is around us; in this formulation, we write *with* the text rather than to produce a text. Such a pedagogy, I submit, is a way to enact the fundamental sense of connection that defines the nondual-ity I explore in Chapter 3. And in that sense it is also a way to take advan-tage of the transformative potential of writing. Ultimately, a pedagogy based on the idea of writing as a way of being is a pedagogy of community: It is a way of being together on the earth and a vehicle for imagining and creating a just and sustainable future together.

It is worth asking whether a new theory of writing can truly matter in a world so profoundly at risk, as the world we inhabit today most surely is. What do writing and writing instruction really have to do with melting gla-ciers, severely compromised ecosystems, intractable ethnic and religious conflict, and unspeakable human misery brought on by profoundly unethi-cal financial practices and the deepest economic crisis since the Great Depression? I hope this book provides a viable—and hopeful—answer to such a question. I hope it reveals that, to paraphrase the National Commission on Writing, at its best, writing truly can transform the world. And I hope it underscores the pressing need to harness the transformative power of writing, for each of us and for all of us, now.

1

WRITING (AND) THE CRISIS OF SUSTAINABILITY

In early 2007, the Intergovernmental Panel on Climate Change (IPCC) released a much-anticipated report on the state of the earth's atmosphere. Based on an analysis of hundreds of scientific studies, the IPCC, considered the world authority on climate change, concluded that "warming of the climate system is now unequivocal" (IPCC, *Physical Science Basis* 5) and that "most of the observed increase in globally averaged temperatures since the mid-twentieth century is *very likely* due to the observed increase in anthropogenic greenhouse gas concentrations" (10). That phrase, *very likely*, was a change from the term *likely* in its previous report, which generated controversy when it was released in 2001. At that time, critics, among them many officials in the administration of President George W. Bush, argued that fluctuations in global temperatures were natural and that available evidence was insufficient to conclude that climate change was a result of human activity. Predictably, they warned that proposed measures to combat climate change, such as reducing automobile emissions, would harm the U.S. economy. But the 2007 IPCC report was difficult for even the most hard-core climate-change deniers to dismiss. A follow-up report released a few months later (*Impacts, Adaptations, and Vulnerability*) described in horrifying detail the likely effects of a warming atmosphere on humans everywhere on earth. It painted an especially grim picture of the future for millions of the world's poorest people, who would suffer most from the more frequent droughts and floods, altered growing seasons, and rising sea levels expected to be caused by climate change.

The IPCC reports received a great deal of play in the popular press, perhaps in part because in his 2007 State of the Union Address, President Bush acknowledged climate change for the first time—a notable reversal in the public stance of a leader whose government had steadfastly refused to sign the most important international agreements intended to address the problem of climate change, including the Kyoto Protocols.[1] A month later, former Vice President Al Gore won an Academy Award for his film about climate change, *An Inconvenient Truth*, and later that year Gore was awarded the Nobel Prize for Peace for his efforts to raise awareness about global warming. Suddenly, it seemed, everyone was worried about climate change.

In the midst of all this attention to what was now widely acknowledged as unprecedented environmental change, Josh, a high school junior living in a suburban town in upstate New York, was quietly preparing to take the SAT exam for the first time. Like millions of other high school students in the United States, he was part of another unprecedented change: a new timed impromptu essay that had been added to the SAT, the most widely used college admissions test. Two years earlier, for the first time in its long history, the SAT began requiring students to write an essay in addition to completing the familiar multiple-choice questions about usage and syntax on the "verbal" sections of the test. The College Board, which develops and administers the SAT, claimed that the addition of a timed essay not only would improve the test's "predictive validity" (i.e., its ability to predict students' achievement in college) but also would encourage high schools to emphasize writing instruction.[2] Indeed, the revised SAT did focus renewed attention on longstanding worries about the perceived poor writing skills of American students and helped put writing instruction on the national education reform agenda. Two years earlier, a quasi-official body called the National Commission on Writing (NCW) released a report titled *The Neglected 'R': The Need for a Writing Revolution* in which the "crisis" in writing was cited as an obstacle both to education reform and to the nation's economic health: "American education will never realize its potential as an engine of opportunity and economic growth until a writing revolution puts the power of language and communication in their proper place in the classroom. Yet, although many models of effective writing instruction exist, both the teaching and practice of writing are increasingly shortchanged throughout the school and college years" (14). The NCW, which was sponsored by the College Board and included several respected scholars as well as the director of the National Writing Project (NWP), warned that students "cannot write well enough to meet the demands they face in higher education and the work environment" (16). The College Board's launch of the new SAT seemed to be part of a national response to The Neglected R.[3]

None of this mattered to Josh. What mattered to him was that he—and the 1.5 million other students who take the SAT each year—would have to write an essay in twenty-five minutes in response to a prompt he had never seen before. As he worked with me (his uncle) to prepare for the test, he practiced strategies that he hoped would earn him a high score on the essay. He had no inkling that his uncle had been part of a brief public controversy over the new SAT when it was first administered two years earlier.[4] By the time he took the test in 2007, the controversy had passed, and the new SAT had already become another established component of the state and national standardized testing regime that has expanded considerably in the past decade, partly as a result of President Bush's No Child Left Behind (NCLB) education reform program.[5] That was no surprise, really, because standardized tests of writing are now not only ubiquitous but also widely accepted as valid. Even in the brief controversy over the new SAT in 2005, little attention was paid to the question of *whether* such a test can actually measure a student's writing ability. But more important, the conception of writing that informs the SAT is so commonplace that it seems completely natural. *Writing* as presented on the SAT is pretty much how *writing*, at least school-sponsored writing, is generally understood in contemporary American society. This version of writing, which focuses on form and convention, is integral to schooling at all levels and, because schooling is essentially an ontological process (as I show later), is a crucial component of the ways in which students come to understand who they are and how they relate to each other and the world around them. Josh and his fellow test-takers were, I'm sure, unaware that as they prepared for the SAT and completed writing assignments in their classes, they were participating in what amounts to a de facto project of mass indoctrination that is part of the reason for the frightening crises we are almost certain to face as a result of the environmental changes that the IPCC has been warning about for nearly two decades. In other words, writing instruction and global warming are related, for writing instruction is implicated in what David Orr has called "the crisis of sustainability" (83).

As I note in the introduction, Orr argues that sustainability "is about the terms and conditions of human survival, and yet we still educate at all levels as if no such crisis existed" (83). To examine current discussions about education reform is to gain a sense of the extent to which Orr's words, first published in 1992, are even more apt today.[6] In 2007, as policymakers were finally beginning to heed the dire predictions from the IPCC about the potentially catastrophic implications of a warming atmosphere, public (and too often professional) debates about education reform remained narrowly focused on matters like standardized testing and "accountability." That focus on testing and accountability remained through 2010 as President Barack Obama's new administration promoted its "Race to the Top" education reform program, which, according to the federal Department of Education's description, encouraged states to "[adopt] standards and assessments that prepare students to succeed in college and the workplace and to compete in the global economy" and "[build] data systems that measure student growth and success, and inform teachers and principals about how they can improve instruction" ("Race to the Top Fund"). These intense discussions about how to "improve instruction" proceeded as if conventional curricula and pedagogies have nothing to do with the looming global crisis. Yet as Orr and others (e.g., Bowers; Giroux) have shown, formal education in the West is built on and promotes the same dualistic Cartesian worldview that has given rise to this crisis in the first place. As philosopher David Loy puts it, "In this century it has become clear that the fundamental social problem is now the relationship between humankind as a whole and our global environment. It is because of our alienation from the earth that we are destroying it" (302). This problem, writes Loy, arises from the "delusive sense of duality between oneself and the world one is 'in.'" Quoting Heidegger, Loy notes that "the same dualism that reduces things to objects for consciousness is at work in the humanism that reduces nature to raw material for humankind" (302). Loy's analysis helps us see that the crisis of sustainability is not an environmental crisis but a social problem that arises from the dualistic way that we understand ourselves as beings in the world. At the root of the crisis of sustainability is the Cartesian sense of the self as an autonomous, thinking being, and that self is fostered and sustained by conventional writing instruction.

To understand this dynamic requires, first, an understanding of the crisis of sustainability as a social problem—that is, a problem that arises from our ways of understanding ourselves in relation to other beings and to the earth itself. Schooling, perhaps the most powerful Western cultural institution, is at the root of this problem because it continues to promote a dualistic Cartesian sense of self. Conventional writing instruction, which is based on a Cartesian view of writing (as I demonstrate in Chapter 2), is central to this process. In other words, in teaching writing in conventional ways, we are teaching a dualistic way of being in the world. Writing instruction is at heart an ontological process, and in order to understand its impact on our sense of self and its role in the crisis of sustainability, we will need to understand writing in ontological terms; we will need to understand the *experience* of writing and of learning to write in order to understand the implications of that experience on students' sense of self. We will need, that is, a theory of writing as a way of being.

In this book I propose such a theory. I argue that we must attend much more directly to the *experience* of writing than we do in mainstream writing instruction. Such a theory can illuminate the connections among mainstream writing instruction, formal schooling, and the crisis of sustainability. In this chapter I examine those connections.

THE CRISIS OF SUSTAINABILITY AS A SOCIAL PROBLEM

In April 2007, as the IPCC was releasing the second part of its report on the state of the earth's climate, there was a celebration of sorts in Albany, New York, where I live and work. Debbie Oatman, a 49-year-old divorced single mother with four sons, was selected to be on the hit television reality show *Extreme Makeover: Home Edition*. The premise of *Extreme Makeover: Home Edition* is to find a family who is down on their luck and build them a new home and, presumably, a better life—to give them an "extreme makeover." The Oatmans seemed good candidates for the show. According to the Albany regional newspaper, Debbie Oatman "struggled financially and got by month to month on government adoption subsidy checks for her three adopted sons" (Grondahl 1). But after being selected to appear on *Extreme Makeover*, Oatman was suddenly sitting on about $1 million in the form of a new 3,700-square-foot home (complete with in-ground swimming pool), full scholarships for her sons to a local college, $6,000 worth of groceries, and donations raised through a local credit union to pay off her existing mortgage and establish a trust fund for her sons. The highlight of the TV episode was what the show's producers call "the reveal," the moment when the Oatmans are brought to see their new home for the first time, surrounded by dozens of volunteers, neighbors, and local businesspeople whose contributions helped make the whole affair possible. There were obligatory close-ups of the teary-eyed Oatman and her excited kids and the satisfied smiles of the producers and volunteers.

In each episode of *Extreme Makeover*, "the reveal" is clearly intended to make you feel good as you witness the good people of a community helping one another. And it is easy to feel happy for the Oatmans, who, like the other temporary stars of *Extreme Makeover: Home Edition*, surely will benefit from appearing on the show. But the factors that led to the Oatmans' difficult circumstances remain intact. We might celebrate their good fortune, but we also can assume that there are thousands of other Debbie Oatmans out there, probably a few in her own neighborhood, which is now graced by her big new house.

I share this anecdote because media events like *Extreme Makeover* can reveal a great deal about how we understand what it means to be part of a community in contemporary American society. On the surface, this show seems to present a community coming together to help a struggling family. That's part of what we imagine a community to be about: a sort of contemporary, media-driven version of an old-time barn-raising. If we look beyond the surface, however, the picture becomes more complicated, and we begin to see that how we, collectively, understand *community* is a problem. We *do* need an extreme makeover, but not the kind depicted on the television show.

As the IPCC has extensively documented, humans have almost certainly caused the unnaturally high levels of CO_2 and other greenhouse gases that are warming the atmosphere, because we have created a carbon-based economy in which the full environmental costs of production and consumption are not taken into account. We rely on carbon-based energy sources (coal, oil, and gas) and, to a lesser extent, hydroelectricity and nuclear power that may be efficient in terms of their capacity to power our consumer-oriented lifestyle on a large scale but are nevertheless destructive in terms of their impact on the air, land, and water. But the problems associated with global climate change are not primarily a result of environmentally harmful technologies, like gas-guzzling SUVs or coal-fired power plants. To the contrary, these problems are ultimately a function of a lifestyle that defines happiness in terms of consumption and commodifies the earth as a source of profit. They arise from a culture that places greater value on 3,700-square-foot homes with inground swimming pools than on living together gently on the land. The Oatmans' problems were not caused by a home that was too small or lacked a swimming pool, but the very idea that a bigger home and more money to buy consumer goods will alleviate the Oatmans' troubles reflects the value contemporary American society places on consumption as a measure of one's viability as a member of a community. In this regard, *Extreme Makeover* is perhaps an extreme example of the problematic way we understand ourselves as members of communities.

Extreme Makeover: Home Edition can serve as a window into what has become the mainstream American idea of a "good life." At the core of this idea is consumption. Historian Gary Cross believes that consumerism, rather than democracy or capitalism, was the victor of the great ideological struggles of the twentieth century: "Visions of a political community of stable, shared values and active citizenship have given way to a dynamic but seemingly passive society of consumption in America, and increasingly across the globe" (1). The American consumer economy is now the global model. And consumerism, which Cross defines as "the belief that goods give meaning to individuals and their roles in society," provides a framework within which we assign value to our lives and our work and make decisions about how to conduct our social, political, and economic affairs. As Cross points out, participation in the consumer culture "is a choice, never consciously made, to define self and community through the ownership of goods" (5). Over the course of the twentieth century, Cross argues, "the self in society came to be defined by consumption" (6).

To some extent, the severe economic crisis that began in 2008 prompted a re-examination of this idea of the good life and led to a rejection of consumption (at least *conspicuous* consumption) among some Americans. *Green* has become synonymous with *good* rather than a sign of membership in the environmental fringe; frugality has made a comeback in some quarters. But even in the midst of extreme economic distress brought on by historic levels of unemployment, housing foreclosures, and business failures, the fundamental idea of consumption as a core value in contemporary culture has not been abandoned. Indeed, some critics have called for consumers to continue consuming in order to bring the nation out of its economic crisis (see Gross, "Stop Saving Now!"). Such exhortations recall President George W. Bush's encouragement to the nation after September 11, 2001 to go on vacation and continue shopping. Consumer culture may have taken a hit in 2008 and 2009, but it remains at the core of contemporary American life.[7]

If consumer culture is "democracy's highest achievement, giving meaning and dignity to people when workplace participation, ethnic solidarity, and even representative democracy have failed" (10), as Cross argues, it also reflects an abiding belief in the primacy of the individual, whose well-being often supersedes that of the community. In this sense, the most basic values of consumer culture are very nearly anti-communitarian. The "good life" that is defined in terms of individual well-being (which in turn is defined as an individual's capacity for material consumption) and valorized in pop-culture events like *Extreme Makeover*, is more or less divorced from a larger sense of the common good. To the extent that we endeavor for a common good, we do so by trying to improve the lots of individuals. As a result, we try to solve social problems in ways that do not necessarily take into account how the problem itself (and, often, our solution to it) may arise from and contribute to the damage we are doing to the earth, in part because the primacy of the individual is never seriously questioned. If it seems completely reasonable to "help" a family like the Oatmans by building them an unnecessarily large new home, that's precisely the point: such a solution is consistent with our ways of understanding ourselves as beings in the world.[8] What is too often described as an environmental problem (global warming), then, is really a function of how we structure and manage our communities in order to maintain a lifestyle that grows out of our dualistic way of understanding ourselves as beings in the world. The crisis of sustainability, in other words, is fundamentally an ontological matter.

Wangari Maathai, the Kenyan environmentalist who won the Nobel Peace Prize in 2004 for founding the Green Belt Movement, describes the movement's mission as "mobilizing community consciousness for self-determination, equity, improved livelihood security and environmental conservation—using trees as the entry point." Significantly, Maathai sees the issue in terms of community and not exclusively as a matter of environmental conservation. She calls for "a new understanding—that self-identity, self-respect, morality and spirituality play a major role in the life of a community and its capacity to take steps that benefit it and ensure its survival." Like some Western scholars, such as C. A. Bowers and David Orr, she challenges us to understand our communities not as collections of individuals whose worth is defined by material possessions but as beings who are fundamentally interconnected to each other and to the earth.

In his famous essay "The Tragedy of the Commons," biologist Garret Hardin uses the example of the traditional common field for grazing livestock to show that if we allow individual community members unfettered access to communal resources, they will serve their own interests first, thereby depleting those resources for the whole community. Hardin concludes,

> We want the maximum good per person; but what is good? ... Comparing one good with another is, we usually say, impossible because goods are incommensurable. Incommensurables cannot be compared. Theoretically this may be true; but in real life incommensurables are commensurable. Only a criterion of judgment and a system of weighting are needed. . . . The problem for the years ahead is to work out an acceptable theory of weighting.

Hardin's analysis shows that for a community to function effectively without destroying the very resources on which its members depend, it must define itself not only in terms of the relationships among its human members but also in terms of the relationship between those members and the earth. That means understanding human communities as encompassing the more-than-human. And it means individuals defining themselves in terms of their relationships to one another and to the land they inhabit. As Bowers puts it, it means "shift[ing] the emphasis away from the traditional liberal concern with using the well-being and self-determined interests of the individual as the basic social unit for determining the moral tenor of social life" (6). It means rethinking how we exist as beings-in-the-world.

If *sustainability* is "the need to ensure a better quality of life for all, now and in the future, in a just and equitable manner, whilst living within the limits of supporting ecosystems," as Julian Agyeman has defined it (6), then our collective inability to fulfill this need has led to the crisis we face in this new century. We have created communities whose very structure ensures that we do not live, individually or collectively, "within the limits of supporting ecosystems." And as long as we continue to conceive of ourselves and the world in Cartesian terms, we will remain unable, collectively, to imagine and create communities founded on the vision of ensuring "a better quality of life for all." But re-imagining communities along these lines requires first rethinking the idea of the self. And that brings us back to the role of schooling.

SCHOOLING AND THE CARTESIAN SELF

David Loy points out that within the Cartesian worldview that characterizes Western culture, "the self is understood to be the source of all awareness and therefore all meaning and value, which is to devalue the world/nature into merely that field of activity wherein the self labors to fulfill *itself*" (303). This also is the fundamental lesson of formal schooling. Significantly, this self is the autonomous self summed up in Descartes' famous line, "Cogito ergo sum": I think; therefore, I am. As the main reference point in conventional education, this Cartesian self also gives rise to the classic Cartesian dualities of self-and-other, subject-and-object, and mind-and-body, which form the epistemological foundation of the modern curriculum. In other words, an understanding of the self as autonomous observer/knower assumes some "other" to be observed or known; that "other" is everything "outside" or apart from the self. Knowing becomes a matter of observing and describing that "outside" world. The basic lesson of conventional schooling, then, is less a matter of learning *what* is outside us than learning *that* there is something outside us that we can see, describe, and understand, a something that is fundamentally separate from our selves. To put it in simpler terms, in school we teach separateness rather than interconnectedness; we see a world defined by duality rather than unity. As a result we promote an idea of community as a collection of discrete, autonomous individuals rather than a complex network of beings who are inherently interconnected and inextricably part of the ecosystems on which all life depends. These lessons are encoded in the institutional structures of schooling, the mainstream curriculum at both the secondary and postsecondary levels, and conventional pedagogies, including writing pedagogies (see Bowers; Giroux; Orr).

Perhaps the most obvious example of this encoding is assessment. At some point, everything in school comes down to a student's individual academic performance and/or achievement, which is measured in various ways. But no matter whether the measures are standardized tests, content-based multiple-choice exams, essay exams, so-called performance-based assessments, or "authentic" measures such as writing portfolios, students almost always are assessed as individuals, and for the most part their individual performances or achievements have no discernible impact on the school as a community. In other words, an individual student can succeed or fail in an academic sense, but the school goes merrily on. Even when schools themselves are evaluated, they are ultimately judged on the basis of the aggregated individual performances of their students, a process that has moved to the center of formal education since the passage in 2002 of the federal NCLB program, which required schools to demonstrate "adequate yearly progress" largely on the basis of standardized test scores. Despite the hand-wringing about the deleterious effects of our growing obsession with standardized testing, it nevertheless seems to be widely assumed that such tests *do* measure students' knowledge and/or skills in various subject areas, including writing. A student *is* who the tests say the student is. The tests are us, so to speak. Similarly, course grades and grade point averages become synonymous with a student's identity within schools—and to some extent outside schools as well (such as when students apply for college or graduate school). Significantly, in this multifarious process of evaluation, the student is implicitly defined as an intellectual entity, a collection of certain cognitive abilities and/or sanctioned bodies of knowledge. The student, in other words, becomes a disembodied intellect. Tests measure certain intellectual capabilities and knowledge, which itself is implicitly defined as exclusively intellectual (as distinct from, say, emotional knowledge or physical skill), as I already noted. Everything else in schools—including behavioral norms, emotional well-being, extracurricular participation, social function or dysfunction, and so on—is subordinate to the academic work that ultimately defines the individual student as an intellectual being. So what counts most in schools—performance on standardized tests and other measures—is the means by which schools define students as beings in the world. Assessment becomes a process of disembodiment that both reflects and reinforces the Cartesian self. In schools, perhaps more than in any other cultural settings, thinking is being. *Cogito ergo sum.*

This fundamental lesson of schooling is encoded not only in conventional educational practices like assessment but also in the social and even spatial organization of schools. Consider, for example, a typical classroom, like the one shown in Fig. 1.1. Such a classroom scene suggests at least three important things about the epistemological and ontological nature of formal education.

First, this scene depicts the kind of knowers that students are encouraged to become. Physically, the students are oriented toward the teacher, not toward each other, which reflects the teacher's position as an authority within the school or university but more importantly an authority for the knowledge that he is conveying to the students. We might think of this scene as a kind of tableau of Paulo Freire's famous "banking concept of education, in which the scope of action allowed to students extends only as far as receiving, filing, and storing the deposits" of knowledge as defined by the teacher (or the curriculum or the discipline) (*Pedagogy of the Oppressed* 58). Students have little (if any) authority for determining what counts as knowledge or how knowledge is used within the institution. Indeed, in most cases, schooling defines "personal" knowledge as distinct from sanctioned "academic" knowledge, thereby establishing a dichotomy between these kinds of knowledge as well as a hierarchy in which the personal is subordinated to "objective" academic knowledge. In addition, students rarely function col-

Fig. 1.1. Typical classroom

lectively as knowers, even in so-called cooperative learning activities. If there is any social interaction among them, it is intended to facilitate individual learning of whatever has been determined they should know. In other words, in such cooperative activities, the students function as collections of individuals who must learn something rather than as communities that have some common purpose or goal and within which individuals have different roles and needs. Ultimately, no matter what subject they are studying, the students are implicitly taught a stance toward knowledge as objective and separate from them, and they come to understand knowledge-*making* as something that does not involve them directly; they are knowledge *receivers*. In these ways, they learn within a positivist epistemology and Cartesian ontology.

Second, this process of learning is separate from the physical environment. As the photograph shows, the classroom as the physical locale of learning is separated from the surrounding landscape—figuratively and literally. The actual location of the classroom is well nigh irrelevant. Whether it is in upstate New York or Manhattan, Costa Rica or Kazakhstan does not substantially affect the learning that is supposed to occur in the classroom. Because knowledge is separate from the knower, it is also portable. Learning thus becomes decontextualized; that is, the student can acquire the requisite knowledge *anywhere*. The students in this classroom might be learning about the local ecology in upstate New York or about the ecology of the rain forest in Costa Rica. It doesn't matter; the process is the same, and it can take place in this or any other classroom without any significant contact with the physical landscape itself. The physical space of the classroom underscores the idea that knowledge is objective and disembodied, separate from both the knower and the physical world.

Third, writing as a technology and literacy as an activity support this learning process by providing a vehicle to convey the knowledge to be learned. In the scene depicted in Fig. 1.1, the students seem to be taking notes, a common use of writing in formal education. Research indicates that the range of the writing students are typically asked to do in schools is limited and focused on either recording and reproducing information or demonstrating (usually on tests) knowledge of specific information, ideas, or rules (Applebee, *Writing*; Applebee and Langer). For the most part, writing in formal education is a basic skill used for recording and communicating specified information or ideas. Literacy thus becomes a process of gathering and conveying objective knowledge about the world as it is, and writing serves as a technology for doing so.

This last point underscores the powerful epistemological consequences of writing in formal schooling. If schooling is a process of cultural reproduction, as many theorists have suggested (e.g., Bourdieu and Passeron; Bowers; Giroux), and if formal education amounts to a vast project of indoctrination into certain cultural values and ways of thinking, as Bowers and others have argued, then writing is a primary vehicle for that process. It is the means by which the knowledge that makes up the curriculum is conveyed; as such it reinforces the positivist epistemology that is the basis of that curriculum.

Bowers points out that "most citizens appear not to recognize the connections between the Western ideas and values they were inculcated with in schools and universities, their consumer-oriented life style, and the depletion of fish stocks, aquifers, old growth forests, petroleum reserves, and the accumulation of toxic wastes at all levels of the biosphere" (1). Confronting the crisis of sustainability, therefore, means challenging the ideological and epistemological foundation of schooling. Bowers believes that "this change in the foundations of taken-for-granted beliefs will require us to develop the same sense of a natural attitude toward ecologically sustainable cultural practices that now characterizes our natural attitude toward a consumer/technologically driven life style" (6). In other words, we will have to teach in ways that foster a sense of self as fundamentally interconnected to all other selves and to the landscape we inhabit, a self characterized by what Orr has described as "the capacity for clear thought and compassion in the recognition of the interrelatedness of life" (100). Given the central role of writing in conveying the fundamental ontological and epistemological assumptions that form the basis of contemporary schooling, that project can usefully begin with writing instruction.

WRITING INSTRUCTION AND THE CARTESIAN SELF

In helping Josh prepare for the SAT in spring 2007, I encouraged him to review the materials on the College Board Web site about the essay portion of the exam. Those materials open a telling window into how we think about writing in contemporary American society. As a widely accepted measure of student "aptitude," the SAT reflects conventional views about learning and knowing, and its timed essay and multiple-choice verbal sections reflect common beliefs about "good" writing. Consider, then, what Josh learns about writing—and about himself as writer and knower—as he prepares for the essay portion of the SAT.

When he visited the College Board's Web site in 2007, Josh found the following sample prompt for the timed essay:[9]

> Think carefully about the issue presented in the following excerpt and the assignment below.

> Many persons believe that to move up the ladder of success and achievement, they must forget the past, repress it, and relinquish it. But others have just the opposite view. They see old memories as a chance to reckon with the past and integrate past and present.
> —Adapted from Sara Lawrence-Lightfoot, *I've Known Rivers: Lives of Loss and Liberation*

> Assignment: Do memories hinder or help people in their effort to learn from the past and succeed in the present? Plan and write an essay in which you develop your point of view on this issue. Support your position with reasoning and examples taken from your reading, studies, experience, or observations.

Leaving aside the questionable value of this kind of writing task, we can learn a great deal about how the College Board understands "good" writing by examining its evaluation of the essays written in response to such prompts. Here, for example, is the explanation for a score of 5 out of a possible 6 that was awarded to one of the sample essays written for the prompt above:

> This essay effectively *develops its point of view* ("Memories and past experiences serve as a rail, a guiding support, for people in an effort to succeed in the present") through the *appropriate examples* of dissent during wartime and grieving for a pet, thus demonstrating strong critical thinking. Well *organized* and *focused*, the essay demonstrates *coher-*

ence and *progression* of ideas ("In seeing the undemocratic ways of an earlier era, America was able to recognize the bad and try to reform it. If the Sedition Acts had been forgotten then what is to say that they wouldn't come back? Remembering the failed times insures that improvement is possible"). The essay also uses appropriate *vocabulary* and demonstrates effective *variety in sentence structure.* To earn a 6, this writer needs to achieve smoother *progression of ideas* by *using language more skillfully* (the phrase "past experiences can only offer a gap between the steps on the ladder of success" seems to express the opposite of what the writer intends). The essay demonstrates reasonably consistent mastery and receives a 5. (emphasis added)

This evaluation highlights characteristics commonly regarded as essential for effective writing—and commonly emphasized in conventional writing instruction: development of an idea (regardless of the merits of that idea), the use of examples or details (although what constitutes an "appropriate" example is never defined), organization, focus (also not defined), coherence, progression of ideas (suggesting some sort of logical sequencing of ideas, although "progression" is never explained), vocabulary, and variety in sentence structure (although why we should desire *variety* is not explained). Often in these explanations poor mechanics are cited as a reason for lower scores. "Critical thinking" also is mentioned, but it too is never defined. Everything else cited as evidence of the essay's quality has to do with structure, style, and mechanics. Rarely (if ever) in these explanations will you find anything about addressing an audience, accomplishing a specific purpose with respect to that audience, making a *valid* point, exploring or presenting a *useful* or *important* idea, conveying *accurate* information, making *ethical* choices as a writer, or any of the other characteristics that reflect the complexities of writing in real-world contexts. In this regard, the College Board's conception of "good" writing is based on the classic binary between form and content.

In learning to produce such "good" writing, Josh implicitly learns that writing is a matter of applying rules and adhering to conventions related to form; the "content" of a piece of writing is implicitly defined as separate from the writing itself and, when it comes to learning to write, ultimately less important than form and correctness. Notice that the College Board's criteria for evaluating writing could apply to *any* kind of essay, regardless of the essay's subject matter, because these criteria have nothing to do with the *subject* of the writing. Indeed, I don't even need to reproduce here the sample essay referred to in the evaluation above, because the "content" of the essay barely matters.[10] In terms of judging these essays, what a student actually says in his or her writing is essentially irrelevant. What matters is not *what* one writes but *how* one writes. In conventional writing instruction, form trumps content. And writing skill is implicitly defined as the ability to produce texts conforming to specific conventions of form and correctness. Writing, in short, is textual production, narrowly defined.

Of course, this lesson about writing as primarily a matter of form is not limited to the SAT. State-mandated writing tests tend to convey this same conception of writing (see Hillocks), and it is consistent with the lessons students learn about writing in school (see Applebee and Langer). Josh shared with me some of the assignments his high school English teacher had given her students as the SAT test date approached, assignments I found painfully familiar: practice essays modeled after the SAT prompts, in-class exercises intended to reinforce the importance of form and structure, refreshers on the rules of standard written English, activities for quickly and efficiently organizing information. With a few exceptions (e.g., a unit on "creative" writing), these assignments and activities were no different from the ones Josh's teacher would typically use during the rest of the academic year—and no different from what the available evidence suggests the vast majority of English teachers do in teaching writing.[11] And the lessons those routine assignments and activities teach students about writing are the same lessons reinforced by the SAT: that writing is primarily a rule-governed activity in which "content" is presented in a sanctioned form according to specific conventions; that there is something called "good" writing that exhibits certain textual features regardless of rhetorical context (which, significantly, is rarely emphasized in conventional writing instruction and almost completely absent from standardized writing tests); that a stable meaning can be encoded in a text by following certain rules and applying certain conventions.

Standardized writing tests like the SAT—as well as typical grading practices—reinforce another of the most basic lessons about writing that students learn at all levels of schooling: that writing is an individual activity. A student's score on the SAT writing test—or any other standardized test—is in effect a description of that student as a writer; ditto for a student's grade in a writing or English class, just as grades become the equivalent of a student's identity in school, as I noted earlier. In this sense, writing as practiced and evaluated in schools is perhaps the most visible expression of formal schooling's focus on the individual. Paradoxically, although writing in school is rarely *about* the self as its subject matter, it is ultimately an expression of the Cartesian self that is the foundation of schooling.

The common conception of "good" writing that Josh and millions of other students internalize through conventional writing instruction is based on what is now an archaic but remarkably resilient view of language as a conduit for meaning, a vehicle for transmitting thought or ideas in a largely unproblematic way. This view of language, which dates back to the ancient Greeks in the Western tradition, remains intact despite theoretical developments in the past fifty years that have profoundly reshaped our understanding of language and challenged longstanding views about how meaning is constructed through texts. It is reflected in the widely held belief that writing is a matter of putting down on paper or a computer screen our already-formed thoughts or ideas or information. If you teach writing, at some point you've heard a student complain, "I know what I want to say, but I just can't find the right words." You also know that it's not true. It feels true because in mainstream education we teach writing as if it were an empty vehicle to carry meaning. We focus on matters of form and style and diction as if to suggest that all a writer really needs to make a point is the right words in the right order. Anyone who has ever written seriously knows otherwise, and much of our scholarship in recent decades has exposed the complexities surrounding the transaction between writer and reader through a text, the instability of meaning, and the situated nature of meaning-making. Yet conventional writing instruction and assessment continue to operate on an assumption that writing is a sometimes challenging but relatively straightforward conduit for meaning. This conduit view of language, which helps give rise to the form-and-content binary that characterizes writing instruction, effectively separates the so-called technical aspects of writing from knowledge-making. So in learning to master these "technical" aspects of writing, students also enact the epistemological lesson that knowledge is separate from them. Writing becomes a practice of the fundamental Cartesian subject–object binary and an expression of the autonomous Cartesian self as knower.

THE ONTOLOGY OF POSTSECONDARY WRITING INSTRUCTION

Everything I have written thus far about writing instruction applies to both secondary schools and postsecondary institutions, despite important differences in how writing functions at each level of schooling and despite the voluminous scholarship in Composition Studies that calls into question much conventional writing pedagogy at all levels of schooling. For one thing, the conception of "good" writing that informs standardized tests like the SAT and most secondary instruction is based on an assumption that college faculty value the same basic characteristics in writing. Some evidence suggests that, despite some differences, high school and college faculty do share basic beliefs about writing. Results of the 2009 ACT National Curriculum Survey, for example, which surveyed a national sample of 1,276 middle, high school, and college English/writing teachers, indicate little significant disagreement about the most important characteristics of good writing. Asked to rank-order six commonly emphasized features of a written text, high school and college teachers gave similar rankings (Table 1.1):

TABLE 1.1. Teachers' Rank-Ordering of Six Features of Written Text

High School English Teachers	College Composition and American Literature Survey Instructors
1. Idea or topic development	1. Idea or topic development
2. Organization, unity, coherence	2. Organization, unity, coherence
3. Sentence structure and formation	3. Sentence structure and formation
4. Word choice	4. Conventions of usage
5. Conventions of usage	5. Word choice
6. Conventions of punctuation	6. Conventions of punctuation

It is revealing that ACT does not include anything resembling rhetorical considerations (related to audience and purpose) in what it calls the "specific content and skills known to be in the English and writing domain" (9) that comprise the list shown in Table 1.1. The implicit definition of writing focuses on form and convention and the "development" of subject matter—once again reinforcing the separation of form from content and ignoring context.

In my work with faculty at my own and other universities, I routinely encounter the same views about what constitutes "good" writing held by high school teachers, despite the different ways in which college instructors use and value writing as compared to secondary school teachers. Although college faculty themselves engage in writing as a sophisticated form of knowledge-making and implicitly understand that they write to participate in the discourses that define their academic fields, they often seem to conceptualize student writing as a basic skill required for the "real" academic work in their disciplines.

Despite a number of promising reform movements over the years, including the process movement (which I discuss at length in Chapter 2), whole-language instruction, and recent efforts to incorporate so-called multiple and digital literacies into writing instruction, the most basic elements of writing instruction at both the secondary and postsecondary levels have remained largely unchanged for most of the history of modern public schooling in the United States. As historians of writing instruction have shown, modern writing instruction arises from a truncated version of classical rhetoric that emerged in the nineteenth century (Berlin, *Writing Instruction*), resulting in the form–content binary that leads to our obsession with form and correctness. Despite some evidence that movements such the writing process movement have influenced instructional methods, the teaching of writing in general remains narrowly focused on specified discourse forms (such as narrative, analysis, and dubious forms like the insufferably resilient five-paragraph essay) and a relatively limited set of conventions related to style and mechanics. In their analysis of data from the National Assessment of Educational Progress (NAEP), Applebee and Langer conclude that "by 1992, process-oriented instruction had become the conventional wisdom" in secondary classrooms nationwide (23), which seems to have influenced how students go about completing a writing task. For instance, in reviewing NAEP data from 1984 through the 2002 administration of the test, Applebee and Langer found that "even with the differences in test administration, students' tendency to do some overt planning before they begin to write seems to have increased across this 18-year time span" (25). However, they also report that "while process-oriented writing instruction has dominated teachers' reports at least since 1992, what teachers mean by this and how it is implemented in their classrooms remains unclear. The consistent emphasis that emerges in teachers' reports may mask considerable variation in actual patterns of instruction" (28). One wonders what might constitute "considerable variation in actual patterns of instruction" when it comes to writing. In their own large-scale studies of writing in secondary schools, Applebee and Langer consistently find that students are asked to write in a relatively narrow range of textual forms, rarely write for audiences other than the teacher, and write mostly for the purposes of assessment; they also find that instructional methods tend to be limited in scope. In their 1987 nationwide study of writing, they note that a curriculum based on "an industrial metaphor," in which the teacher is "a provider of information" responsible for "providing instruction directed at [students'] missing skills and testing to see if the instruction has been effective, … continues to undergird contemporary approaches to schooling," despite what they call the "process- and context-oriented research" of the 1970 and 1980s (Langer and Applebee 138). They warn, "Though persistent and widespread, this [industrial] model of teaching militates against many of our goals for writing and learning" (138). More than two decades after they published that warning, available evidence suggests that little has changed. Indeed, in raising questions about the nature of classroom instruction in writing in their 2006 analysis of NAEP data, Applebee and Langer specifically refer to concerns they highlighted in their 1987 study. Their studies paint a consistent picture of form-driven writing instruction with virtually no attention to the matters of audience and purpose that are emphasized in classical rhetorical theory or to the complexities of language highlighted by poststructuralism and related theoretical movements in the past several decades. Nor does mainstream writing instruction attend to the experience of writing. (I say much more about this lack of attention to the experience of writing in Chapters 4 and 5.)

At the postsecondary level, large-scale studies of writing instruction such as Applebee and Langer's are virtually nonexistent, and the growing body of scholarship in Composition Studies may skew our sense of what actually happens in college writing classes. Although some college composition programs seem to reflect the influence of contemporary composition theory, we have little systematic data to help us see what students are being taught in their writing classes and elsewhere in the college curriculum. As noted previously, we have evidence that faculty in disciplines other than rhetoric and composition continue to hold—and reinforce—the same functionalist view of writing that we see at the secondary level. Despite the maturation of Composition Studies as an academic discipline characterized by a robust scholarly literature on writing theory and pedagogy, writing instruction at the postsecondary level may be much more narrowly focused on form and convention than the scholarship would suggest. The best-selling composition textbooks, for example, continue to be handbooks, which tend to focus on the forms and conventions of writing. So-called "modes-based" composition readers, which categorize readings according to traditional genres such as narrative and argument, continue to outsell "thematic" readers, which seem to reflect the emphasis in contemporary composition theory on the social nature of writing.[12] This is not to say that postsecondary writing instruction is a simple matter of rules, forms, and conventions; it is clear that many faculty outside the field of Composition Studies appreciate the complexities of written discourse in the academic disciplines and understand the challenges facing undergraduates seeking to develop competence as participants in discourse communities in which they are, in the end, novices at best and probably more like "visitors." Many studies of students' experiences as writers across the curriculum indicate that at least some faculty understand these challenges and try to accommodate students accordingly (e.g., Carroll; McCarthy; Sommers, "Across the Drafts"; Walvoord & McCarthy); however, these same studies also suggest that many faculty view writing rather narrowly and reinforce a view of writing as a "basic skill" devoid of content and somehow separate from the "real" knowledge-making that characterizes the academic disciplines.

These attitudes among faculty mirror the narrow view of writing that informs much of the public discourse on education reform. In their argument to replace the traditional first-year composition course with an "Introduction to Writing Studies—a course about how to understand and think about writing in school and society" (558)—compositionists Downs and Wardle identify what they call a "systemic misconception" about writing that undermines the effectiveness of writing programs—a misconception based on the following specious assumptions: "writing can be considered independent of content; writing consists primarily of syntactic and mechanical concerns; and academic writing skills can be taught in one or two intro-

ductory general writing skills courses and transferred easily to other courses" (554–55). They go on to point out that

> [t]hese assumptions are reflected in public policy reports such as
> *Standards for Success* by the Center for Educational Policy Research,
> which focuses primarily on the need for grammar instruction—even
> sentence diagramming—in writing instruction. The "blue ribbon"
> National Commission on Writing in America's Schools and Colleges
> has produced two reports, *The Neglected R* and *Writing: A Ticket to
> Work . . . Or a Ticket Out,* both of which favor college professors' and
> business professionals' impressions of students' writing over actual data
> developed by writing studies scholarship. Not surprisingly, those
> impressions focus on syntactic and mechanical concerns and assume
> that "writing is writing," involving "learn-once/write-many" basic
> skills. The content-versus-form misconception—as old as FYC itself—
> appears in standardized testing, with the SAT "writing" test giving bet-
> ter scores to longer essays and completely discounting factual errors. It
> also finds its way into *New York Times* editorials, where no less a pub-
> lic intellectual than Stanley Fish argues that it is possible to, and there-
> fore that FYC should, focus strictly on writing's grammatical forms and
> disavow interest in its content. (555)

Downs and Wardle's characterization of the problematic assumptions
informing attitudes about writing both within and outside academe reinforces my point that writing continues to be understood largely as a basic
skill and primarily a matter of form and correctness. I am arguing, however,
that these assumptions do not reflect "misconceptions" so much as a
Cartesian view of writing. That is, these assumptions about writing reflect
the Cartesian worldview that is encoded in the conventional school curriculum. They are consistent with the epistemology and the dualistic sense of
self fostered by schooling, which may account for their resilience both within formal education and society in general.

   If my analysis of the Cartesian nature of writing instruction is valid,
then it seems clear that what students learn about themselves and the world
through conventional instruction is antithetical to an idea of community
based on "the recognition of the interrelatedness of life," as Orr puts it (100).
The focus of formal schooling on measuring individual ability, intellectual
achievement, and/or academic performance presents a significant obstacle to
even the most modest pedagogical reforms that might be seen as working
toward a more substantive sense of community (to the extent that schools
even see such a goal as part of their mission). Even promising pedagogical
developments like collaborative writing and community service learning are
undermined by the institutional requirement to assign grades to individual
students; moreover, because such pedagogies diverge from the basic assump-

tions about writing and the self that inform writing instruction in schools, they often are resisted by faculty, administrators, parents, and students. Ultimately, what is valued in writing instruction in schools is the individual student's capacity to conform to a narrow set of rules and conventions for written texts. Effective communication is reduced to a kind of decontextualized clarity and correctness. As a result, to be a successful writer in school does not require a student to gain an understanding of the complexity of writing within various rhetorical situations, for varied audiences, within specific historical moments, or different cultural contexts. Nor does it require that students necessarily understand themselves as members of communities working toward some common good.

This disconnection is perhaps even more apparent at the postsecondary level, where even the ostensible characteristics of a community (e.g., the students and their families all living physically within the same town or school district) are largely absent (see Mauk, "Location") and where students tend to be temporary members of the university "community," however it is defined. In this regard, the fundamental lesson of schooling about the autonomous self seems to be reflected in the material conditions of the typical undergraduate student, who experiences school in ways that reinforce a sense of separation and dichotomy. And this sense of separation may, paradoxically, be deepened by the growing role of online activities, including "social networking," that for many students become integral to their lives yet may have no significant relation to the physical location of their school or the school community, such as it is. Thus, students' ways of being in postsecondary schools seem to extend the basic lessons about who they are and how they relate to the world around them that they learned in secondary schools.

No one described the epistemological and ontological nature of schooling in the West more compellingly than Freire, whose metaphor of schooling as "banking education" poignantly captures the Cartesian foundations of modern education. At the heart of Freire's analysis is a critique of what is really the ontology of conventional schooling: "Implicit in the banking concept is the assumption of a dichotomy between human beings and the world: a person is merely in the world, not with the world or with others" (*Pedagogy* 75). As Freire demonstrated, literacy as practiced in schools is implicated in this process of teaching students how to be *in* rather than *with* the world, for conventional ("banking") education is based on the "unauthentic word," which results from a dichotomy between action and reflection. Deprived of the essential dimension of action, "the word is changed into idle chatter" (87). Dialogue, which Freire sees as an "existential necessity" (88), is thus impossible, "reduced to the act of one person's 'depositing' ideas in another" (89). From this perspective, to teach writing as a basic technology for communication, as mainstream schooling does, is to reinforce the dichotomy between self and world and therefore foster a dualistic way of being in the world.

Ultimately, then, writing instruction, like schooling in general, is an ontological process; it is part of how we learn to *be* in the world. And although such a statement may strike many readers as so much theorizing, our conceptions of ourselves matter. As Crispin Sartwell has noted, "How we think of ourselves in relation to the earth actually effects ways of being on the earth" (122). Sartwell offers a provocative challenge to our conventional ways of thinking about ourselves and our sense of the purpose of our lives. These, he argues, grow out of a Western intellectual and cultural tradition that "conceives of a separation, conceives of the earth as inanimate and unintelligent, and of ourselves as animate and intelligent. It conceives of the earth as means, persons as ends. It conceives of human action technologically, or according to the canons of practical rationality" (122–23). Such a dualistic worldview, of course, also gives rise to our sense of human exceptionalism, a view that philosopher John Gray has assailed as both recent and absurd: "For much of their history and all of prehistory, humans did not see themselves as being any different from the other animals among which they lived. . . . The humanist sense of a gulf between ourselves and other animals is an aberration. It is the animist feeling of belonging to the rest of nature that is normal" (17). The intense reaction to Gray's critique[13] may reveal how deeply our experience of ourselves is shaped by our Western dualistic sense of self. But although Gray sees little possibility for a world in which humans exist in some kind of harmony with other species and with the earth itself ("What could be more hopeless than placing the Earth in the charge of this exceptionally destructive species?"), for others the recognition that humans are not exceptional is a source of hope. A rethinking of an anthropocentric perspective is a step toward re-examining the Cartesian dualistic worldview. For Sartwell and a few other thinkers (e.g., Loy), the realization that duality is but one mode of existence opens up the possibility for alternatives to the Cartesian worldview. Gray may believe that there is no going back to earlier ways of thinking and being, but alternatives to our mainstream worldview exist, as Sartwell and Loy demonstrate. (I explore a nondualistic alternative worldview in Chapter 3.) However, as long as schooling, so potent a cultural institution, continues to foster a Cartesian sense of self, it remains an obstacle to realizing alternative ways of being that might enable us to confront the crisis of sustainability. And as long as writing instruction, a central component of schooling, continues to be based on a Cartesian view of writing, it will remain implicated in this crisis.

Gunther Kress has argued that the "design for a future social subject" and "a design for a future society" should be the framework for English Studies as both a curriculum and a scholarly project (16). Because of its claim to *writing* as its area of inquiry and expertise, Composition Studies should be at the center of this project and indeed has the potential to lead such a project—but only if it first acknowledges that potential and, second, embraces the related project of replacing the Cartesian view of writing that informs current composition theory.

COMPOSITION AND THE CRISIS OF SUSTAINABILITY

When Al Gore released his film about global warming, *An Inconvenient Truth*, in 2006, some critics charged that the film was alarmist. But by the time he was awarded the Nobel Peace Prize a year later, many of the nightmare scenarios depicted in the film seemed close to becoming alarmingly real. In *Field Notes from a Catastrophe*, one of the most carefully researched works on global warming, journalist Elizabeth Kolbert describes a situation much scarier than what Gore depicts in his very scary film: "Since this book first went to press, in the fall of 2005, dozens of important new studies on global warming have appeared. An uncomfortably large proportion of them point to the same conclusion: the world is changing more quickly and more dramatically than had been anticipated" (194). As Kolbert shows, the available evidence makes it is increasingly clear that climate change will define human existence in the coming century. She describes studies of the disappearance of past civilizations that scientists have explained as the result of environmental destruction and climate change, and she concludes that the scale of the change we are now facing may exceed anything humans have confronted in the past.[14] In view of overwhelming evidence and a growing consensus that climate change is the most pressing problem facing humankind in the twenty-first century, Kolbert provocatively asks,

> As the effects of global warming become more and more difficult to ignore, will we react by finally fashioning a global response? Or will we retreat into ever narrower and more destructive forms of self-interest? It may seem impossible to imagine that a technologically advanced society could choose, in essence, to destroy itself, but that is what we are now in the process of doing. (189)

Reading Kolbert's challenge, I could not help but recall a similar one posed by Mary Rose O'Reilley in *The Peaceable Classroom*. Describing her formative experiences as a new graduate teaching assistant at the University of Wisconsin during the social upheaval of the late 1960s, O'Reilley tells us that for her and her inexperienced colleagues, the Vietnam War profoundly complicated the already complicated matter of grading student writing, because in the context of the military draft, "grading was a life-or-death proposition" (9):

A bad grade could mean dismissal from college for a student, which in turn could mean being drafted. So when one of her professors posed the following question, it haunted O'Reilley: "Is it possible to teach English so that people stop killing each other?" (9). In view of Kolbert's challenge and the growing crisis of sustainability, I want to amend O'Reilley's question slightly: How can we teach writing so that we stop destroying ourselves?

O'Reilley notes that "second only to what happens between parent and child, what happens in the classroom determines the shape of culture and evolution of consciousness" (7–8). That statement takes on great weight considering that today virtually all children in the United States between the ages of 5 and 16 attend school (indeed, for the most part, school attendance is required by law), and nearly two-thirds of those who graduate from high school go on to some kind of postsecondary schooling.[15] It seems safe to say that no other social or cultural institution has as great a potential influence in shaping our sense of who we are. And because all states require students to study English through high school and almost every college and university requires some version of composition of all students, regardless of major, it also seems safe to say that the potential impact of writing instruction on our sense of ourselves as beings in the world is vast. Freire was indeed right: We do have the capacity to change the world through literacy education. To put it somewhat differently, writing instruction can be a potent vehicle for addressing the crisis of sustainability.

For the past few decades, since its so-called "social turn" in the 1980s, Composition Studies has increasingly focused on important concerns related to gender, race, social class, sexual identity, and social justice. The field's understanding of the writer has become more complex, evolving from a more traditional Romantic notion of the writer and the cognitive view that informed its scholarship in the late 1970s and early 1980s to a fundamentally social view of a writer shaped by language and culture. Questions of identity and agency moved to the fore of the field's concerns, and critical pedagogy, based in large part on Freire's theories, with its overt concerns about social justice and social change, became part of the field's mainstream. Yet despite these developments, Composition Studies has not been directly concerned with the role of writing in the crisis of sustainability, even though this crisis is consistent with the field's social concerns and (at least for some compositionists) its sense of mission. This is so, I believe, not because scholars in the field do not care about such issues but because the prevailing Cartesian theory of writing has made it difficult for compositionists to reconcile their work as teachers of writing with the seemingly "external" matters of living together on the earth. Certainly many in the field have written about such matters, and the recent emergence of "eco-composition" as a recognized subspecialty within the field attests to the strength of these concerns among scholars (see Dobrin and Weisser; Owens; Weisser and Dobrin). However, the peripheral status of eco-composition within the field reflects not the lack of importance of concerns like global warming or environmental racism but the inability of our prevailing conception of writing to encompass such concerns as integral to the act of writing—indeed, as part of our very being-in-the-world. When Derek Owens, for instance, compellingly argues that "the composition classroom offers a unique intellectual space to experiment with sustainable pedagogies" (29), he also implicitly acknowledges a view of writing as an intellectual activity in need of "content," a view based on the Cartesian dichotomy between subject and object that, as I have already argued, gives rise to the form-versus-content binary that characterizes mainstream writing instruction. According to Owens, "what students actually write, think, and talk about [in composition courses] . . . is determined locally by the teacher and by the students." Within the prevailing Cartesian view of writing, Owens must argue that sustainability should become the subject matter of the writing course, because that view of writing understands the subject matter as external to the writer and separate from *writing*. From this perspective, a writer writes about something. In this case, sustainability becomes that *something*. The very act of writing thus reinforces (unintentionally) the writer's separateness from that something, despite the focus in Owen's pedagogy on students' connection to their local communities. This is so no matter how much we emphasize the social nature of writing, because our understanding of writing rests on the idea of the autonomous Cartesian self. Writing in school is an enactment of that conception of the self.

We need a theory that enables us to see writing as something other than a dualistic act of communicating a subject matter that is external to the writer. A theory of writing as a way of being can help us accomplish that goal. It can illuminate how the experience of writing shapes our conception of ourselves and our ways of living together on the earth. It can enable us to see the role of writing in our ways of being as our prevailing theories do not. And it can help expose the Cartesian dualisms that have defined ways of being in the world that have led to the crisis of sustainability. In this sense, a theory of writing as a way of being might also help us *be* differently.

ENDNOTES

1. Although experts disagree about whether the provisions of the Kyoto Protocols and follow-up international agreements will actually achieve the goal of reducing greenhouse gas emissions, all but a few of the world's industrialized nations signed the Kyoto Protocols in 1997. The United States was not among the signers, although, as many critics have pointed out, the United States, which has 5 percent of the world's population, remains the world's largest producer of

greenhouse gases, although in recent years China seems to be vying for that dubious honor (see Graham and Fagotto; Raupach et al.).

2. For a review and critique of the College Board's own studies of predictive validity, see NCTE Task Force, "The Impact of the SAT and ACT Timed Writing Tests."

3. For example, see also Graham and Perin, *Writing Next*.

4. In April 2005, one month after the College Board administered its new version of the SAT for the first time, the National Council of Teachers of English (NCTE) released a report of a special task force on the SAT and ACT writing tests. I was chair of the task force, which examined the new timed essay portion of the SAT as well as the ACT timed writing test and evaluated the claims made for these tests by their authoring organizations. The NCTE task force reviewed studies conducted by the College Board to support its claims about the validity of the test. The results of the task force's study are available in its report, "The Impact of the SAT and ACT Writing Tests." After the release of the report, articles about the new SAT appeared in numerous regional and national publications, including *The New York Times*, *USA Today*, *The Chronicle of Higher Education*, and *Education Week*. Many of these articles included criticisms of the new SAT by the NCTE task force as well as the College Board's responses to these criticisms. Several task force members (including me) as well as NCTE officials were interviewed by reporters, and articles about the "controversy" continued to appear for several months after the release of the task force report.

5. See Hillocks, *The Testing Trap*, for an analysis of the proliferation of state-mandated writing tests. Although Hillocks does not link the increase in state writing tests directly to the federal NCLB program, other observers have shown that NCLB, which requires schools and districts to show "adequate yearly progress" in several subjects, including English Language Arts, has prompted states to increase their uses of standardized tests to measure student progress. See Lynn Olson, "State Test Programs Mushroom as NCLB Mandate Kicks In."

6. In 2007, the debates surrounding the reauthorization of the Bush Administration's NCLB education reform program tended to focus on two issues: first, the definition of "adequate yearly progress" that schools are required to make, which is determined almost exclusively by standardized test scores; and second, the authority of the federal government to impose educational standards on the states.

In 2006 the U.S. Department of Education released the so-called Spellings Report, which warned that American postsecondary education has not fulfilled its promise as a vehicle for social mobility and economic competitiveness. In the report, postsecondary education, described as "increasingly vital to an individual's economic security" (x), is compared to a flagging business enterprise in need of revitalization; little attention is paid to other purposes of postsecondary education, such as educating citizens for democracy, and no mention is made of the connection between education and the nation's social and environmental well-being (U.S. Department of Education, *A Test of Leadership*).

As I noted earlier, in *The Neglected 'R': The Need for a Writing Revolution in America's Schools and Colleges*, the National Commission on Writing explicitly cited the nation's economic growth as the primary justification for a "revolution" in writing instruction. Although the report offers a complex view of writing as inquiry and social engagement, it defines the purposes of writing instruction in terms of the nation's economic health.

The debates surrounding President Barack Obama's "Race to the Top" education reform initiative in 2009 and 2010 reflected this same focus on economic concerns. Matt Miller, a columnist for *The Washington Post*, offered a typical perspective in a commentary about the program that was published in 2010: "[T]he real race we're in is not a 'race to the top' within the United States but a race to maintain middle-class living standards in a world where rising, hungry powers such as China and India now threaten them. It's a race against other advanced nations whose school systems routinely outperform ours" (Miller, "Race to the Top").

In these examples, which reflect the tenor of the discourses of education reform in the United States, education is explicitly connected to maintaining a consumer-oriented capitalist economic system.

7. It has been an article of faith in the United States that economic growth, fueled by consumption, is necessary for the increased prosperity that Americans and the citizens of other developed nations enjoy. However, this unquestioned belief in consumption has come under increased scrutiny as pressure on the land and on natural resources has intensified in the wake of globalization. See, for example, Benjamin Friedman, *The Moral Consequences of Economic Growth*, in which Friedman, an unabashed proponent of economic growth as a means to improving society, acknowledges the need for strict environmental policy and greater efficiency in using natural resources, measures that he acknowledges may necessarily inhibit economic growth. See also Bill McKibben, *Deep Economy: The Wealth of Communities and the Durable Future*. McKibben argues for a zero-growth economy on the basis of the contention that continued growth at current rates will lead to greater inequality and insecurity.

8. The size of the average American house has increased inexorably in the past half century. In 1950 the average American family home had 290 square feet per person living there. In 2003 the average home had 900 square feet per person. In 1970 the National Association of Home Builders did not keep statistics on the number of homes with three bathrooms because such homes were so rare; by 2005, one out of four new houses had three or more bathrooms. See Cox, "Big Houses Are Not Green."

9. On its Web site, the College Board provides a great deal of information about its writing tests for students preparing to take the SAT. As I was finishing this manuscript in winter 2011, those materials were essentially the same as what Josh encountered as he prepared for the exam in 2007. See http://sat.college-board.com/practice/writing-sat-essay

10. Here is the essay in its entirety (available at http://sat.collegeboard.com/practice/writing-sat-essay?pageId=practiceWritingEssay&tabValue=scoring):

Memories and past experiences serve as a rail, a guiding support, for people in an effort to succeed in the present. People not only learn from the past, but the very act of going through something provides experience for a person who is to "move up the ladder of success and achievement."

Some view failed experiences as a hinderance to future success. This is very untrue because history has a tendency of repeating itself, and in recognizing past failures, one can learn how to successfully approach similar situations in the future. An example of this is looking back in history to World War I. Sedition acts at this time allowed for the imprisonment of anyone who voiced an opinion against the president, or against the war. America recognized this shady time in its past, and instead of covering it up in a movement toward a more democratic nation, these acts were published in textbooks and taught to students. Americans saw the poor judgement of this situation and later with the war in Iraq, approached "patriotism" differently. With this present war, those adverse to the war are able to voice their opinions without fear of imprisonment or death. In seeing the undemocratic ways of an earlier era, America was able to recognize the bad and try to reform it. If the Sedition Acts had been forgotten then what is to say that they wouldn't come back? Remembering the failed times insures that improvement is possible.

In my personal experience, I have found that the very act of living through something not only matures me, but also provides skills and knowledge. In remembering past events, I am able to use them as reference, and sometimes assurance. A personal example, somewhat juvenile, but also effective, is when my first pet died. I was devastated and wanted to just clear my mind of the event, but I didn't. After time, I recovered, but maintained the memory of this horrible tragedy. Later in life, another pet died. I looked back to that memory as a guide and learned from it that in time I would be fine and to just hang on. In this situation, a memory served as a reference and catalyzed in my personal growth and recovery.

Memories, good or bad, assist people in obtaining success. Whether used as reference for guidance, or lessons on what not to do, past experiences can only offer a gap between the steps on the ladder of success. Forgetting the past can and will only erase experience and knowledge from a person and in affect hinder one in seeking achievement. In looking at historical repeats and personal events, it is clear that old memories can only aid in success.

11. I base this claim on the few available studies of writing in secondary schools and especially on data collected as part of the National Assessment of Educational Progress (NAEP). There are precious few large-scale studies of writing instruction in schools, and those we do have are by now dated, such as Applebee's *Writing in the Secondary School* (1981) and Langer and Applebee's *How Writing Shapes Thinking* (1987). (Applebee and Langer were in the process of conducting a large-scale national study of secondary school writing instruction as I was completing this manuscript in 2010, although their full results were not available before this book went to press, preliminary studies support many of the findings of the earlier studies mentioned here.) However, every four years when the NAEP writing test is administered, survey data are collected from both students and teachers about their experiences with writing instruction in schools. These data, which are reviewed by Applebee and Langer in *The State of Writing Instruction in America's Schools*, suggest that although "process-oriented instruction had become the conventional wisdon" by 1992 (23), what students write and how they are taught have remained largely unchanged since

Applebee's 1981 study. For example, in his earlier study he noted the lack of practice students receive in various kinds of analytical writing. In a review of data from the 2004 NAEP writing test, Applebee and Langer noted that "over 40% of the students at Grade 8 and a third at Grade 12 report writing essays requiring analysis or interpretation at most a few times a year" (8). They also note that data collected between 2002 and 2005 "indicate a small but consistent reduction in the amount of time devoted to writing [in secondary schools]. . . . This decrease may be related to the increased focus on high stakes test performance, which sometimes leads to a focus on more restricted tasks" (6). My own two decades of experience with professional development in secondary schools in several different states and through the NWP supports the general conclusions that Applebee and Langer are able to draw from the NAEP data about the lack of variety in much writing instruction, the lack of practice students receive in writing extended texts, and the impact that the increased focus on standarized tests has had on writing instruction.

12. Curiously, this is true almost three decades after Robert Connors proclaimed the "fall" of the modes as reflected in the most popular composition textbooks of the late 1970s. In tracing the history of the four main discourse forms (narration, description, persuasion, and argument), Connors concludes, "Of the fifteen or so most widely-used freshman rhetoric texts, only one still advances the modal classes as absolute. Though the modes still retain a shadow of their old puissance as an organizing device in certain freshman anthologies of essays, their importance in modern pedagogy is constantly diminishing, and the only teachers still making real classroom use of the modes are those out of touch with current theory" (453). The continued strength in the sales of modes-based readers so many years after Connors' declared the modes to be "expiring" (453) suggests that they still likely play a significant role in contemporary composition instruction.

13. In a review of *Straw Dogs* for *The Guardian*, for instance, well-known literary theorist Terry Eagleton called Gray "a full-blooded apocalyptic nihilist" who "has passed from Thatcherite zest to virulent misanthropy." Like many reviewers, Eagleton cannot accept Gray's argument that humans have no greater inherent value than any other species and thus pronounces Gray's book "a dangerous, despairing book, which in a crass polarity thinks humans are either entirely distinct from bacteria (the sin of humanism) or hardly different at all" (Eagleton). Similarly, Carlin Romano's dismissal of Gray as a smug "know-it-all" who wallows in "self-indulgent apathy" seems to grow as much out of his embrace of the idea of human progress, which Gray rejects, as it does out of the contradictions and unsupported generalizations that he charges characterize Gray's writing (Romano B5). (I do not disagree entirely with either of these reviews or similar ones; I am merely offering them as support for my contention that Gray's rejection of human exceptionalism provoked a shrill response from many readers, who embrace the idea that humans are indeed exceptional.)

14. See also the Technical Summary of the IPCC's *Climate Change 2007: Impacts, Adaptation, and Vulnerability*, which examines the many different possible impacts of climate change on different regions and different sectors of human society. The report concludes that "[v]ulnerability to specific impacts of climate

change will be most severe when and where they are felt together with stresses from other sources. Non-climatic stresses can include poverty, unequal access to resources, food security, environmental degradation and risks from natural hazards" (813) For example, "adverse health impacts will be greatest in low-income countries" (393). Also, "Some poor communities and households are already under stress from climate variability and climate-related extreme events; and they can be especially vulnerable to climate change because they tend to be concentrated in relatively high risk areas, to have limited access to services and other resources for coping, and in some regions to be more dependent on climate-sensitive resources such as local water and food supplies" (46–47; available at http://www.ipcc.ch/pdf/assessment-report/ar4/wg2/ar4-wg2-ts.pdf). These assessments underscore my point earlier in this chapter that climate change is a social problem. For an overview, see Revkin.

15. See *Digest of Education Statistics, 2009,* Table 6, National Center for Education Statistics (http://nces.ed.gov/programs/digest/d09/tables/dt09_006.asp?referrer=list). Nationwide, school attendance for children ages 5–15 is virtually university (approximately 98 percent); for adolescents ages 16–17, it drops slightly to 95 percent. Approximately 62 percent of high school graduates attend postsecondary schools (*Digest of Education Statistics, 2009,* Table 203 (http://nces.ed.gov/programs/digest/d09/tables/dt09_203.asp?referrer=list). For further discussion of these figures, see footnote 7 in Chapter 5.

2

THE CARTESIAN VIEW OF WRITING

Jack was unusual among the students in the master's program in general education studies in my department at the State University of New York (SUNY) at Albany. Most students in the program are either practicing teachers seeking to retain their state certification or career-switchers seeking certification to teach. Jack, however, was explicit—and passionate—about his interest in studying rhetoric and composition and, more specifically, critical pedagogy. Typically, a student with those interests would enroll in the master's program in English, the traditional institutional home of Composition Studies. But Jack, who entered our program in fall 2007, already had a master's in English. A degree in education, he believed, would enable him to learn more about pedagogy, something he felt he was lacking after a year of teaching basic writing as an adjunct at the City University of New York (CUNY). That experience not only enflamed Jack's already intense passion about teaching students who were labeled "remedial" by their institutions but also convinced him that he was ill prepared to help those students. His willingness to address his self-perceived limitations as a teacher stood out among the other 20-somethings I regularly encounter in our program, mostly hard-working and academically successful students whose embrace of cultural myths about education tends to discourage them from asking the kinds of hard questions that preoccupied Jack.

During his first semester in our program, I supervised Jack's independent study of critical pedagogy, a topic he could not find among available courses on campus. During our biweekly meetings, he would express frustration about his classmates' seemingly uncritical acceptance of the educational status quo, and he complained about what he saw as the diminishing interest in critical pedagogy in the field of Composition Studies. In one of his papers, he wrote of the stigma that he felt was "attached to associating oneself with critical pedagogy" (Morales). "There is an overwhelming sense," he continued, "that to speak of the place of politics in education is to commit an unforgivable offense." He cited an essay in which Stanley Fish admonished college professors to "teach their subjects" (Fish did not use the term *subjects* in a postmodern sense), and he referred to academic journal articles that seemed to share Fish's sentiment (Fish, "Save the World"). Throughout that academic year, Jack wrestled with the question of whether Composition Studies' apparent embrace of Paulo Freire's liberatory pedagogy was something more than just the field "trying to assert its identity." Reviewing the scholarship on critical pedagogy since Freire's death in 1997 (e.g., Durst; Greenbaum; J. Hardin; R. Miller; Ronald and Roskelly), Jack concluded, reluctantly, that Composition Studies had abandoned critical pedagogy in favor of what he called a liberal pragmatism, a kind of loyal opposition to the institutional status quo. This development dismayed him, because it suggested that the field had narrowed its sense of the aims of writing instruction to method.

My conversations with Jack in 2007 and 2008 took me back to my own first years as a graduate student in the early 1980s, when I was caught up in the heady sense that Composition Studies was emerging as an exciting academic discipline. The teaching of writing, it seemed to me, was being transformed by visionaries like Donald Murray and Peter Elbow and by groundbreaking researchers like Linda Flower. As someone who had earned a partial living as a freelance writer, I found it easy to embrace Murray's argument that we should teach writing based on how writers write. Murray was still in his prime when I was a teaching assistant in the program he built at the University of New Hampshire (UNH), and I enthusiastically adopted his approach. Teaching writing to first-year students was challenging, yes, but I accepted that challenge with a fervor born of the belief that we writing teachers were doing good work in the interests of the student writers sitting before us.

Unlike Jack, I was slow to see my classroom as part of a vexed history of writing instruction, inextricably connected to social, cultural, and economic developments that helped shape the program I taught in, the field I was seeking to enter, the pedagogy I was learning, and indeed the world we live in. Like the other instructors on the UNH composition staff, I strove to make my classroom an energizing but relatively safe space for my student writers. I did not understand that the safety of my classroom, such as it was, resulted less from my efforts to employ a student-centered pedagogy than from my own blissful lack of attention to these larger connections. Like many other aspiring writing teachers energized by Murray's process-oriented ideas, I was blind to the political genesis of his pedagogy, and so I remained focused on method: the writing workshops and one-on-one conferences and freewriting exercises that characterize the process approach to writing instruction and seemed so effective in getting students to do the hard work of learning to write. It wasn't until a few years later that I came across Murray's essay "Teaching Writing in an Age of Dissent," which places his pedagogy in political and historical context.[1] By then I had finished the program at UNH and I was trying to adapt Murray's techniques to my English classes in the independent high school where I was teaching. My experiences there led me to question what I was hoping to accomplish in my classroom, and I was starting to feel the same kind of uneasiness that Jack would feel in his first year as an adjunct instructor at CUNY so many years later.

My struggles to formulate a workable pedagogy consistent with my evolving sense of the larger purposes of writing instruction eventually led me to Freire. Like Jack, I encountered Freire early on, although the little of Freire's work I read initially had little impact on my teaching. While at UNH, I overheard some doctoral students discussing, almost in reverential terms, Freire's *Pedagogy of the Oppressed*, and I picked up a copy soon after. Laboring through the book, I was alternately excited and confused, understanding little of the theory and philosophy that were the foundation of Freire's critique of conventional education. But his famous banking metaphor resonated with me. I knew nothing about Hegelian dialectic or Marxist theory, which deeply inform Freire's problem-posing pedagogy, but I highlighted lengthy sections of the book that seemed to describe a truly empowering way to teach. As I gained more experience and continued to wrestle with increasingly complicated questions about education, I returned time and again to Freire for guidance. Slowly I tried to incorporate his ideas into my classroom, adjusting my Murray-esque techniques accordingly. My assignments evolved into versions of Freire's belief that we must start with the material conditions of our students' lives, and I developed my own approach to identifying the "limit-situations" that Freire uses as the starting point for his problem-posing pedagogy (Freire, *Pedagogy of the Oppressed* 99). These became the focus of my attempt to foster in students what I understood as the critical consciousness that Freire believed was necessary for humanization. Semester after semester, my efforts led to the mixed results so well documented in the professional literature (e.g., Ellsworth; Tassoni and Thelin).

Undaunted, I remained committed to the belief that teaching writing should foster good, that it should result not only in benefit for students but betterment for all. So I continued to wrestle Freire's rich, round ideas into the squared-off confines of my classroom. Only after many more years of teaching, in both high school and college classrooms, did I begin to see that Freire's liberatory approach, no matter how much it might energize my own teaching, was ultimately ineffective because it remained in that box that my classroom would always be. In her critical study of the administration of schools, Linda McNeil describes the "loosely coupled" organizational structure of schooling (which some critics have called the "egg carton" structure of schooling; see Goodlad 374). In such a structure, teachers and administrators function semi-autonomously but administrators retain their status as teachers' superiors (McNeil 21). My struggles to develop a Freirean pedagogy helped me appreciate the genius of this industrial structure of schooling as a way to maintain control. Freire's banking metaphor didn't completely capture what McNeil's research reveals: that the organization of schooling helps perpetuate the educational status quo by isolating teachers but still relying on their commitment to their students. In this way, student-centered pedagogies may energize individual teachers and transform individual classrooms, but such pedagogies do not threaten the status quo and may in fact strengthen it by allowing those individual teachers to feel that they are making a difference for their students without effecting any broader systemic change. It simply wasn't enough, I began to conclude, to embrace Murray's student-centered pedagogy or to adapt Freire's liberatory method in my own classroom.

By the time I met Jack, I was on record as unapologetically Utopian in my belief that education has a progressive social mission and that English, and particularly writing instruction, should be at the center of that mission.[2] So Jack's agonizing about the purposes of writing instruction was more to me than just another sobering example of a bright and earnest young teacher coming to understand the sometimes overwhelming complexities of education. In him I could see my own ongoing struggle to enact the progressive vision that has always driven my sense of the importance of writing instruction. It was all the more dismaying to see this passionate, promising young scholar-to-be slipping so soon into resignation as he surveyed the academic field he had chosen to enter and saw it, in his mind, capitulating to a deeply troubling status quo.

I'm not sure the field of Composition Studies *has* capitulated in quite the way Jack believed, but it certainly seems less enamored of the liberatory possibilities of literacy today than it felt to me in the 1980s. I don't believe that's necessarily because the field has narrowed its focus to method in the interest of gaining institutional legitimacy, as Jack argues, though I do think there is merit to that argument. No doubt the field's maturation and its now well-established place in the academy have shaped its debates about the purposes of writing instruction and, more specifically, the role of first-year composition. The field today is the establishment in ways it has never been. But if Composition Studies now seems more comfortable as part of the educational status quo, it isn't necessarily because those of us teaching composition have become completely consumed by our roles as "boss compositionists"[3] or have given up the good fight that Jack sees himself fighting on behalf of his students; rather, it is, I believe, because our writing theories and pedagogies and the programs based on them continue to be driven by a Cartesian view of writing that serves the status quo that many of us seek to change.

My purpose in this chapter is to expose the Cartesian view of writing as an obstacle to change, both in the teaching of writing as an academic discipline and in terms of the broader sense of education as a vehicle for social change. Because it continues to work within a Cartesian view of writing, Composition Studies plays a central role in an educational status quo that, as I explained in Chapter 1, is implicated in the crisis of sustainability. In exploring this role, I argue that the field's debates about critical pedagogy and the purposes of writing instruction are part of the larger ongoing struggle over the purposes of education in American society. Implicit in this argument is the belief that writing instruction *should* serve progressive ends. I also examine the current state of writing theory in Composition Studies, focusing on the recent emergence of post-process theory. The debates about whether the field has moved "beyond process" are important for two reasons. First, they are part of the field's continuing struggle to define itself and to identify a direction for its scholarship. Second, these debates about the writing process can bring into relief the Cartesian view of writing that continues to be the basis of our prevailing understanding of writing and pedagogy. Despite differences among the various approaches to writing instruction, and despite the effort by post-process theorists to redefine writing theory and pedagogy, writing continues to be broadly understood within a Cartesian framework. My contention is that this prevailing Cartesian view of writing is a primary reason that the robust debates about what Lester Faigley once called the "competing theories of process" seem to have had so little effect on mainstream writing instruction. Post-process theorists make a compelling case for rethinking our understanding of writing, but the Cartesian view of writing prevents change on this front. More important, we will have to move beyond this view if writing instruction is to become part of a larger project of imagining and creating a just and sustainable future.

REVISITING THE CARTESIAN VIEW OF WRITING

The Cartesian view of writing is much like Poe's purloined letter: hiding in plain sight and obscured by its ordinariness. But it is not difficult to see in our classrooms.

Except for the startling cleanliness of its corridors and rooms, Canajoharie High School, with its big-box architectural style, looks like just about every other school I've ever visited. But the building's symmetrical lines, perfect brick facade, and glimmering metal trim look out of place on the hillside above the town of Canajoharie, which sits in sullen industrial decline along the banks of the Great Erie Canal in upstate New York. Kristen Montgomery, an earnest young English teacher, has invited me to work with her students on their latest writing assignment, a profile of a resident of "Canjo." Kristen devised the assignment as a way for her students to examine the history of their town through the personal story of an elderly relative or acquaintance. She hopes the assignment will help make writing more relevant to her students than the conventional assignments that, she says, routinely bore them.

The dozen seniors in Kristen's class sit in a semi-circle in her tidy classroom. We are discussing Karen's profile of her grandmother, who was born and raised in Canajoharie and spent much of her adult life working at the giant Beechnut factory that defines the town's modest skyline and looms over the canal alongside the crumbling downtown. In her draft, Karen describes her grandmother's childhood on a farm outside of town and the excitement her grandmother felt about working in the Beechnut factory mailroom as a young woman. She reveals that her grandmother's dream was to visit Arkansas, a detail that seems to say much more about her grandmother than do the many biographical facts in the draft. As I read it, Karen's draft offers provocative glimpses of a young woman whose world was defined by that hulking factory and the mental and physical confines of a tiny canal town that seems so far from anywhere else. I ask Karen about these sections of her essay, and she dutifully shares a few more details about her grandmother's early life. But most of what seems to lie tantalizingly beneath the surface of her description of her grandmother seems invisible to Karen.

Doing my best to draw the other students into the conversation, I share the possibilities I see in Karen's draft: what her grandmother's story reveals about how we live together in our communities, about how our lives can be defined by operations like a factory or a family farm, about how we relate to the landscape that is part of who we are, about choices that lead to a life spent entirely in a small town. But like her classmates, Karen seems unable or unwilling to imagine these possibilities. She listens deferentially to my comments, but instead of writing her way into her grandmother's (and thus her own) world, she wants to know where to "develop" her description of her grandmother, which sections of her essay to condense or delete, how to organize her chronology of her grandmother's life, whether this sentence or that is "clear." She and her classmates, like their teachers, are comfortable with this way of talking about their writing, because that is generally how we talk about writing in schools and encode it in our textbooks and tests (as I discussed in Chapter 1). We zero in on textual features as if the writing were not really about anything, as if Karen's writing is not about her grand-mother at all, as if it has nothing really to do with the ground on which we are all sitting at that very moment, a few miles from the factory that shad-ows the unnaturally straight canal running alongside the town where Karen's grandmother spent her life—as if that ground and the people living on it were abstractions.

And they *are* abstractions. That is precisely the point. One of the great powers of writing is its capacity to abstract—to separate speech from the speaker, writer from writing, and both writer and writing from place. As Marshall McLuhan, Eric Havelock, and Walter Ong famously theorized, writing is a technology that transforms the spoken word into visual form and makes it possible for that word to be transported across time and space. In this way, writing enacts the Cartesian mind–body split by making the body irrelevant to the words the body produces. In this formulation, those words are the product of the mind, which is understood to be separate from the body and the physical world. Writing is thus an expression of Cartesian ontology. It is a physical artifact of the Cartesian self declaring itself to be and defining itself as metaphysical entity. Writing is a visual, tangible record of the abstract, metaphysical being that we become as writers. It is a concrete reminder of what Descartes believed: that thinking is what makes us who we are.

Although this "strong text" view of writing associated with Ong and others has been vigorously critiqued and our sense of the role of social and cultural context in writing is now much more nuanced than what Ong sug-gested (see Brandt), the fundamental components of this view of writing remain intact in mainstream writing pedagogies, in conventional schooling, and in the culture more generally. There are three such components: an understanding of language as a relatively unproblematic conduit for thought; an essentially positivist conception of knowledge as separate from the knower; and a sense of the self as an autonomous, thinking being.

As I noted in Chapter 1, the understanding of language as a conduit for meaning and a vehicle for thought continues to inform common conceptions of "good" writing, especially as those conceptions are reflected in standard-ized tests, educational standards, and pedagogical techniques. This under-standing of writing is related to the positivist epistemology that is built into the conventional curriculum at all levels of education. Within this epistemology, the world exists "outside" us, and knowledge is a function of our efforts to describe that world. Language is the means for describing the world but, as a conduit for thought, it cannot be the source of knowledge. So writing becomes a technology for communication, not a means of inquiry or an act of knowledge-making. To employ this technology as a means of communicating requires adherence to convention. In mainstream schooling, to write is to apply convention for the purposes of conveying knowledge. Knowledge (content) is thus fundamentally separate from writing itself. Kristen's students write *about* their community; the act of writing is a matter of fitting their knowledge of their community into the appropriate textual form according to the conventions of written discourse. The same is true of almost all school-sponsored writing.

Although Kristen's assignment for her students is ostensibly about their hometown of Canajoharie, their writing has nothing substantively to do with Canajoharie—or any other place. Within the context of schooling, the assignment's only real purpose is to demonstrate a certain (limited) kind of writing competence and an ability to apply the conventions of academic writing. What students actually write about is tangential to their ability to produce a sanctioned form according to the criteria for "good" writing that I examined in Chapter 1. Kristen's admirable goal of encouraging students to write about something that matters in their lives is largely irrelevant to the primary goal of teaching students the conventions of writing. By the time they move into college classrooms, the students have already learned that their school-sponsored writing has no significant purpose outside the classroom and is relevant only to the extent that it earns them academic credit. In this regard, Kristen's students might as well be writing about Tanzania or Amsterdam. The act would be the same, because it has nothing to do with any place. It is an act of separation from place.

This idea of separation points to the third feature of the Cartesian view of writing: the conception of the writerly self as an autonomous, thinking being existing separately from other beings and the wider world. This idea of the self is central to my analysis of contemporary theories and pedagogies of writing in the rest of this chapter. In effect, the Cartesian view of writing rests on a set of ontological assumptions that inform the mainstream view of the writer. Among these assumptions are the fundamental dualities that distinguish the Cartesian worldview: subject as separate from object, mind from body, self from other. These dualities are understood hierarchically, so that mind supersedes body. It is intellect that matters: The writer in the Cartesian view is fundamentally a metaphysical entity.

These three assumptions, then, constitute the basis of the Cartesian view of writing. First, language, including written language, is a largely unproblematic conduit for meaning. Second, knowledge exists separately from us and is essentially a function of a reality that is external to us. Third, the writerly self is based on a Cartesian conception of the self as an autonomous, thinking being. Although few scholars in Composition Studies today would embrace these assumptions, they continue to inform mainstream education, and as I show here, the Cartesian conception of self remains central to our understanding of the writing process. Despite the dramatic theoretical developments in the last century that have profoundly reshaped our collective thinking about language, literacy, knowledge-making, and subjectivity, we inhabit a status quo that continues to be driven by a Cartesian worldview. And the teaching of writing is an integral part of that status quo.

THE STATUS QUO AND THE PURPOSES OF WRITING INSTRUCTION

In 1992, Maxine Hairston created a stir with her article "Diversity, Ideology, and the Teaching of Writing," in which she warned about an emerging model for first-year composition that "envisions required writing courses as vehicles for social reform rather than as student-centered workshops designed to build students' confidence and competence as writers" (180). Hairston decried this apparent politicizing of the writing classroom, which she attributed to the "cultural left suddenly claim[ing] writing courses as their political territory" (183). Interestingly (although perhaps not surprisingly, given the contentious history of rhetoric and composition in English departments), Hairston saw this development as an effort by composition-ists to claim academic respectability within English departments that are populated by (as she saw it) literary critics enamored of "fashionable" theories like poststructuralism, deconstruction, and Marxism. And although she admitted to being "sick over the condition of our country" and shared the desire to "to bring about a fairer, more compassionate society" (187), she argued forcefully that "as writing teachers we should stay within our area of professional expertise: helping students to learn to write in order to learn, to explore, to communicate, to gain control over their lives. That's a large responsibility, and all that most of us can manage. We have no business getting into areas where we may have passion and conviction but no scholarly base from which to operate" (186). She advocated "a student-centered classroom in which the teacher doesn't assume, as our would-be forcers of conscience do, that he or she owns the truth. Rather the students bring their own truths, and the teacher's role is to nurture change and growth as students encounter individual differences" (192). From such a classroom, Hairston argued, "students can emerge with confidence in their ability to think, to generate ideas, and to present themselves effectively to the university and the community" (192). To put this point in different terms, students can take their places in the status quo for which they have been competently prepared.

Implicit in Hairston's diatribe against the "radical few" who she believed were taking over first-year composition courses is a widely held view of schooling as an inherent good and an integral part of a status quo that is fundamentally acceptable—our wishes for "a fairer, more compassionate society" notwithstanding. Schooling has always been a political battleground, but those battles have tended to be about how best to prepare students for the world we know. From the very beginnings of mass schooling in the United States, cycles of reform have left schools essentially unchanged. That's because most school reform is an effort to make schooling as we know it "better" rather than different—that is, to make it more like it already is rather than change it in any fundamental way. Most school reform tends to rest on the assumption that the primary purpose of schooling is maintaining a more or less "good" status quo, which in more concrete terms is our market-based, consumer-oriented capitalist economic system and its related democratic political system. We may need to make this system fairer and more compassionate, but its foundations—individualism, consumerism, and democracy—are generally assumed to be sound.

Efforts to reform literacy education and writing instruction are driven by this same assumption. For example, in its high-profile report *The Neglected 'R': The Need for a Writing Revolution in America's Schools and Colleges*, the National Commission on Writing warns that "American education will never realize its potential as an engine of opportunity and economic growth until a writing revolution puts language and communication in their proper place in the classroom" (3). Such an exhortation overtly connects writing instruction to the economy: We teach writing in order to help our students eventually make the economy work better. The idea of economic growth, not justice or equity or tolerance (although these are sometimes invoked), is assumed to be at the center of schooling's mission. Economic growth—and, by extension, the consumer-oriented economic system in general—is never questioned as a desirable goal. Few would reject the idea that effective writing instruction is necessary for educational success and therefore connected to America's economic well-being, but the NCW's call for a writing "revolution" seems disingenuous, since it envisions no fundamental change in anything but curriculum and pedagogy—not in the structures or purposes of schooling or in the larger society of which schooling is a part. The NCW's unquestioned connection between formal education and our capitalist economic system implicitly rejects the possibility that writing instruction—and education more generally—can serve larger progressive or even Utopian ends that may diverge from the values of a consumer-driven culture. Although *The Neglected 'R'* acknowledges other traditional justifications for writing instruction, it subordinates these to the seemingly paramount economic mission of writing instruction.

The rather conservative perspective on education that informs the NCW's reports seems to be widely shared among educators at all levels. The vast majority of teachers and administrators I work with accept as self-evident the assumption that schooling is ultimately about preparing students for the job market—so much so that this assumption usually is beyond question. Like Hairston, these educators often are genuinely "sick over the condition of our country," worried about racism, sexism, and (these days) global warming, among other such ills. But like Hairston, they also assume the classroom to be a relatively safe, more-or-less neutral space within which students prepare to meet the challenges such ills present within a status quo that seems fundamentally right. Like Hairston, they see their role as helping prepare students for that status quo, not changing it. "Radical" is not a label most educators I know would willingly embrace.

Hairston's challenge to "radical" composition scholars came at a time when the field of Composition Studies seemed to be moving toward a consensus that writing is an inherently social activity by which identities are constructed and through which agency can be claimed in a postmodern world characterized by unequal power relations and struggles over meanings. The scholars she criticized—Bizzell, Knoblauch, Berlin, Trimbur, Ohmann, among others—generally reject the view that their role as writing teachers is to prepare students for the society we know; rather, they espouse various versions of a progressive vision of education as a vehicle for social change. I recall Richard Ohmann's keynote address at the 1989 Penn State Conference on Rhetoric, a pointed critique of President George H. W. Bush's "thousand points of light" education policy. Few in that audience would have rejected Ohmann's talk as inappropriate for a gathering that was ostensibly focused on the scholarship of teaching writing. In that regard, Ohmann, Berlin, Bizzell, and the other "radicals" Hairston criticized are heirs to a tradition of American progressive education that stretches back even before John Dewey, the often cited "father" of progressivism, for whom the connection between education and a healthy democracy was self-evident. In a sense, Hairston redrew battle lines that Ohmann described fifteen years earlier in his seminal *English in America*, which cast college English and first-year composition programs essentially as elements of the military-industrial complex and issued a stirring call-to-arms for academics to join a revolutionary effort to change what he described as a corrupt and oppressive political and economic system. As Ohmann acknowledged in a 2002 essay, the battle over the purposes of English education that he joined in the 1960s and 1970s goes on, changed somewhat by globalization and a new geopolitical world order but ongoing nonetheless (Ohmann "Afterword"). Indeed, the debate about the purposes of writing instruction that Hairston energized in the 1990s was Composition Studies' version of the larger, never-ending debate in American society about the purposes of education in general—a debate the field largely seems to have lost interest in today.

More than thirty years ago, sociologists Samuel Bowles and Herbert Gintis, in their famous critique of American education, *Schooling in Capitalist America*, "advanced the position that schools prepare people for adult work rules, by socializing people to function well, and without complaint, in the hierarchical structure of the modern corporation. Schools accomplish this by . . . structuring social interactions and individual rewards to replicate the environment of the workplace" ("Revisited" 1). In their study, Bowles and Gintis analyzed statistical data to show that "the United States fell far short of the goal of equal economic opportunity and that genetic inheritance of cognitive skill—as measured on standard tests— explains only a small part of the intergenerational persistence of status within families" (2). Their research suggested that "the evolution of the modern school system is not accounted for by the gradual perfection of a democratic or pedagogical ideal" but emerged from "the transformation of the social organization of work and the distribution of its rewards" such that "the interests of the owners of the leading businesses tended to predominate but were rarely uncontested" (2). Schooling, in other words, did not lead to a more just and equitable social order; instead, it served the purposes of the few who, for the most part, controlled capital. Bowles and Gintis gave the lie to the widespread American faith in education as a means to a better life. They showed that the fervent belief in the economic rewards of hard work and self-discipline is part of a value system that ultimately benefits those who manage the economy, despite data showing a correlation between schooling and income. Their analyses reveal that while schooling can indeed improve the lot of some, in general it tends to help maintain a stratified system whose hierarchical structure enables those already in positions of economic power to thrive.

In 2002, Bowles and Gintis used newer data to re-examine this connection and concluded that

> [i]n light of the outpouring of quantitative research on schooling and inequality in the intervening years, the statistical claims of the book [*Schooling in Capitalist America*] have held up remarkably well. In particular, recent research by us and others using far better data than were available in the early 70s has entirely vindicated our once-controversial estimates of high levels of intergenerational persistence of economic status, the unimportance of the heritability of IQ in this process, and the fact that the contribution of schooling to cognitive development plays little part in explaining why those with more schooling have higher earnings. ("Revisited" 2)

To put it more plainly, Bowles and Gintis's original conclusion that schooling seems to have little impact on the socioeconomic status of most students—that it helps maintain an already stratified status quo—was reaffirmed. As they put it, "In the United States, knowing the income or wealth of someone's parents is about as informative about the person's own economic status as is the person's own years of schooling attained, or score on a standardized cognitive test" (3). Family wealth is as good or better a predictor of a student's future wealth as educational attainment. In fact, educational attainment is predicted by family wealth. Students from wealthier families tend to have both higher levels of educational attainment and higher incomes than students from lower socioeconomic groups. In general, schooling doesn't change that dynamic.

What Bowles and Gintis call "intergenerational persistence of economic status" has been supported by other recent studies, which, according to a 2008 report by the Brookings Institution and the Pew Charitable Trusts, "suggest that there is less economic mobility in the United States than has long been presumed" (Sawhill and Morton 1). The authors of that same report show that "income inequality has been widening for nearly three decades in the United States" (3), that "absolute [economic] mobility is declining for a significant group of Americans" (5), and that family income growth has slowed (6). In that same time period, overall wealth has increased, but the proportion of that wealth held by those in the highest income brackets also has increased. The rich get richer, as the saying goes.[4] These data suggest that the raging success of capitalism during this period has not necessarily resulted in widespread improvement in the material lives of most of us—at least not in terms of the primary measure of well-being in our economic system: wealth.

In their retrospective essay on *Schooling in Capitalist America*, Bowles and Gintis also noted, "The same conflict-ridden evolution of the structure and purposes of education was strikingly evident in higher education at the time we wrote *Schooling in Capitalist America*, and we devoted a chapter to what we termed the contradictions of higher education" (2). In their view, higher education is just as fully implicated in maintaining the socioeconomic order as is K–12 schooling. More than three decades after they published their original study, their conclusions seem even more apt as public higher education is becoming increasingly privatized in ways that they could not have anticipated in the 1970s. Indeed, the sense of the mission of public higher education as a vehicle for social mobility that emerged in the wake of the G.I. Bill after World War II has given way to a market-oriented vision. Despite well-publicized efforts by the nation's most elite institutions in 2007 and 2008 to make themselves more accessible to low-income students, the median income of students attending college has risen in the past three decades and is now well above the national median.[5] Postsecondary institutions now seem ever more fully integrated into the emerging monolith of global capitalism. And given the now well-established role of the required composition course as a mainstay of the general education curriculum in most colleges and universities, it would seem that writing instruction also is configured to serve the interests of the corporate capitalist state.

It's hard to know whether most writing teachers and scholars would assent to such a statement, but even if they would, there is apparently little agreement on what to do about it, if anything. Hairston's plea to leave politics out of the composition classroom would very likely seem reasonable to many practitioners in the field today, even as a review of major journals and recent conference programs makes it clear that the views of "radicals" like Bizzell and Trimbur and Berlin live on. For all the attention composition scholars devote to issues of power and identity and social justice, the field seems to have developed a silent consensus about why we teach writing that diverges from the concerns addressed in much of its scholarship. Many compositionists continue to embrace a progressive vision for their work, and the field often seems uneasy about its increasingly entrenched place in the institutional status quo (an uneasiness evident in the sustained—and warranted—attention to the exploitation of part-time or contingent composition faculty). Yet as Jack detected in the scholarship on critical pedagogy, many compositionists seem just as uneasy about heeding the call of those "radicals." Thus, Richard Miller's complaints about the field's puzzling (to him) embrace of a Freirean sense of mission and the liberatory possibilities of pedagogy seem as fresh today as when he first published them more than a decade ago. As paeans to Freire's influence appeared after his death in 1997 (see, e.g., the "special cluster in memory of Paulo Freire" in *Journal of Advanced Composition*, vol. 17.1), Miller wondered about the appeal of a pedagogical approach whose "inutility" he claims had long been demonstrated "by our own experiences" (12). Noting that Freire's critique casts educators as most likely to suffer from the very same false consciousness that they seek to combat in their students, Miller asks, "Why, as a profession, would we be drawn to an approach that depicts professionals in such a negative light?" (15). He ultimately concludes that "however tempting it may be to describe our work as teachers as being pursued in the interests of 'liberation' or 'consciousness-raising' or 'resistance,' the truth is that this [critical pedagogy's] rhetoric's appeal is so attractive because it covers over our more primary role as functionaries of the administration's educational arm" (18). If that conclusion feels unsatisfying, it probably reflects the sense of many in the field about what is—and is *not*—possible through the teaching of writing. Indeed, the field seems to have accepted Miller's view that our primary role "as teachers who have years of experience in this frequently capricious and indifferent system" is "to assist our students in acquiring the skills necessary for persisting in the ongoing project of navigating life in a bureaucracy" (27).

I find it hard to argue with Miller that "between the poles of these two representations of schooling as either radically liberating and empowering or ceaselessly oppressive and instrumentalist, one finds a vast, unexplored territory—the fraught, compromised world where all of our classes are actually convened" (23). And I can even follow him where he goes next: In order for students to "formulate a more nuanced understanding of how power gets exercised in the social sphere,"

> we must provide them with opportunities to discover the virtues of discursive versatility, by which I mean the ability to speak, read, and write persuasively across a wide range of social contexts. Lest this sound like a refurbished but thinly disguised call to renew our commitment to rhetorical instruction, let me make clear that I am interested in promoting a fluency in the languages of the bureaucratic systems that regulate all our lives; a familiarity with the logics, styles of argumentation, repositories of evidence deployed by these organizational bodies; a fuller understanding of what can and cannot be gained through discursive exchanges, with a concomitant recalibration of the horizon of expectations. (23)

But Miller seems content to stop there, pragmatically (as I think he would say) arguing that that is perhaps the limit of what is possible for us to achieve: teaching students "how to work within and against discursive constraints simultaneously, thereby helping them to experience the mediated access to 'authenticity' that social action allows" (27). Such a goal seems consistent with Joe Hardin's provocative argument in favor of a critical pedagogy that does not "see itself as the emancipator of students" but rather "empowers students to articulate their own values through the conventions of cultural, academic, and disciplinary rhetoric once those conventions are demonstrated to be powerful, available, and useful" (5). Acknowledging that such a goal will not "necessarily produce supporters of the kind of social justice Freire envisions," Miller proposes "the more modest goal" of providing students "the opportunity to speak, read, and write in a wider range of discursive contexts than is available to them when they labor under the codes of silence and manufactured consent that serve to define the lived experience of subordinates in the culture of schooling" (27). That goal is itself ambitious and, I daresay, even noble. And it is, understandably, enough for Miller—and, it would seem, for most teachers and scholars of writing. It isn't enough for me, however. For such a goal seems too comfortable with (perhaps "resigned to" is the more accurate phrase) a status quo that sickens many of us more than it did Hairston nearly two decades ago. More important, it subordinates our collective well-being to a well-intentioned but problematic belief in the primacy of student autonomy and self-determination, thereby reifying the same focus on the individual that is at the heart of consumer culture and therefore at the center of the crisis of sustainability.

This is tricky terrain, for as Miller, Hardin, and others have pointed out, progressive pedagogies, including Freire's, have been critiqued (rightly, in my view) for assuming that students are passive, unwitting pawns who must be liberated from false consciousness by enlightened educators; in other words, the very agency that Freire posits as necessary for becoming "fully human" seems impossible for students to realize without an enlightened educator to make it available to them. Such a vision of the student leads to charges that critical pedagogies offer indoctrination rather than liberation. Susan Miller voices this concern in reference to the social-epistemic pedagogy that James Berlin advocates in *Rhetorics, Poetics, and Cultures*, which is based on Berlin's belief that English "has a special role in the democratic educational mission" (Berlin, *Rhetorics* 54); in order to fulfill that role "in preparing critical citizens for participatory democracy" (97), Berlin writes, critical educators must challenge the discourses and linguistic codes that "can define subjects as helpless objects of forces—economic, social, political, cultural—that render them forever isolated and victimized by the conditions of their experience" (98). These codes "that define individuals as helpless ciphers, must be replaced by narratives that enable democratic participation in creating a more equitable distribution of the necessities, liberties, and pleasures of life" (98). Complaining that Berlin posits a "fatherly" teacher who "infantalize[s]" students, Susan Miller resists the idea that "institutional claims to teach a universal moral sense should supplant families, regional customs, class, or ethnic politics, to normalize and covertly coerce conscience" and that "institutions can or should install a universal vision of 'democratic' subjectivity" (Susan Miller 498). This is a valid concern, and critical pedagogues have taken pains to address it. Hardin, for instance, emphasizes that teaching resistance, which he believes is both "ethical and necessary, . . . can protect the autonomy of both student and teacher without endorsing a specific set of values, other than the view that language, discourse, and rhetoric are always interested and always value-laden" (5). His approach is sensitive to concerns such as Miller's about imposing values on students; at the same time, it assigns to students an agency that often seems absent in pedagogies like Berlin's.

But agency is a complex matter. As I argued elsewhere (see *Literacy Matters*), agency is a function of overlapping and sometimes competing discourses that both open up and constrain possibilities for action and self-determination. Hardin seeks to "encourage students to appropriate and use the rhetoric and conventions of academic and cultural discourses to inscribe their own values" (5), (which is akin to Richard Miller's goal of enabling students to "navigate life in a bureaucracy"), but students' values are not separate from the academic and cultural discourses to which they are subject; indeed, their values are in large part a *function* of those discourses, and their autonomy is both enabled and circumscribed by those same discourses. Susan Miller is right to worry about institutions promoting ("installing" is her term) "a universal vision of 'democratic subjectivity'" that supersedes "families, regional customs, class, or ethnic politics," but educational institutions at all levels (kindergarten through college) already promote a more fundamental subjectivity that undergirds all manner of political ideologies: the Cartesian sense of self. The dualistic Cartesian ontology at the heart of schooling inevitably shapes student agency. We act on the basis of how we understand ourselves as beings in the world. Thus, the Cartesian ontology that is the foundation of schooling is prior to the ideological differences that have often been the focus of debates about critical pedagogy. We may be appropriately vigilant about indoctrinating our students into certain political ideologies, but as part of the educational system, writing instruction is implicated in an ontological process that fosters a dualistic way of being in the world, regardless of ideology. Whatever our politics, that is, we reinforce a status quo based on Cartesian duality.

It may well be, then, that the vigorous debates about critical pedagogy and the larger discussions about the purposes of writing instruction miss the point. Berlin's passionate advocacy for a pedagogy that foregrounds "the student's position as a political agent in a democratic society" (112); or Hardin's pedagogy of resistance, in which "writers negotiate the spaces between their own values and the values of other writers in a way that exposes and critiques the power imbalances of that particular moment and space" (112); or Susan Miller's argument "for enabling students to act through language, first by placing its differential modes of making in the center of our teaching" (499); or even Richard Miller's "modest goal" of giving students "the opportunity to speak, read, and write in a wider range of discursive contexts than is available to them when they labor under the codes of silence and manufactured consent" (27)—all these are in the end various versions of the same thing, for none of them necessarily challenges the Cartesian sense of self that schooling fosters. Despite the powerful influence of postmodern theories that have illuminated the often oppressive workings of language and literacy and challenged positivist beliefs about knowledge-making and the related Enlightenment narratives of progress, educators continue to convey the same basic way of thinking about *being* in the world, a way of thinking founded on Cartesian duality. That, more than anything else, may be the biggest obstacle to change, whether that change is pedagogical, curricular, social, political, or cultural. Paradoxically, as transformative pedagogies are promoted—by Berlin and Susan Miller and Hardin and others—on the basis of a belief in the central role of writing in our lives and its power to transform, we may continue, through those same pedagogies, to reinforce the status quo we seek to change. We teach writing, to borrow Susan Miller's phrase, as a technology of self-formation, but one steeped in a Cartesian worldview, within which our separateness is reinscribed with every act of writing.

In recent years, some theorists have begun to map out an alternative to this mainstream Cartesian view of writing. Notably, Couture has advocated a phenomenological rhetoric that "abandons the Western sophistic tradition of arriving at truth through conquering and consensus, and grounds it instead in conscious commitment to collaboration with others in truth-seeking" (4); significantly, such a rhetoric imagines "a construction of self that stakes identity on . . . acceptance of an integral relationship with the world" (4). Thomas Kent's paralogic rhetoric, which informs Couture's work, may offer the most promising challenge to the mainstream view of writing. I turn to Kent's work later. First, however, I review the current state of writing theory in the field—specifically, the recent efforts of some scholars to move "beyond process"—in order to show that a mainstream Cartesian view of writing continues to inform writing theory and pedagogy. Understanding the place of that view of writing in our theories and pedagogies is the first step toward developing alternatives to it. For my purposes, it is a step toward a theory of writing as a way of being.

THE CURRENT STATE OF WRITING THEORY

In his influential 1986 article, "Competing Theories of Process: A Critique and a Proposal," Lester Faigley disavowed the use of the term paradigm to describe the role of the idea of the writing process in the field of Composition Studies but nevertheless acknowledged the widespread influence of that idea: "Even though the claim of a paradigm shift is now viewed by some as an overstatement, it is evident that many writing teachers in grade schools, high schools, and colleges have internalized process assumptions" (527). Two decades later it seems fair to say that *most* writing teachers "have internalized process assumptions." In K–12 classrooms, the idea of writing as a process now amounts to a nearly monolithic belief and shapes much writing instruction, at least in terms of pedagogical technique (i.e., student–teacher conferences, requiring multiple drafts of assignments, etc.).[6] And although process cannot be described as a formal theory in a strict sense, its influence on postsecondary writing instruction and the great deal of scholarship that has been devoted to it seem to warrant describing it as a paradigm. Despite the more recent use of the term post-process to describe the current state of the field, the idea of the writing process remains the central concept in the field and in much of the teaching of writing at all levels of schooling.

The effort by some scholars to move "beyond process" has rekindled discussion of the writing process that energized the field in the 1980s. Specifically, scholars have debated the usefulness of the idea of writing as a process and advocated various alternatives. Unlike earlier debates about process and "expressivism" (which is sometimes conflated with process-oriented pedagogies), which tended to focus on how best to understand writing as a process (or which version of process is best), the discussions about "post-process" theory emerge from the contention of some scholars that "writing is a practice that cannot be captured by a generalized process or Big Theory," as Thomas Kent puts it (*Post-Process Theory* 1). Acknowledging that post-process theory is a nebulous term—that there is no "party line regarding post-process theory"—Kent asserts that post-process scholars "display a fresh and enthusiastic engagement with crucial issues that have become moribund in a field still dominated by the nearly forty-year-old tradition we all know as the process movement" (6).

But even if we do move "beyond process," we will still be in more or less the same place—not because we still employ pedagogies based on some idea of writing as a process but because both the advocates of process-oriented approaches and the post-process theorists challenging those approaches imagine a writer based on the Cartesian self. And *writing* as generally understood in the field continues to be taught within a Cartesian worldview. Despite the post-process challenge, process "theory" and the post-process theory that seeks to supplant it rest on the same fundamental Cartesian dualisms that provide the foundation for modern schooling.

To understand this dynamic it is helpful to revisit the debates about the different versions of the writing process that helped shape the field of Composition Studies and the teaching of writing in the 1980s. These debates matter today not only because they serve as a kind of reference point for the post-process movement but also because the vision of the field that they present remains essentially intact. When Faigley identified three "competing theories of process"—the expressive, the cognitive, and the social—he called them the "dominant theoretical views of composing" (528). These three "competing theories" and Berlin's corresponding three main "rhetorics" ("Rhetoric and Ideology") became the standard taxonomy of the field. Although Faigley and Berlin have different agendas and somewhat different emphases in their analyses, they describe the field in essentially the same way. What each offers is a description of three different versions of the same basic idea of writing as a process of composing a text.

For both Faigley and Berlin, the differences among these versions of process grow out of the epistemological assumptions that inform each version. For example, Faigley describes the social view of process as resting on "one central assumption: human language (including writing) can be understood only from the perspective of a society rather than a single individual" (535). The key implication of this assumption is that meaning is contingent, socially determined, and therefore unstable (and here the influence of post-structuralism on Faigley's thought, so clear in his later book, *Fragments of*

Rationality, is evident). Knowledge becomes a function of discourse and the writerly self a construction of discourse: "The focus of a social view of writing, therefore, is not on how the social situation influences the individual, but on how the individual is a constituent of a culture" (535). More important, a social view of writing "rejects the assumption that writing is the act of a private consciousness and that everything else—readers, subjects, and texts—is 'out there' in the world" (535). Rather, "everything else" essentially exists within discourse and therefore as a function of our interactions with and through language.

Berlin takes this analysis further. In explaining the dialectical nature of knowledge as understood within what he calls "social-epistemic rhetoric," he writes,

> Our consciousness is in large part a product of our material conditions. But our material conditions are also in part the products of our consciousness. Both consciousness and the material conditions influence each other, and they are both imbricated in social relations defined and worked out through language. In other words, the ways in which the subject understands and is affected by material conditions is circumscribed by socially-devised definitions, by the community in which the subject lives. The community in turn is influenced by the subject and the material conditions of the moment. Thus, the perceiving subject, the discourse communities of which the subject is a part, and the material world itself are all the constructions of an historical discourse, of the ideological formulations inscribed in the language-mediated practical activity of a particular time and place. ("Rhetoric and Ideology" 489)

In this analysis, the self is constructed through interaction with other selves, mediated by language. The constitutive role of language is central to knowledge-making in this view. The writer constructs him or herself—and is constructed—through discourse. Indeed, the writer exists within discourse. Even though Berlin includes the "material world" in his analysis, that world is essentially a function of discourse.

Both Faigley and Berlin contrast this social view of writing and rhetoric with what they see as the epistemological underpinnings of the expressivist and cognitivist views. According to Faigley, "a social view of writing moves beyond the expressivist contention that the individual discovers the self through language and beyond the cognitivist position that an individual constructs reality through language. In a social view, any effort to write about the self or reality always comes in relation to previous texts" (536). To put it somewhat differently, in all three views language is necessary for knowledge-making but only in the social view is language ultimately the source of knowledge, for the social view is informed by a postmodern understanding of a contingent reality constructed through language. For

Berlin, cognitivist rhetoric is characterized by the assumption of a stable external reality that can be known and described rationally: "The existent, the good, and the possible are inscribed in the very nature of things as indisputable scientific facts, rather than being seen as humanly devised social constructions always remaining open to discussion" (484). By contrast, expressionistic rhetoric is characterized by the idea of a transcendent self, which is the source of truth: "For this rhetoric, the existent is located within the individual subject. While the reality of the material, the social, and the linguistic are never denied, they are considered significant only insofar as they serve the needs of the individual" (484).

In short, these views of the writing process rest on slightly different conceptions of knowledge and the role of language in knowledge-making. Each also rests on a seemingly different understanding of the relationship of the self to the world. Yet all three of these views conceive of the self as primarily an *intellectual* entity; that is, they understand the self in a fundamentally Cartesian way. The expressivist view may conceive of the self as stable, autonomous, and "discoverable" through language, but that self remains a kind of metaphysical being. The same is true for both the cognitive view, for which mind is paramount, and the social view, which understands the self as a function of discourse. These are, in the end, different versions of Descartes' I ("I think; therefore, I am."). The differences among these views lie essentially in the mechanisms by which the self comes to know the world—through self-exploration (expressivist), through descriptions of the external world (cognitivist), or through discourse (social)—and in where knowledge is located—in the self (expressive), in an external reality (cognitive), or in language-mediated interactions with other selves (social). But in the end, they are ontologically similar: They all assume that we exist in the world as intellectual beings separate from other beings and the world around us.

Post-process theory has been characterized as an effort to move beyond the idea of the writing process and thus beyond disagreements over different versions of process. Joseph Petraglia describes post-process theory as "a rejection of the generally formulaic framework for understanding writing that process suggested" (53). According to Sidney Dobrin, "post-process in composition studies refers to the shift in scholarly attention from the process by which the individual writer produces text to the larger forces that affect that writer and of which that writer is a part" (132). For many post-process theorists, this shift is driven by the view that, as Lee-Ann Kastman Breuch puts it, "process (prewriting, writing, rewriting) is no longer an adequate explanation of the writing act" (119). But as Kent himself acknowledges, exactly what "post-process" means is open to some question (*Post-Process Theory*). Richard Fulkerson points out in his review of Kent's *Post-Process Theory* that "there is not a 'post-process' movement, any more than there was a 'process' movement. If these authors are united, they are united only by what they oppose" (104). What they oppose is the idea that writing is a process that can be fully understood and taught as such (Kent; Gary Olson) or the position that the idea of the writing process is rich enough to be pedagogically and theoretically useful (Clifford and Ervin; Petraglia) or that any theory of writing should be linked to pedagogy in the first place, as process is perceived to be (Dobrin). Fulkerson may be right that what characterizes post-process theory is opposition to the idea of the writing process, but that opposition rests on an understanding of writing based on the assumptions that "writing is public, thoroughly hermeneutic, and always situated" (Kent, *Post-Process* 5). In other words, the opposition of post-process theorists to the idea of the writing process grows out of a general theoretical understanding of writing.

In her helpful overview of post-process theory, Breuch argues that "post-process theory encourages us to reexamine our definition of writing as an activity rather than a body of knowledge, our methods of teaching as indeterminate activities rather than exercises of mastery, and our communicative interactions with students as dialogic rather than monologic" (98–99). She points out that Kent's rejection of the idea that writing can be taught, a contention that has been a focus of debate among post-process theorists, is based on the position that "neither writing nor reading can be reduced to a systemic process or to a codifiable set of conventions, although clearly some of the background knowledge useful for writing—like grammar, sentence structure, paragraph cohesion, and so forth—can be codified and reduced to a system" (Kent, *Paralogic*; qtd. in Breuch 100). For Kent, writing and reading are "kinds of communicative interactions" requiring "us to make hermeneutic guesses about how others will interpret our utterances" (Kent 161); thus, writing cannot be taught as a codified system. As a result, Kent rejects process pedagogy as an effort to systematize what cannot be systematized. As Breuch points out, however, Kent does not reject pedagogy entirely; rather, he reconceptualizes the teaching of writing so that

> we would stop talking about writing and reading as processes and start talking about these activities as determinate social acts. This shift from an internalist conception of communicative interaction—the notion that communication is a product of the internal workings of the mind or the workings of the discourse communities in which we live—to an externalist conception . . . would challenge us to drop our current process-oriented vocabulary and to begin talking about our social and public uses of language. (169; qtd. in Breuch 101)

This "dialogic pedagogy requires two-way rather than one-way communication, suggesting that teachers move away from a transmission model of education and toward a transformative model that includes active participation from both teachers and students as collaborators" (Breuch 102). Like other post-process advocates, however, Breuch wants to resist the "peda-gogical imperative," a term she borrows from Dobrin to refer to "the idea that a theory must have direct classroom application" (102). Instead of describing a specific post-process pedagogy, Breuch seeks to redefine *writing* as an "indeterminate activity" that "cannot be predicted in terms of how students will write (through certain formulas or content) or how students will learn (through certain approaches)" (110). This view of writing doesn't necessarily make pedagogy impossible, but as Kent suggests in the passage quoted above, it means changing how we talk about acts of writing in our classrooms and how we approach the writing of our students.

For my purposes in this chapter, the specific positions within this debate about the possibilities for a writing pedagogy are less important than the fact of the debate itself. (I say much more about the possibilities for pedagogy in Chapter 5.) The question of whether (and how) writing can be taught is a crucial one that can only be answered with reference to a specific conception of writing. As Breuch demonstrates, a post-process conception of writing limits the possibilities for writing instruction and makes some pedagogies impossible. Conceiving of writing as inherently interpretive and situated, post-process theorists must necessarily reject the possibility that students can be taught *the* writing process through which they can communicate a stable meaning in writing. Thus, the idea of mastery is explicitly rejected by post-process theorists. Instead, writing instructors must make the indeter-minate nature of writing itself the focus of instruction, becoming not experts who share their insights and guide students but, as Breuch puts it, mentors who spend "time and energy on our interactions with students—listening to them, discussing ideas with them, letting them make mistakes, and pointing them in the right direction" (120). Pedagogy becomes a matter of dialogue among students and teachers, ideally (for Breuch) in one-on-one settings.

The key point here is that a pedagogical vision emerges from a deter-mined effort to articulate a theoretically sound conception of writing. Some post-process theorists complain that there is no such thing as "process *theo-ry*," no coherent theoretical explanation of writing that undergirds process-oriented approaches to writing (see Gary Olson 8). I agree. Instead, as I sug-gested previously, the implicit conception of writing that informs discussions of process is what I have been calling the Cartesian view of writing, charac-terized by an understanding of the writer as a version of the autonomous Cartesian self and by the classic dualities that constitute the Cartesian world-view (subject–object, mind–body). Kent argues that the "classical paradigm" that "treats discourse production and discourse analysis as codifiable processes" (18), which emerges from Plato and Aristotle, "still controls our conception of discourse production, and it appears regularly as the constitu-tive schema from which the entire field of rhetoric takes its shape" (20). He goes on to say that "our contemporary metadiscourse of rhetoric—the language we employ to talk about rhetoric—has remained the same for two thousand years" (20–21). I am arguing that the contemporary version of this "classical paradigm," which Kent rejects on the basis of his view that discourse production is "paralogic and unsystematic in nature" (22), rests on a Cartesian ontology and its concomitant positivist epistemology.

Post-process theory purports to move beyond this Cartesian framework. But despite the emphasis in post-process theory on the indeterminate nature of meaning-making through written language, writers (and readers) as conceived in post-process theory remain in a Cartesian world, as they do in process accounts of writing. Post-process theorists may draw heavily on postmodern theory to reject the foundationalism they see as informing process pedagogies, but their writer is ontologically the same as the writer imagined in process-oriented approaches. Kent, whose *Paralogic Rhetoric* provides the theoretical foundation for much (if not most) post-process theory, overtly seeks to reject Cartesian dualisms—and the Cartesian conception of language as a medium for representing or describing the world—that he sees undergirding contemporary composition theory and pedagogy (*Paralogic* 17). But post-process theorists seem to focus on Kent's arguments about the hermeneutic nature of writing as a process of meaning-making (and the impossibility of teaching writing as a codifiable process) and largely ignore his appropriation of Donald Davidson's ideas about "triangulation," which foregrounds the role of others and, significantly, knowledge of the world, in communicative interaction. In other words, they fail to emphasize Kent's epistemological project and focus instead on his ideas about meaning-making. To an extent, this is understandable, because although Kent draws heavily on Davidson's notion of triangulation (about which more in a moment), he tends to emphasize the inherently interpretative nature of meaning-*making* through language rather than the problem of *knowledge*-making. He therefore focuses on discourse production and the implications of the continued embrace of the classical paradigm in contemporary composition theory and pedagogy. Although he rejects the idea of the Cartesian subject, he tends to direct his attention to *writing* rather than the *writer*. Not surprisingly, then, scholars embracing Kent's analysis tend to ignore his sense of the subject (writer) in written communication and especially the role of "the world" in that analysis. As a result and despite Kent's stated goal of undermining Cartesian duality, the post-process theory that grows out of Kent's work remains mired in a Cartesian framework when it comes to understanding the writer.

Understanding this problem requires a more careful look at Kent's analysis of discourse production, and in particular his reliance on Davidson's key concept of triangulation. Kent actually does push in promising ways beyond the Cartesian dualities that continue to inform contemporary composition theory, but post-process theorists who draw on his work mostly do not.

THOMAS KENT'S ANTI-CARTESIAN PARALOGIC RHETORIC

In *Paralogic Rhetoric*, Kent challenges the idea of "interpretive communities," popularized by Stanley Fish, that informs what Kent calls "reader-ori-
ented reception theory" and "communitarian" theories of interpretation
(77), which he believes characterize the understanding of meaning-making
in contemporary composition theory and pedagogy. Communitarians
"claim that knowledge comes into being only within the incommensurate
interpretative communities in which we live" (76). The problem with this
view, according to Kent, is that the idea of interpretive communities rests on
what he calls "internalism," the view that an "internal realm of mental
states—beliefs, desires, intentions, and so forth—exists anterior to an external realm of objects and events" (98). Internalism is based on "the Cartesian
idea of a split between mind and world" (97). What Kent calls internalism
incorporates the same basic conception of the self that emerges from Plato's
discussion of the soul and the realm of absolutes, the same conception that
becomes Edmund Husserl's idea of "solitary mental life" that Derrida critiques (see Neel 142). For Kent, the Cartesian split that is assumed in communitarian perspectives such as Fish's dooms knowledge-making and truth-
seeking to endless relativism:

> To hold such a Cartesian position means that Fish possesses no convinc-
> ing response to the skeptic or to those who charge him with relativism.
> When Fish accepts a Cartesian epistemology and imagines that a subjec-
> tive conceptual framework exists that constitutes all that we can know
> about the world, he obviously may never be sure that his claims about
> the world—the propositional attitudes he holds—refer to anything out-
> side his own subjective conceptual framework. (80)

In the end, "we are cast into a world where truth is unknowable and rhetoric is king" (80).

Kent seeks to replace internalism with "externalism," which he defines
as "the position that no split exists between an inner and outer world and
claims that our sense of an inner world actually derives from our rapport
with other language users" (104). His externalism is based on Davidson's
analysis of meaning-making, which replaces the shared conceptual schemes
of the communitarian view with "hermeneutic guessing": "For Davidson,
satisfactory communication depends on our ability to interpret the beliefs
and intentions of others, and interpretation depends on the efficacy and
felicity of our hermeneutic guesses," which "never correspond to a linguistic code or framework that we know before we begin the process of communication" (88). In other words, "When we communicate, we make

informed guesses about meaning" (87). In Davidson's analysis, those guesses are made more or less on the fly as we try to communicate with another in interaction with them and with the world. In drawing on that analysis, Kent emphasizes that "knowledge of our mind cannot be separated from knowledge of another's mind and knowledge of the world" (108). He goes on,

> Without the other, we can have no thoughts, no language, no cognizance of meaning, and no awareness that we can possess something called mental states. Public and external communicative interaction, through our ability to triangulate, forms the basis for internal mental states, and not the other way around. Internal cognitive processes, mental schemata, or conceptual schemes do not create an external world; instead, the external world creates our sense of the internal one. (108)

This is Kent's crucial move in rejecting a Cartesian framework. In Chapter 3, I pursue in detail this matter of the relationship between mind and world, but the key point here is that in Kent's formulation, and in Donaldson's theories on which Kent relies, "the world" is an integral part not only of meaning-making but also *knowing*. Language is essential for this process but it isn't the sole ground for knowing or meaning-making. Indeed, Kent routinely emphasizes that language is exclusively communicative and essential for knowing but is not the source of meaning.[7]

As I noted earlier, central to this analysis is Donaldson's conception of triangulation, which is essentially the process by which we make sense of the world. Significantly (and as many post-process theorists have noted), "it takes two to triangulate" (Davidson 159; qtd. in Kent, *Paralogic* 89). That is, we do not make sense of the world alone, within our own minds; we require others in order to know. Thus, the I and the other are two corners of the triangle; "knowledge of the shared world" is the third corner (Kent, *Paralogic* 89). Davidson describes the process as follows:

> Each of two people is reacting differently to sensory stimuli streaming in from a certain direction. If we project the incoming lines outward, their intersection is the common cause. If the two people now note each others' reactions (in the case of language, verbal reactions), each can correlate these observed reactions with his or her stimuli from the world. (Davidson 159; qtd. in Kent, *Paralogic* 89)

In this formulation, "stimuli from the world" constitute an essential component of the process. In other words, meaning is not made exclusively within discourse but through a three-way interaction that requires *two* "others": another person/communicator and the phenomenal world. This third apex of Davidson's triangle is crucial in two respects. First, it undermines the Cartesian idea of the autonomous self knowing the world on its own, because an other is always required for knowing. Second, it moves the process of meaning-making out of the realm of discourse exclusively and out of an internal mental realm, because "the world" is an integral component of meaning-making. Kent sees triangulation as the key step toward eliminating the Cartesian dualities that continue to inform writing theory and pedagogy. He emphasizes that "Davidson's argument takes the radically anti-Cartesian position that no subject/object split exists" (90). Cartesian subjectivity—the Cartesian sense of self as an autonomous, thinking being—"emerges only when we imagine that language can be used for something other than communication" (90). Davidson rejects that notion. As Kent explains it, "When we understand that language's raison d'être is communicative interaction, radical subjectivity—in the form of a private language or a conceptual scheme—makes no sense. In order to surmise if our marks and noises create any effect in the world, we require at least an-other language user and objects in the world we know we share" (90).

For Kent, triangulation means that communication (and therefore writing) is inherently nondualistic. Therefore, writing does not demarcate boundaries between the writer and others, because we cannot make meaning without others; furthermore, it begins to erase the boundary between writer as subject and the world as object, because the world is integral to meaning-making: "We cannot know our own minds—the concepts that form our thoughts—without knowing the minds of other language users; consequently, no split exists between our minds and the minds of others or between our minds and objects in a shared world" (91–92). The key point is that Kent's approach conceives of a writer making meaning within a matrix of self–other–world that eliminates the "inside–outside" binary. Kent's primary complaint about mainstream theories of the writing process is that they all approach writing and meaning-making as "internal" matters, thus retaining the Cartesian subject–object split that he seeks to deny. Consequently, they propose what he calls "conceptual schemes"—that is, an "internal realm of mental states" or "beliefs, desires, intentions, and so forth" (98)—as ways to understand and teach discourse production: "They take the epistemological position that knowledge of the world and of other minds is relative to some sort of conceptual scheme, and they propose that discourse production can be reduced to a process that represents, duplicates, or models these conceptual schemes" (101). By contrast, Kent and the postprocess theorists who follow him reject the possibility that discourse production can ever be reduced to a codifiable (and teachable) process. Instead, "[t]o produce discourse, we must continually triangulate in a public way with other language users and with objects in the world" (124).

Post-process theorists have seized on Kent's views about the interpretative, uncodifiable nature of communication in their challenge to the idea of the writing process. They also have embraced Kent's analysis of the essential role of the other in meaning-making. In effect, they have focused on the first two points of the hermeneutic triangle (knowledge of our mind and knowledge of another's mind), pursuing Kent's argument that writing is always "public," which means that another's mind is essential to the process of meaning-making that takes place through writing. But they seem to have missed the third point of the triangle. Few post-process theorists incorporate "knowledge of the world" fully into their analyses, and few seem to have pursued the ontological and epistemological implications of Kent's radical anti-Cartesian approach. Crucially, without the third apex of the triangle, Kent's theory of communicative interaction is reduced to a dialogic process of meaning-making between writer and reader. As a result, post-process theorists continue to work within a poststructuralist realm of discourse without significant reference to "the world" that is an inherent part of Kent's analysis of meaning-making.

In her overview, for example, Breuch appropriately summarizes Kent's use of Davidson's conception of triangulation and correctly points out that this concept is at the heart of Kent's contention that writing is inherently public. She explains that this idea of writing as public "is already apparent in some writing pedagogies; however, these pedagogies are often described as 'dialogic' instead of 'post-process' because they emphasize communicative interaction in the teaching of writing" (112). In pursuing this point, Breuch reviews the work of several theorists whom she considers post-process (e.g., Kay Halasek), emphasizing the central role of dialogue in their approaches. She concludes, "The assumption that writing is public, therefore, incorporates the idea that meaning is made through our interactions. Terms used to describe this emphasis include language-in-use, communicative interaction, and dialogue, but they all point to the idea that writing is an activity—an interaction with others—rather than content to be mastered" (113). Here, dialogue replaces triangulation, and the third point of Davidson's triangle (the world)—with its anti-Cartesian ontology—is missing. Thus, the writerly self implicit in this understanding of a dialogic approach to writing may be inherently social but is largely conceived as existing within discourse—an intellectual being constructed through language.

Similarly, in reviewing Kent's assertion that communication is inherently interpretative, a key assumption in post-process theory, Breuch again seems to leave out the third corner of the hermeneutic triangle. She reviews "competing conceptions of interpretation [that] characterize a recurring debate within current hermeneutic theory" (114) and emphasizes the anti-foundationalism that emerges from these debates and informs post-process theory, concluding that "[t]o understand writing as a thoroughly interpretive activity (in the spirit of hermeneutic universalism) means accepting that no foundational knowledge is the basis for writing as a discipline" (115). Therefore, post-process theory rejects "process as a foundational body of knowledge" and embraces "the indeterminate nature of the writing activity" (115). However, the definition of writing that grows out of these assumptions seems to exclude the third apex of the interpretative triangle: "Writing becomes an activity that requires an understanding of context, interaction with others, and our attempts to communicate a message" (115). Here, "context" seems to be the setting for the communicative interaction rather than the phenomenal world that Kent points to as integral to meaning-making. And when Breuch goes on to review the key post-process assumption that writing is situated, an assumption she describes as "discussed most frequently by scholars interested in postmodern or anti-foundationalist perspectives" (115), she again seems to downplay the role of "the world." Post-process theorists, she writes, assume "that writing should change with the situation, that students interact with the world through dialectical interaction, and that rhetoric involves interpretation of social and historical elements of human discourse" (116). Note that although "dialectical interaction" with others and the world is not necessarily incompatible with Kent's use of Davidson's idea of triangulation, it isn't the same kind of process. Dialectic, as I understand Breuch's use of the concept here, implies a sense of the writer as subject interacting with an other or an object; thus, the Cartesian split between self and other is retained. In Davidson's analysis of communicative interaction through triangulation, by contrast, the interaction between two communicators integrates the object/world, eliminating the split between self and other and subject and object, as I noted earlier. Moreover, in the conventional understanding of dialectic, knowledge of the world emerges through the interactive inquiry between two knowers who are separate from the world; thus, knowledge is ultimately abstract. In triangulation, however, knowledge emerges as a function of the effort to communicate with another knower *in the context of* the world that is inherently part of the communicative process. Without that crucial element, the knower or communicator remains within a Cartesian binary, even if knowledge is assumed to be contingent rather than objective (as post-process theorists assume); the knower or communicator, therefore, is still a Cartesian subject and knowing a Cartesian process.

A review of the work of other influential post-process theorists reveals this same lack of attention to the "triangular" nature of meaning-making that characterizes Kent's theory of paralogic rhetoric. Indeed, the contributors to his edited collection, *Post-Process Theory*, all more or less share the basic understanding of meaning-making that Breuch puts forth in her overview of post-process theory. Like Kent, they all reject the idea of writing as a codifiable process of meaning-making. Like Kent, they embrace the postmodern view of the instability of meaning and the "public" nature of communication. But unlike him, they remain stuck in the Cartesian subject--object binary and continue to conceive of the writerly self in Cartesian terms.

In the end, although Descartes' goal of objectivity may have been rejected in this brave new anti-foundationalist world of post-process theory, his idea of the autonomous thinking self has not. It remains the foundation of writing theory. For both the advocates of process theory and post-process theorists, writing is primarily an intellectual activity through which we make sense of ourselves and the world around us. That world, however, remains separate from us. We write as Cartesian beings in the world, not *of* it. Ultimately, then, post-process theory attempts to move "beyond" process theory by incorporating insights from poststructuralist theory (and other theoretical movements) but without entirely rejecting the Cartesian self that is implicit in process theory and continues to inform mainstream writing instruction.

Still, Kent's paralogic rhetoric points in a promising direction toward an epistemological and ontological alternative to Cartesian duality. Ultimately, it is nonduality that will enable us to replace the Cartesian self with a different conception of the writer so that writing can become an act of connection and an expression of wholeness rather than an enactment of separation. Understanding writing as a way of being is a necessary step in that process. The next chapter takes up that project.

ENDNOTES

1. I discuss the political origins and implications of Murray's approach in "'Radical to Many in the Educational Community': The Process Movement After the Hurricanes."
2. See Yagelski, "English Education" and "Stasis and Change."
3. See Joseph Harris, "Meet the New Boss, Same as the Old Boss," and James Sledd's response, "On Buying in and Selling Out: A Note for Bosses Old and New." These exchanges reveal some of Composition Studies' uneasiness about its role in the modern university and its struggles to define its sense of mission.
4. Although there is disagreement among economists and other social scientists about the specific figures, there is general agreement that income disparity in the United States has increased in recent decades. Currently, approximately half of the total wealth in the United States is controlled by the top 5 percent of income earners, and the percentage of wealth controlled by the top income earners has grown since the 1970s. See "The Wealth Divide: The Growing Gap in the United States Between the Rich and the Rest. An Interview with Edward Wolff." See also Timothy Noah, "The United States of Inequality." For an

opposing analysis, see Rector and Hederman; their analysis, however, does not address trends in income distribution since the 1970s.

5. In 2007, Harvard announced changes in its financial aid policies that would dramatically reduce the required contribution of students whose families earned less than $120,000 annually, and it would continue its policy of not charging any tuition to students whose annual family income was less than $60,000. See "Harvard Announces Sweeping Middle-Income Initiative." Several other elite institutions followed suit with similar policies. The actions by these institutions may have been motivated by concerns about the rising costs of college; however, available data suggest that college is increasingly less accessible to lower- and middle-income students and that the gap between such students and their more affluent peers is growing. In 2005, the median household of entering first-year college students was $74,000, which was 60 percent higher than the national average household income ($46,326). In 1971, by comparison, students' median family income ($13,200) was 46 percent higher than the national average household income ($9,028). See Pryor, J. H. et al. "The American Freshman: Forty-Year Trends, 1966–2006."

6. In summing up trends in writing instruction in secondary schools in the 1980s and 1990s, Applebee reported that by 1992, about half of teachers surveyed for the NAEP reported using process-oriented approaches to writing instruction (see Applebee, *Alternative Models*); in a follow-up study Applebee and Langer reported that "process-oriented writing instruction has dominated teachers' reports at least since 1992" (Applebee and Langer i). A quick review of current college composition textbooks reveals the extent to which the writing process has become a fixture of writing instruction at the postsecondary level. This is not to say, however, that what I am calling a process approach to writing instruction is monolithic among teachers, for "process" pedagogies vary dramatically. What I am suggesting is that the *idea* that writing is a process has become firmly established in secondary and postsecondary writing instruction and is embraced by most writing teachers.

7. At first glance, this formulation looks similar to Berlin's analysis, as quoted earlier; however, the difference is that for Berlin knowledge emerges exclusively from discourse, whereas Kent understands language as communicative and not epistemological, although it is an integral part of the process of knowledge-making. In other words, in Berlin's analysis, the world is always already conceptualized through discourse, whereas for Kent the world is an integral part of the process of meaning-making. To put it somewhat differently, in Berlin's analysis, the external world is filtered through discourse and is thus once removed, as it were, from the process of meaning-making; for Kent, the world is engaged directly with another communicator in any communicative act.

3

WRITING, BEING, AND NONDUALITY

A human being is part of the whole, called by us "Universe," a part limited in time and space. He experiences himself, his thoughts and feelings as something separated from the rest—a kind of optical delusion of his consciousness. This delusion is a kind of prison for us, restricting us to our personal desires and to affection for a few persons nearest to us. Our task must be to free ourselves from this prison by widening our circle of compassion to embrace all living creatures and the whole nature in its beauty. Nobody is able to achieve this completely, but the striving for such achievement is in itself a part of the liberation, and a foundation for inner security.
—Albert Einstein

In *The Tao of Physics*, Fritjof Capra describes a moment of epiphany:

I was sitting by the ocean one late summer afternoon, watching the waves rolling in and feeling the rhythm of my breathing, when I suddenly became aware of my whole environment as being engaged in a gigantic cosmic dance. Being a physicist, I knew that the sand, rocks, water and air around me were made of vibrating molecules and atoms, and that these consisted of particles which interacted with one another by creating and destroying other particles. I knew that the Earth's atmosphere was continually bombarded by showers of "cosmic rays," particles of high energy undergoing multiple collisions as they penetrated the air. All this was familiar to me from my research in high-energy physics, but until that moment I had only experienced it through graphs, diagrams and mathematical theories. As I sat on that beach my former experiences came to life; I "saw" cascades of energy coming down from outer space, in which particles were created and destroyed in rhythmic pulses; I "saw" the atoms of the elements and those of my body participating in this cosmic dance of energy; I felt its rhythm and I "heard" its sound, and at that moment I knew that this was the Dance of Shiva, the Lord of Dancers worshipped by the Hindus. (11)

When I first read that passage, I immediately thought of a moment a few years earlier when I was improbably perched on a small ledge on the Grand Teton in Wyoming. I was climbing the mountain with two partners, and at that moment I was resting a few hundred feet below the summit as one of my partners stood next to me, managing the rope, which led down the mountainside to our third partner, who was climbing toward our airy ledge. It was a spectacular July day, bright and clear, a few scattered puffs of cloud intensifying the stunning blue of the sky. We had been climbing since 3 a.m., and now the late morning was bringing forth the full brilliance of the day. As my partner worked the rope beside me, I sat motionless, gazing west, my back leaning against cold rock, the hood of my parka pulled tightly over my head. I looked down at the steep ridge we had just climbed, which extended for thousands of feet in a dramatic downward sweep toward the high plains of Idaho. The wind, which had been steady all morning, suddenly abated. In an instant, everything seemed to grow quiet except for the sound of the rope sliding over rock, the clink of metal climbing gear, and an occasional grunt from our partner below as he climbed toward us. In that same instant, I was overcome by an intense feeling of well-being such as I had never before experienced. Despite our precarious stance, I felt utterly safe. I felt a deep connection not only to my two climbing partners—to whom, in fact, I was literally connected by the climbing rope—and to that spectacular spot on that mountain but also to something else, something inchoate and much bigger. I thought of my wife and two young sons, who at that moment were camping in the valley far below, and of friends and other family members hundreds of miles away. I felt connected to all of them. I was enveloped by a palpable sense of their warm presence. I felt another presence as well: the mountain, perhaps, or the plains that stretched to the horizon, or the sky, or something even bigger. As an atheist, I did not believe I was feeling the presence of God, but what I experienced was perhaps something like what a believer might feel as that kind of sacred presence. The sensation was almost physical, and it was overwhelming.

A smile broadened on my face as I sat waiting for my climbing partners to finish the pitch. My own sense of self seemed to dissolve into the moment, into the mountain, into the brilliance of the day itself. As a climber, I often had experienced the exhilaration that can well up as you reach a remote summit or pause on a steep mountainside to take in a view that only mountains provide, but this moment was different. The feeling had nothing to do with the sense of accomplishment that accompanies a successful climb or the happy relief of finishing a challenging pitch of climbing. At that moment, on that exposed ledge thousands of feet up on a steep mountainside, there was no climbing. There was just the moment and that intense feeling of connectedness.

In the years since I first read Capra's description of his epiphany on the beach, I often have tried to capture in writing my moment on the Grant Teton. You can judge whether my description somehow resonates for you, but whether you find this passage compelling, cliché, vague, or something else is irrelevant. For there is no possibility that my words can fully convey the experience of that moment on the mountain—just as Capra's words can accomplish nothing more than describing what he felt or reminding me (or you) of what I take to be a similar experience that I had. Both Capra's epiphany and mine (if such a term is even appropriate, no matter how inadequate it might be) are beyond words. And trying to render such an experience—or any experience—into words is itself a separate experience.

I am interested here in the relationship between the two: the experience itself (on the beach or the mountain) and the telling (writing) of it, the rendering into language of the experience.

Rendering in this context connotes a transformation of the experience itself, suggesting that language makes or remakes the experience. I want to suggest, however, that whatever else language can do when it comes to our experience of ourselves in the world, it does not change the experience itself. The experience is prior to the telling, which is necessarily separate from the experience. It is certainly possible, perhaps even inevitable, that language— my ability to speak, to read, to write, and to think in words—somehow figured into the moment I experienced on the Grand Teton by shaping the self that was experiencing that moment (e.g., my reading about climbing or spirituality might have influenced how I understood what I was doing at that moment), but even so, the moment stands apart from the telling of it. The telling can give meaning to the experience, but it cannot change the experience itself, because the meaning made in language of the experience is subsequent to the experience itself. In the end, the moment simply was, and I was at that moment. The telling does not change that, no matter what significance you or I or others might construct through the telling.

In this chapter I explore this relationship between experience and the telling of it. My purpose ultimately is to work toward a theory of writing as a way of being. The first step is to address the question of how writing figures into our being in the world in order to understand—and move beyond—the Cartesian view of writing and its implications for our sense of ourselves as beings in the world. In doing so, I revisit the longstanding philosophical question of the relationship between language and being. That relationship is important because contemporary theory has essentially cast language as the realm of truth, which in turn has led to the thorny problem of relativism. To put it simply, if we can know ourselves only through language, then our sense of being depends on language; furthermore, if language is necessary for being, then meaning and truth reside not in our experience but in our telling of it. Truth and meaning thus become relative. From this perspective, the truth or meaning of my moment on the mountain emerges only in the telling of it, and because there can be multiple tellings, we must find a way to judge among them; otherwise, all tellings are equally "good" or "true." However, because there is nothing outside language to ground these various tellings, we must in effect use language itself to evaluate its own truth value. Barbara Couture has succinctly articulated this dilemma: "We are trying to use language as if it can be truthful while believing it cannot be" (8). Couture elaborates: in contemporary theory, she asserts,

> [t]here is no truth that binds us all; therefore, the objective to find such truth through speaking or writing is moot. Given that truth cannot be found, the best we can do is believe the most credible or strongest argument *as if it were* true and dismiss our search for the truth. (8)

Within this framework, writing becomes an agonistic act of constructing and justifying meaning, an endless contest of meaning-making. And within the Cartesian worldview that I described in Chapter 2, that contest is exclusively intellectual, located within the realm of the Cartesian self that is conceived as fundamentally separate from the world around us. To put it in slightly different terms, my actual experience on the mountain is irrelevant; it is the telling of it, which is a linguistic act, that brings it into being and gives it meaning. The telling, not the experience, is what matters.

Obviously, such a conception of language as the locus of meaning or truth gives writing enormous power. As I point out later, the extreme version of this view is Derrida's assertion that writing is necessary for being itself. But even less extreme versions of contemporary theory conceive of meaning and truth as socially constructed through language. For example, the neo-Sophists have been at pains to reconcile this view of the role of language in meaning-making and truth-seeking with the desire to avoid relativism; as Couture implies, contemporary theorists like the neo-Sophists reject foundationalism while seeking some foundation for truth, or at least for judging among truths. Jasper Neel, Susan Jarratt, and others continue to seek that foundation in language itself.

My sense of my experience on the mountain suggests, however, not only that language (written or otherwise) is somehow inadequate to convey the experience itself but also that the experience matters without the telling. In other words, there is meaning in our experience outside language. If so, then experience itself holds the promise of becoming a grounds for truth-seeking. Language becomes not the grounds for truth but a vehicle for truth-seeking. And writing becomes part of that process. That's the dynamic I explore in this chapter.

My experience on the Grand Teton, like Capra's experience on the beach, points to another key issue that I take up in this chapter: the possibility of experiencing ourselves nondualistically rather than existing within a world defined by Cartesian duality. My experience—like Capra's and many others that have been shared in various literatures[1]—seems to point toward nonduality; it suggests a way of being in the world that is different from the dualistic Cartesian worldview that dominates mainstream schooling and writing instruction. Although such a notion is often dismissed in scholarly discussions in Western culture as spiritual rather than rigorously academic, nonduality as a way of being enjoys a strong tradition in Eastern philosophy as well as in some non-mainstream Western schools of thought. Exploring this possibility of nonduality is important in order to identify alternatives to the Cartesian worldview that informs current writing theory.

THE PROBLEM OF LANGUAGE AND BEING

How do we know that we are?

This question, which has preoccupied philosophers at least since the ancient Greeks, matters for those of us interested in writing and literacy because language is implicated in the many attempts to answer it. We might amend the question as follows: Is language essential for us to know that we exist? For much of the intellectual history of the West, the answer has been no. In the twentieth century that changed, and the ramifications for our understanding of the role of language and literacy in our sense of being have been significant.

Derrida famously used the term the metaphysics of presence (*Of Grammatology*) as shorthand for the idea in the Western intellectual tradition that reality—or *a* reality—exists outside of and unchanged by human perception and consciousness. In this metaphysics of presence, reality can be described by human language, both spoken and written (with written language traditionally understood as a representation of oral language), but reality and our sense of ourselves as separate from that reality exist apart from language; they are, that is, "prelinguistic." Language may be necessary for us to describe reality, however imperfectly, and to communicate our descriptions of it to others, but language itself is not essential for us to exist or to know that we exist. This formulation is evident in Plato's discussions of the soul and Truth, which lead to his distinction between philosophy and rhetoric (especially in *Phaedrus*). For Plato, philosophy (or more properly, dialectic) is the means to Truth, the vehicle by which our true selves, our souls, achieve the realm of the Absolute; rhetoric, which is little more than the use of language to discuss the affairs of the relative world, has nothing directly to do with Truth. In this formulation, we see the fundamental duality between self and other, between the physical and the metaphysical, that has come to define the Western intellectual tradition. We also see the beginnings of the idea of the self as essentially intellectual, an idea summed up in Descartes' line, "I think; therefore, I am."

For Plato and Aristotle, who, as Sharon Crowley puts it, "have generally held the field" (283) when it comes to our understanding of self, knowledge, and language, language was a largely unproblematic vehicle for communicating ideas, which were understood to be separate from language. The thorny questions for them had to do with the relationship between Truth and our perception of the physical world, not whether our perceptions of the world *could* be communicated through language. As Susan Bordo explains, in Plato's understanding "the typical human process of perceiving is not taken as suspect, but as a norm of one of the ways human beings make contact with the world. Looking at the process of sense-perception reveals something about the *world* of 'becoming,' it is a 'clue' to metaphysical distinctions" (36). But that changed with Galileo and then Descartes, who transformed our perceptions of the world—that is, the reality we perceive through our senses—into "mental states" that are "related to the world only causally"; in other words, the "relocation of tastes, colors, odors, and so forth, on the side of the subject" (rather than outside the subject) creates "a human capacity which, rather than being suited to apprehend a world of transient reality, is *itself* a world of transient reality: fluctuating, relative, and impermanent" (Bordo 37). Whereas for Plato the senses provided information or knowledge about the physical world, after Descartes the world essentially exists as a function of our consciousness. Human consciousness becomes the locus of reality and truth.

With Descartes the disconnection between human beings and the world is thus redefined. From the perspective of Plato and Aristotle, humans can mistake the sensible world for the realm of the Absolute, but the sensible world remains intact. For Descartes, the problem becomes the relationship between consciousness and the outer world: Because the world is not reflected but represented—constructed—in the human mind, how do we know whether that representation or construction truly corresponds to any external reality? Bordo describes this problem as one of subjectivity, that is, "the notion of the influences proceeding from 'within' the human being—not supplied by the world 'outside' the perceiver—which are capable of affecting how the world is perceived" (50). In other words, our perception of what is outside us (the world) is shaped by what is inside us (our consciousness, our intellect). This problem leads to "epistemological anxiety," or "the possibility that our human capabilities may be such that we may never be able to reach the ordinary, changing world unless, as Dewey puts it, 'the mind were protected against itself'" (51).

What is significant here is, first, that the separation between the human self (as an intellectual entity) and the physical or phenomenal world (as an external reality) that emerges from Plato is reified, and second, that human consciousness becomes the locus of all meaning. The Cartesian self is now the main reference point in our efforts to understand reality, who we are, and how we relate to the world around us. Bordo refers to the resulting "deep epistemological alienation that attends the sense of mental interiority" that emerges from Descartes, "the enormous gulf that must separate what is conceived as occurring 'in here' from that which, correspondingly, must lay 'out there'" (55). The divide between the self and any external reality, which is now essentially a mental state, is complete: "Under such conditions, *cogito ergo sum* is, indeed, the only emphatic reality, for to be assured of its truth, we require nothing but confrontation with the inner stream itself" (55).

Language thus becomes ever more important to the most fundamental epistemological and ontological questions. If reality, meaning, and truth reside within human consciousness, then the capacity of the human mind to make sense of and communicate experience becomes paramount and the question of the relationship between knowing and language becomes central to any effort to seek knowledge or truth. In other words, we must now ask to what extent our knowledge of reality is a function of language, and we must ask whether our experience of ourselves as beings in the world is possible without language. This is where Derrida's influence becomes especially important.

Probably more than any other major thinker, Derrida challenged the idea that language is subsequent to our sense of ourselves as beings in the world. As Jasper Neel has explained, Derrida "shows that solitary mental life does not precede and inform systems of indication; instead, systems of indication create the possibility of solitary mental life by replacing it, representing it, and showing that it is gone. Further, pure self-presence, rather than the originary medium in which solitary mental life exists, itself depends on a prior medium" (143). For Derrida, of course, writing is that medium. As Neel puts it,

Through an enormous and painstaking set of readings ... Derrida has
tried to show that all the characteristics of writing in the narrow sense—
all the deficiencies that make it tertiary, repetitive, metaphoric, and
metonymic—also exist in speaking, also exist in thinking, exist even in
Being. In other words, what Derrida calls writing-in-general ... already
constitutes everything that would present itself as prior to and purer
than writing. (112–13)

To state it baldly, we do not exist without writing.

As Neel rightly notes, this is an audacious assertion that "invites scorn,
if not contemptuous ridicule" (112). Yet Derrida's conception of writing as
necessary for being is not a terribly long step from Descartes' view that the
human mind contains all reality; it is a daring but not entirely surprising
answer to Descartes' question of "whether any of the object of which I have
ideas within me exist outside of me" (qtd. in Bordo 55). Part of Derrida's
answer is that it doesn't matter. That is, if all we really have is our representation of an object, then the object can only exist as a representation; ultimately, all we have are the signs by which we represent the signified. For
Derrida, there can be no pure meaning because meaning can never be
reduced to the object itself (the signified); the expression of the thing is
always already removed from the thing itself: "the representative is not the
represented but only the representer of the represented; it is not the same as
itself" (*Grammatology* 297). The result is the now familiar endless play of
signification.

So language is all we have, not only to know ourselves but also to know
the world, which exists as a mental representation constructed through language. Derrida argues that the self can never be present to itself without a
way to describe itself, which is language. But as soon as any attempt to
describe the self enters the realm of language, the self is immediately dis-
placed by the inherently referential nature of language. Language is thus
necessary for the self to know itself, but language cannot allow for the pure
"solitary mental life" that Edmund Husserl sought to describe. Meaning
that resides in that "solitary mental life" could only exist beyond language if
it were "present to the self in the life of a present that has not yet gone forth
from itself into the world, space or nature" (*Speech and Phenomena*, pp.
40–41; qtd. in Neel, p. 143), which for Derrida is not possible. Note that
Derrida's analysis rests on a fundamental separation between that human
self and the "world, space or nature." The self attempting to know itself, in
Derrida's formulation, exists apart from the world, just as it does for
Descartes. In fact, the relationship of that self to any sort of external reality,
physical or otherwise, is largely irrelevant to Derrida's analysis of the role of
language in being, because for Derrida being is an exclusively intellectual
(indeed, *linguistic*) matter. He is not concerned with any sort of correspondence between the self—essentially, the mind—and an external reality, for

such a correspondence is not, in his analysis, possible. The main point here is that the separation between mind and world is a foundational assumption that enables Derrida to pursue his analysis.

Many compositionists, notably Neel, Crowley, Victor Vitzanza, and Jarratt have embraced this line of analysis in their efforts to revive what they see as a promising alternative to the mainstream Platonic and Aristotelian versions of rhetoric. That alternative lies in the Sophists. As these neo-Sophists have shown, the Sophists anticipated the poststructuralist analyses of language and meaning by rejecting the Platonic idea that we can know Absolute Truth. Thus, they also rejected Plato's distinction between philosophy and rhetoric and his denigration of rhetoric as relegated to the ordinary world of appearances—that contingent, day-to-day reality that Plato believed is not where Truth resides. For the Sophists, the impossibility of knowing the Absolute, even if it exists, elevates rhetoric to an essential vehicle for pursuing the contingent truth that is the only truth available to us. Gorgias, a key Sophist (and a focus of Plato's condemnation), asserted in *On the Nonexistent* that "even if anything exists, it is unknowable and incomprehensible to man" (Sextus, *Against the Schoolmasters* vii, 65–87, 77). Moreover, even if we could know reality, "it would be incapable of being conveyed to another" (83). For Gorgias, *logos*, which roughly corresponds to language, is "that by which we reveal" the world, "but logos is not substances and existing things. Therefore we do not reveal existing things to our neighbors, but logos, which is something other than substances" (84). To put that statement in more contemporary terms, the signifier is not the thing signified. As Crowley points out, "What Gorgias does here is to release logos from adherence to any other reality; the word has no necessary correlation to the world of Being" (281). Like Derrida, Gorgias essentially embraces language as all we really have.

Resurrecting the Sophists is part of an effort to challenge the dominance of Platonic and Aristotelian versions of rhetoric but also to confront the specter of radical relativism that accompanies a postmodern perspective on knowledge and truth. Neel, for example, argues for a "strong discourse" based on Sophistic principles, especially the indeterminacy of truth and the centrality of language in our understanding of ourselves within the world of probability; strong discourse, according to Neel, assumes "the power of rhetoric to shape all things human" but also assumes "that humans could make better or worse choices and that the value of rhetoric, in spite of its capability of being misused, was to make the better choices prevail" (208). Rhetoric becomes the vehicle for determining good in an inherently contingent world, thereby displacing philosophy as the means to Truth in Plato's longstanding hierarchy. Like Neel, Jarratt finds in the Sophists "a usable model for contemporary historians of rhetoric" (*Rereading* xxi); for Jarratt, "analyzing the relationships among the first sophists' social theory, their pedagogy, and the functioning of the democracy in their time can help us evaluate the political dimensions of the composition pedagogies in our own" (82). In her view, the power of a sophistic rhetoric lies in the possibilities it represents for combating relativism: "Through reference to the formation of ethical norms within communities, the sophists go beyond total relativism— a hedonistic self-interest—to a discourse about enlightened self-interest based in the notion of 'self' constituted by the community" (96). In other words, truth lies in an ethical practice of rhetoric, which is essentially the social process of truth-seeking through language.

These are compelling, if by now familiar, arguments that speak to the view, which I believe is widespread among compositionists, that teaching writing is intimately related to the functioning of our communities and institutions, as I noted in Chapter 2; they reflect the progressive hope that writing instruction can be part of a larger effort to create a more just society. I share this view. However, the Cartesian worldview that remains at the foundation of contemporary composition theory, including neo-sophistic rhetoric and post-process theory, undermines these progressive goals. For in developing theories and associated pedagogies that rest on a Cartesian worldview, we also continue to promote the dualisms that characterize that worldview and perpetuate the Cartesian self that is implicated in the crisis of sustainability, as I explained in Chapter 1.

It is important to emphasize here the value of the insights that neo-sophistic and post-process theorists have brought to the teaching of writing. For example, the widely accepted view of the contingency of meaning and the inherently referential nature of language helps us understand not only how language—and especially writing—functions but also how our conventional approaches to writing instruction can shortchange students. Neel, for example, uses Derrida's analyses to show how conventional writing instruction perpetrates a fraud on students by reinforcing the false idea that individual writers can encode a stable and intentional meaning in their texts that any reader can then decode: "Most writers seek an algebraic writing in which inscription functions as an equation between the author's intended meaning and the reader's comprehension of that meaning" (163–64). This "inscription" is the kind of writing we claim to teach students. But "the more deeply the student becomes enmeshed in the writing process, the more surely that process places the finitude of meaning outside itself" (164). In the end, "encouraged by the composition teacher's insistence on the framing mechanisms and usage patterns of edited prose, students attempt to construct a pure outside with no inside at all, a group of marks having nothing to do with writing and announcing themselves as correct" (165).

I think Neel is right. In this regard, we would do well to apply Derrida's insights and stop promoting the myth that writing is a matter of form and convention that give us control over meaning. Writing may enable us to act, to claim agency in the social realm (as Freire argued), but writing cannot give us control over meaning. To write is to know that; to write is continually to confront the impossibility of control, as Neel suggests. Yet we teach the opposite lesson. In doing so, we not only perpetrate on students the fraud that Neel describes but we also reinforce a greater (and more problematic) belief about the extent of control we humans can exert over the world around us. At the same time, we reinforce the Cartesian binaries and resulting hierarchies that characterize the Western worldview, especially the valuing of the intellect over the physical, which leads to a denigration of the non-human world. In this way, through mainstream writing instruction we enact a dualistic way of being in the world that has contributed to the structures and practices that characterize our destructive, wasteful, and inequitable contemporary lifestyle.

If Composition Studies is to be part of a larger effort to imagine and build a just future together, it must move away from the Cartesian worldview that informs its current theories. Although dominated by Platonism and, later Cartesianism, the Western intellectual tradition does include alternative philosophies that lay a foundation for a nondualistic worldview, including schools of thought such as transcendentalism and some versions of phenomenology (e.g., Martin Heidegger and Maurice Merleau-Ponty). Some composition scholars, notably Couture, have drawn on these traditions to argue for theories based on connection, empathy, and negotiation (about which I say more later.) But Eastern intellectual history offers a much stronger tradition of nondualism, especially in Zen Buddhism. I turn now to that tradition as a foundation for the nonduality that I believe should characterize our understanding—and practice—of writing.

NONDUALITY AS A FRAMEWORK FOR UNDERSTANDING WRITING AS A WAY OF BEING

Eihei Dogen (1200–1253), one of the most significant thinkers in the Eastern tradition, is studied as a great Zen Buddhist teacher, but he also is regarded as a brilliant and innovative philosopher who offers sometimes startling insights into the timeless problems of philosophy, including the nature of being. As Thomas P. Kasulis notes, it is common although misguided to "make the assumption that being a Zen Buddhist and being a philosopher are mutually exclusive projects"; Kasulis points out that Zen "does make certain claims about the structure and pattern of human experience" and addresses the same fundamental questions that have preoccupied Western philosophy (354).[2] Despite being absent from most philosophical discourse

in the West, Dogen recently has been the focus of study by Western scholars, in part because of the perceived similarities between his thinking (and
Zen thought in general) and postmodern theory (see Carl Olson).

For my purposes, Dogen's significance grows out of his radical nondualistic approach to the problem of the self as well as his characteristic Zen
skepticism about language. His insights, which converge with some of the
most important ideas informing neo-sophistic rhetoric and post-process
theory, offer a powerful way to undermine the Cartesian worldview that is
the foundation for our prevailing understanding of writing. If we replace the
fundamental separation of self and world (and the related Cartesian binaries
of subject–object and mind–body) with a view of the basic interconnectedness of all beings, we can revise the problem of language and being. Instead
of language being all we have and therefore the source of whatever truth we
can find, as contemporary theory holds, language becomes a vehicle for
understanding our experience of the phenomenal world as a foundation for
truth. Writing can then be redefined as part of a nondualistic way of being
in the world. As I demonstrate here, such an approach is not "foundational" in the sense of that term that emerged from the theoretical debates in
Composition Studies in the 1980s and 1990s (e.g., Bizzell; Cooper), because
it redefines truth-seeking as a dialectical process in which language plays a
key role and preserves the idea of contingent truth that has energized the
neo-Sophists; moreover, nonduality enables us to negotiate the problem of
the relationship between language and reality that I discussed earlier in this
chapter.

The key to Dogen's philosophy lies in what Masao Abe calls Dogen's
"radical Buddhist deanthropocentrism" (44), his idea of "whole-being,"
which includes "sentient as well as nonsentient beings" (42). The implications of such a radical nonduality are profound, but they are especially relevant to our efforts to reconceive of the self. As Abe notes, Western philosophy valorizes humans over things, which leads to a "reification of the
human self" (32). By contrast, "[i]n Dogen, people are not essentially distin-
guished from other beings, but are grasped as part of the realm of beings.
People and other beings are equally subject to impermanence, or transien-
cy" (32). In Dogen's understanding, then, the self cannot be purely intellectual, because the self emerges from a oneness that encompasses all beings,
both sentient and nonsentient; moreover, Dogen's emphasis on impermanence leads to a rejection of the ideas of a genuine or metaphysical self—that
is, "the immutability of *atman*, or selfhood"—and "the perishability of the
body, a view whose Western equivalent may be the Platonic immortality of
the soul or the Cartesian thinking ego" (Abe 44). Dogen sees whole-being as
"human, sentient, and non-sentient beings within the limitless universe,
which is radically deanthropocentric and constitutes the ultimate ontological ground" (44).

Through an extremely complex analysis founded on the basic idea of impermanence, Dogen thus eliminates the problematic Platonic hierarchy of the
intellectual (the mind or soul) over the physical (the body) as well as the
familiar Cartesian subject–object duality. Because all beings, both sentient
and insentient, are subject to the inherent impermanence of existence, there
is no fundamental distinction among them; moreover, impermanence
extends to any ideas of selfhood or ego, which means that there is no transcendent self or individual soul that exists apart from the body. In explaining Dogen's understanding of realizing Buddha-nature, which we might
translate roughly as truth (or, to put it in more spiritual terms, enlightenment), Abe emphasizes Dogen's insistence that

> to attain Buddha-nature, one must transcend one's egocentrism, anthro-
> pocentrism, and sentient-being centrism, and thereby ground one's exis-
> tence in the most fundamental plane, that is, in the being dimension,
> which is the dimension of Dogen's *shitsuu*, that is, whole-being. The
> realization of the impermanence of *shitsuu* is absolutely necessary for
> the attainment of Buddha-nature. (50)

Abe sums up this crucial idea: "For Dogen, all beings, impermanence, and the
Buddha-nature are identical, with the realization of impermanence as the
dynamic axis" (64). Within such a framework, there can ultimately be no distinction between the physical and the intellectual, between self and other.[3]

Characteristically, Dogen's understanding of nonduality encompasses
the kind of paradox that many people associate with Zen. With respect to the
self, as Abe notes, "while all subjects and objects are mutually reversible, the
subject is always the subject and the object is always the object. Self and
other are nondual but do not lose the distinction between them" (89). This
sense of nonduality resembles the idea of dialectic familiar to us in Western
philosophy, but it differs from dialectic in that it assumes that the distinction
between subject and object is irrelevant because ultimately both are defined
by the same oneness. (Strictly speaking, in Zen thought, these distinctions
are human-constructed categories, which by definition are delusions and
therefore do not correspond to truth; they are simply imperfect tools by
which we try to describe existence.)

Dogen's nonduality leads to an approach to the question of being that is
dramatically different from the approach that Western philosophy has taken.
Whereas Western philosophers after Descartes have focused on the nature of
the human self as an "interior" matter, Dogen emphasizes the *experiences* of
duality and nonduality (or in traditional Zen terms, delusion and enlightenment). For Dogen, realizing duality is necessary in order to overcome it;
nonduality therefore becomes both an explanation and a way of being. In
Zen terms, Dogen presents a path to "realization," or the experience of nonduality, rather than an analysis of it in the Western sense:

The boundary of realization is not distinct, for the realization comes forth simultaneously with the mastery of buddha-dharma [i.e., Zen teachings]. Do not suppose that what you realize becomes your knowledge and is grasped by your consciousness. Although actualized immediately, the inconceivable may not be distinctly apparent. Its appearance is beyond your knowledge. (Tanahashi 15)

We can understand "the inconceivable" roughly as truth (in Zen terms, enlightenment). This truth is beyond our grasp, because truth cannot be understood intellectually; it must be "realized"—that is, experienced as a way of being. That experience is, paradoxically, an outcome of a study of the self in order to realize the ultimate emptiness of the self—to experience what in Zen is known as "no-self." Tanahashi explains that "'Self' immediately opens into selflessness. . . . Thus, the teaching of no-self is not nihilism, not an assertion that nothing exists. Rather, it is an awareness of the interdependence of all things—the reality of things as they are," unfiltered by human conception (17). The idea of *self* thus becomes a realization of nonduality; experience and conception converge and then disappear (in Dogen's famous phrase, "mind and body fall away").

This kind of approach often is dismissed by Western scholars as so much spiritualism or mysticism, but Dogen addresses the same fundamental issues examined by Western philosophers and, like many Western philosophers, relies on empirical evidence gleaned from experience. "The major difference between the appeal of the Western empiricist or phenomenologist and the appeal of the Zen master," according to Kasulis, "is that the former very often appeals to experiences we have all had, but the latter appeals only to the experience that his disciple is having at that very moment" (356). Zen is characterized by "a dogged refusal to manufacture realities that are not directly experienced and a critical vigilance against both the idling of language and the acceptance of hidden, unjustified presuppositions lurking within our commonly held conceptualizations" (355). Or as David Loy puts it, "All philosophy is an attempt to understand our experience, but here the critical issue is the type of experience that we accept as fundamental, as opposed to the type of experience that needs to be 'explained'" (8). Loy argues that "those educated in the Western empiricist tradition are more likely to be skeptical of such [nondualistic] experience and prefer to 'explain away' nonduality in terms of something else that they are able to understand" (8). But the possibility of experiencing nonduality is well documented, as Loy goes on to show, and not only in Eastern traditions; indeed, there is in the Western tradition similar descriptions of nonduality, such as Emerson's "Over-Soul" (see also Capra; Sartwell, esp. 122–28).

Here we are back to the problem of language, for if Zen is vigilant against "the idling of language and the acceptance of hidden, unjustified presuppositions lurking within our commonly held conceptualizations," as

Kasulis puts it, how do we get beyond language to access a reality untainted by human delusion, which is reflected in language? The answer lies in Dogen's rejection of language and thought as *the* sole means to truth.

Dogen exhibits Zen's traditional skepticism about language, which in many ways resembles the poststructuralist view that there is no stable relationship between the signifier and the thing signified. As I noted earlier, for Derrida (and other postmodern theorists), the indeterminacy of meaning is a given, because there is always a distinction between the sign and the thing signified; ultimately, the signifier is not the same as the thing signified but always a representation of the thing signified. Dogen shares the view that meaning is unstable and therefore unreliable as a vehicle for truth. As Kasulis describes Dogen's ideas about expression, "the occasion determines the perspective that any given expression will take. In short, the meaning of an expression always has a contextual dimension" (360). The difference is that for Dogen there is the possibility of an "extra-linguistic" reality. This possibility must be understood in terms of Dogen's radical nonduality, in which our being as well as our consciousness of ourselves and the physical world are one and the same. There is no distinction between the world of appearance, the world of delusion, and the realm of truth. In this sense, Dogen rejects the most important duality established by Plato and reified by Descartes. I quote Kasulis' helpful explanation of this dynamic at length:

> Dogen would not want to say that he is describing "Zen consciousness" or "enlightened consciousness" to the exclusion of "ordinary consciousness." Fundamentally, our experience as experienced is not different from the Zen master's. Where we differ is that we place a particular kind of conceptual overlay onto that experience and then proceed to make an emotional investment in that overlay, taking it to be "real" in and of itself rather than to be an "expression" of the "occasion" in which we think or talk about the given experience. In a sense, we have a double-layered description. First, there is the prereflective, not yet conceptualized, experience—what we all share, Zen master and the rest of us alike. Second, there is the expression or characterization of any experience within a particular situation or occasion. If the speaker brings no personal, egotistic delusions into this expression, the occasion speaks for itself, the total situation alone determines what is said or done. Thus, in the case of the Zen master, what-is-said is simply what-is. In the case of the deluded person, however, the "what-is" includes his excess conceptual baggage with its affective components, the deluded ideas about the nature of "self," "thing," "time," and so on that constitute the person's own particular distortion of what actually is. (359–60)

In this formulation, language ceases to be an obstacle to truth because truth is extra-linguistic.

Dogen's nonduality thus enables us to redefine the problem of language and being. Whereas for Derrida and other postmodern thinkers language is all we have, for Dogen language is both necessary and irrelevant. This understanding may strike many compositionists, steeped as we are in postmodern theory, as smacking of foundationalism, given that it assumes a kind of transcendent truth that can be accessed. But the assumption that language is all we have is itself foundational and based on the same Cartesian dualisms that Derrida claims to undermine. In fact, Loy charges that Derrida's critique is "not radical enough" because it does not go far enough in deconstructing itself (249). Loy argues that Derrida's notion of *differance* stops short of erasing the dualities it seems to undermine: "Derrida, although aware that each term of a duality is the differance of the other, does not fully realize how deconstructing one term (transcendental signified, self-presence, reference, etc.) must also transform the other (differance, temporization, supplementation, etc.)" (249).[4] As a result, Derrida disrupts the hierarchy of thing to signifier but remains trapped "in the halfway-house of proliferating 'pure textuality'" (249). A "complete deconstruction of such dualities," according to Loy, can lead to "a mode of experience which is not governed by them" (249–50). As a nondualist, Loy agrees that

> such dualities are ineluctably inscribed in language and thus are fundamental categories of thought; however, *this means not that they are inescapable, but that their deconstruction points finally to an experience beyond language*—or, more precisely, to a nondual way of experiencing language and thought. (250; emphasis added).

Loy draws on the same radical nonduality that Dogen posits to call for the deconstruction of "the apparent objectivity of the world": "the relationship between names and things is the archetypal signifier/signified correspondence, and the nondualist goal is nothing else than its complete deconstruction" (250). Philosophy, Loy argues,

> cannot grasp what it seeks in any of its categories, but, as language becoming self-conscious of its function, it can learn to "undo" itself and cease to be an obstruction, in that way allowing what we have long sought to manifest itself. This "origin-that-cannot-be-named" has always been the most obvious thing, but all ways of thinking about it— whether metaphysical or deconstructive—can only conceal it by dualistically separating us from it. (250–51)

In short, the duality we assume and enact through language prevents us from realizing the nonduality we seek. Conversely, an assumption of nonduality—and the acceptance of the possibility of experiencing nonduality as a valid mode of being, or in Loy's phrasing, "a nondual way of experiencing language and thought"—holds open the possibility that we can overcome (or circumvent) the inherent duality of language as we work toward meaning and truth, even as we recognize the contingency of both.

Part of what makes Dogen's nondualistic perspective so challenging for Western readers is that its basic premises seem to fly in the face of what Western philosophy assumes to be valid. As Loy explains, "The Western belief that only one type of experience is veridical is a post-Aristotelian assumption now too deeply ingrained to be easily recognized as such by many" (8); that experience is "our usual dualistic experience (or understanding of experience)," which Western philosophy accepts as valid and therefore worthy of study; nonduality and experiences associated with it (such as Zen enlightenment) are usually dismissed as "philosophically insignificant aberrations" (8). Like Loy, I often see that impasse as insurmountable: "Because it is a matter of premises, at this level there are no neutral or objective criteria by which we can evaluate these two views—indeed, the very concept of 'objective criteria' is itself under question" (8). That statement should sound familiar to those of us trained in the postmodern era. We can see this problem in neo-sophistic terms and assume that because objectivity in the Western sense is impossible, we must seek contingent truth, through rhetoric, in the world of probability. This is now more or less how we in Composition Studies tend to view the problem. At the same time, some cross-cultural work in anthropology (see Abram) as well as theoretical developments in modern physics suggest that the idea of nonduality is not merely a spiritual belief or so much philosophic debate but rather a legitimate description of the physical world and a valid way to understand what it means to be human (see Capra).

One simple example comes from Lisa Delpit's description of her literacy work in Native Alaskan villages. Explaining some of the difficulties that mainstream literacy teachers encounter as a result of cultural differences, Delpit shares the comment of a Native Alaskan teacher about "one of the most senseless rituals of schooling," the roll call: "'We ask the children if they are here while looking at them!'" Such a practice may not seem senseless to those of us raised in mainstream American society, because, as Delpit notes, it "conforms to the decontextualizing rituals of school: we insist that children assert their existence through the *word*, their actual presence is insufficient" (99).[5] Delpit goes on to discuss "our insistence that children verbally mediate any action. The action itself is not evidence of its existence—it must be put into words." She then questions the imposing of Western pedagogical methods and values on other cultures: "Could we be asking them [non-Western students] to ignore knowledge they've acquired through a variety of nonverbal sources and to limit their understanding of the world to the word?" (99). Leaving aside the valid point that writing (or speaking) about an action is a legitimate means of fostering a certain kind of reflection in students (which is itself reflective of Western values), the answer to Delpit's question is yes. Her question underscores not only the emphasis we in the West place on the *word* as an expression of our being but also the possibility that other cultures experience the world differently—in ways that are not always mediated by the word.

Earlier in her essay Delpit relates an anecdote about visiting Denali National Park. Before her visit an Aleut friend told her, "When you see the mountain, say 'Hello, Grandfather'" (91). That request, writes Delpit,

> stopped me in my tracks: I had been going, as the superior human, to look at the lifeless, inanimate mountain. She [her Aleut friend] reminded me ... that the mountain and I were part of the same world, that it had lived infinitely longer than I, that it would "see" me, even as I thought I was looking at it, and that I must approach this grandfather with due respect, a respect deserved for all that it had seen. (91)

Delpit's anecdote highlights a way of being in the world (that of the Aleuts) that, although seeming exotic to Westerners, seems quite consistent with Dogen's radical nonduality, in which both the sentient and insentient are the same reality, in which human *being* is fundamentally a part of the physical world, in which oneness is part of one's lived experience. Her story opens up the possibility not only that we can grasp nonduality but also that it can become a way of experiencing ourselves in the world. It also underscores the ambivalent role of language and literacy in that process, which contrasts sharply with the postmodern preoccupation with language.

WRITING (IN) AN EXTRA-LINGUISTIC REALITY

My analysis thus far might suggest that writing is less relevant, less important, than those of us who have devoted our lives to the study and teaching of writing would like to believe. If truth is extra-linguistic, as Dogen believed, and not a function of discourse—and thus not the exclusive realm of rhetoric—but rather resides in experience that can never be fully captured in language, what role does writing play in truth-seeking? What role can it play in our efforts to know ourselves and the world? If the Cartesian dualities that I have argued are at the root of the crisis of sustainability are "inscribed in language and thus are fundamental categories of thought," as Loy holds (250), how can writing be part of our efforts to move beyond those dualities? If Loy is right that we should seek "a nondual way of experiencing language and thought," what would that be? More to the point, how would writing figure into it? And where might such a way of experiencing language and thought leave Composition Studies? Where does it leave the writer? The writing teacher?

I have suggested in this chapter that we abandon the idea that language and writing are essential for truth-seeking and accept Dogen's view that language is, at best, an imperfect tool for truth-seeking rather than the grounds for truth itself. Such a view obviously requires revising some of our beliefs about the value of writing. The idea that writing is important—indeed, essential—is so deeply ingrained in contemporary schooling, in mainstream culture, and in the field of Composition Studies that it is virtually beyond question. The centrality of the written word in Western culture has given rise in the modern era to an almost universal emphasis on literacy (I think it's fair to call it an *obsession* with literacy, as some critics have) as a crucial tool for progress—so much so that it seems downright nutty to question the role of writing in formal education or to propose displacing writing from the center of any project concerned with truth-seeking. I would even go so far as to say that a subtle (if unintentional) arrogance infects the field of Composition Studies—an arrogance based on our deeply held belief that writing not only lies at the heart of learning in formal schooling but also is essential for our effective functioning as citizens, workers, and consumers; writing, we like to say, is a form of agency, a powerful and essential means of making our way in the world. (The wonderful irony here is that Composition has long been dismissed in the academy as Literature's poor stepsister, yet ultimately it is Composition that wears the gown to the postsecondary ball in the form of virtually universal undergraduate general education writing requirements.) I am guilty of this arrogance, having argued for even greater emphasis on writing in conventional secondary and postsecondary curricula and having theorized the role of writing as central to the process of constructing the self (Yagelski, *Literacy Matters*; "Literature and Literacy"). Indeed, in the book you are now reading I rest my argument for a new theory of writing and its role in creating a just and sustainable future in large part on the centrality of writing in schooling and the near-universal experience of school-sponsored writing instruction in modern American (and Western) society. Yet my analysis suggests that writing may be, if not irrelevant to truth-seeking, then at least something less than central to it; moreover, writing as practiced and taught in mainstream schooling may well be antithetical to truth-seeking.

So as the New Englander in the old joke says to the tourist asking for directions, "Ya can't get there from here." If "here" is a world facing a crisis of sustainability in which writing is implicated, as I argue in Chapter 1, and "there" is a more just and sustainable future in which writing is part of the process of truth-seeking, we will need to take a few detours along the way. The first I have already noted: the acceptance of the idea of extralinguistic experience.

In what he calls his "discourse against discourse" (3), Crispin Sartwell challenges "our obsession with language" (3) and emphasizes "what, in our everyday experience and in our everyday world, escapes linguistic articulation: at a rough estimate, almost everything" (5). Acknowledging that "[p]erhaps what we do frame into words constitutes our awareness at any given moment," Sartwell avers that "some things (most things) always stand in excess to language" (5); that is, language can never capture the totality of our experience or even partially render it in a way that is adequate: "Try providing an exhaustive description of your own visual experience at any given moment, and you will see how much of what we experience, even if it could in principle be cast into language, isn't" (5). Sartwell's larger purpose is to show that there is no purpose, to challenge what he calls the "teleological order" (12) that he sees characterizing the Western worldview. This impulse to see human life as project and the individual human life as defined by a project, which originates in Aristotle and provides the framework for mainstream Western intellectual history, leads to narrative, the idea that "our self-understandings and our understandings of others are articulated as stories" (9). Narrative, writes Sartwell, "is a principle of or a strategy for organization" (9), and he wishes to "sketch the limits of narrative as a category" and "question whether and to what extent human experience and human life are organized narratively" (10). In Western culture, Sartwell argues, "narrative is bound up with the teleology of human life, a teleology that lends life intelligibility or makes it meaningful" (11). He rejects that idea—"I will question whether human experience and human life are meaningful" (10)—and seeks to "develop or discover ways out of the linguistic and narrative teleological order" (8), which, he asserts, essentially make us miserable in pursuit of socially constructed goals that are, in the end, chimerical at best.

We need not embrace the idea that human life is meaninglessness, as Sartwell does, to achieve the well-being, the release, he seeks (although it would probably eliminate much of our individual and collective anxiety about our individual and collective futures), but his critique of the poststructuralist obsession with language that has characterized contemporary theory can help us better grasp the idea of extralinguistic experience. For example, in rejecting the notion, which emerges from Alasdair McIntyre and Paul Ricoeur, that a coherent narrative of human life is necessary, Sartwell asks us to consider how poorly language allows us to describe or account for how we actually experience ourselves in time:

> Think seriously for a minute about what you do and what you experience in a day. Better, think about the richness contained in a single glance. Then think, first, about the impoverished character of any human sign system with regard to the content of any glance: how far we are from being able to describe it, how far we are from wanting to, how far we are from needing to. Look at a wall, and think seriously for a moment what would be

involved in attempting to squeeze that experience, all of it, into the order of the sign; now add the other sense modalities and their contents; now add the feelings within your body. Now think about the act you are performing: intentionally looking at a wall, in fact, looking at it for certain ends. Now try to rank that experience on a hierarchy of values. Even if something comes to mind here, think about whether you usually do that with glances at a wall, think about whether you want to do that with all such glances and whether you could. Think seriously about the torturous obsession that would ensue from taking that approach to life. (44)

Here Sartwell illuminates the inadequacy of signs—of writing—to capture experience at the same time that he exposes the power of language to oppress. We use language to (try to) impose order on the world and give meaning to our experience of it; at the same time language imposes an order on our experience of the world. Either way, we are removed from our experience, which can never be adequately rendered in language. Paradoxically, then, our efforts to make sense of the world through language leave the world less intelligible to us.[6]

Part of the point here (and one that Sartwell emphasizes) is that there is no need to impose such a linguistic regime on our experience of ourselves in the world. I am reminded of a friend who refuses to talk about the novel he is writing, as if his spoken words will somehow corrupt his written ones or, more to the point, his experience of producing them. For him it is enough to write, to *be* in his writing. What happens to the text he creates after he is finished with it is, in large measure, irrelevant to his experience of writing it now. And he need not understand that experience (or try to) by talking about it with me or anyone else. Even if he wanted to, he could not convey the experience adequately to others; he could only construct a version of it by telling it to another. That version would not be the experience itself, and it would not change the experience (although it might change his subsequent sense of it or the meaning he tries to make of it). In the end, his experience and the telling of it are two different things, and telling it does not make it more or less real nor does it enhance the experience, because the telling will always be subsequent to the experience itself—in the same way that my telling of my experience on the Grand Teton at the beginning of this chapter does not change the experience I had then. (I can, of course, say the same thing about the writing I am engaged in right now—about which I will say more in Chapter 4.) Some things are better left to silence. And that, Sartwell argues, is what's missing from the analyses offered by Foucault, McIntyre, Lyotard, and other poststructuralist theorists: "the moment of silence, the moment of death, the moment of inarticulate orgasm" (4). To illustrate, he points to ecstasy, that "extraordinary experience of letting-go into the divine, or into the lover, or into death." To this extraordinary experience, Sartwell says, language seems radically insufficient. He continues,

This movement is present in all great spiritual traditions (with regard to which it is often called "mysticism"), as when the *Tao Te Ching* says that the Tao that can be spoken is not the real Tao, or when the Zen master, asked for the one word of power, replies by burping. (4–5)

Thus, Sartwell acknowledges extra-linguistic experience and rejects what he sees as our obsession with trying to impose order and meaning on that experience through language. This is a first step toward an ontology of writing that is consistent with the hope for a just and sustainable future.

A second step is to redefine writing itself: not as the grounds for truth or the expression of truth, for these conceptions of writing grow out of the Cartesian dualisms that I wish to undermine, but as *part of the process of truth-seeking*. Writing, as a way of being in the world, must become, as Loy puts it, part of "a nondual way of experiencing language and thought" (250). Such a conception of writing is a significant departure from current theory, which defines language as the grounds for contingent truth and writing as a means of constructing and conveying knowledge. But it is a necessary step toward replacing the mainstream Cartesian view of writing. For this step, Couture's phenomenological rhetoric provides an especially useful framework.

In *Toward a Phenomenological Rhetoric*, Couture seeks to counteract "the exclusion of truth from writing" (2), which she believes has resulted from Composition Studies' embrace of poststructuralist theory and Derrida's version of deconstruction; she wishes to restore truth to writing by adopting a phenomenological rhetoric that "abandons the Western sophistic tradition of arriving at truth through conquering and consensus, and grounds it instead in a conscious commitment to collaboration with others in truth seeking" (4; emphasis added). Drawing on Husserl, Heidegger, and other philosophers in the tradition of phenomenology, Couture proposes a rhetorical practice of profession in which the writer "attends to the world with open acceptance ... [and] reconciles the objective world with one's self assessment of it"; in this formulation the writer "transforms both the world as seen and the 'I' within it" (5) through a collaborative process of regeneration that "establish[es] new ground for shared understanding" (131). Couture's effort to reclaim "rhetoric as a truth seeking practice" (63) rests on three principles of phenomenology: "1. all essences or truth are located in subjective experience; 2. truth is an outcome of intersubjective understanding; and 3. intersubjective understanding progresses toward truth through expression (writing/speaking)" (64). Thus, writing can be an integral part of the process of truth-seeking, which is grounded in subjective experience: "rhetoric works or ought to work to further our endeavor of making sense of the world" (64). According to Couture, "we see purpose ... in participating together in *writing* the world; and it is in doing so that we move together toward writing truth" (83).

Couture's rhetoric is thus inherently social and deeply ethical; it rests on a notion of truth not as transcendent and thus "separate from the present life we experience" but as residing in the personal, in our lived experience of the world (23). In this view, writing is not the locus of truth but a necessary means for *expressing* lived experience as part of the collaborative process of making sense of the world—of seeking truth. Significantly, Couture recognizes the "difference between particular experience and generalizations about it, acknowledging the dif-ference between experience lived and experience writ, as it were" (124).[7] This is a crucial point that is akin to the Zen understanding of the relationship between experience and language. As I noted earlier, experience and the rendering of it into language are not the same thing, but language can be *a* means (not *the* means) to understanding experience. As Couture puts it, "language ... does not represent our consciousness but rather manifests it" (108). This conception of the relationship of language and consciousness enables us to begin to reconceptualize writing as an expression, rather than the locus, of truth.

Couture's understanding of language provides the foundation for her critique of the philosophical relativism that emerges from current textual theories. According to Couture, philosophical relativism leads to the dilemma that I identified at the beginning of this chapter: "We are trying to use language as if it can be truthful while believing that it cannot be" (8). As a result, rhetoric, instead of being part of a process of truth-seeking, "merely provides a tool to distinguish the difference between one way of seeing and another, a perception that, if left unguided by some ethical stance, could lead either to endless and unresolvable bickering over which position holds greater value or to a *truth* accepted on the sole basis of a rhetorical argument that proved most powerful" (8). For Couture, such a condition is untenable: "If human activity is directionless, then seeking the truth through writing is essentially purposeless and merely substitutes change for progress, as one discourse continually replaces another through besting an other" (23).

Leaving aside the vexed idea that human life should be defined by progress (a notion that Sartwell adamantly rejects, as I noted above), we can see in Couture's rhetoric a crucial move to wrest truth from the realm of discourse and relocate it in shared human experience: "We must reclaim truth as an essential function of our subjectivity, of our daily interaction with one another, and of our constant effort to reflect on ourselves in order to understand one another" (10). For Couture, truth can be found in "the very phenomenon of continuous human interaction" (10). And that move enables us to redefine writing as part of a process of truth-seeking: "The consequence of reconstructing truth in this way is not to separate our rhetoric—that is, our writing and speaking of truth about the world—from philosophy, but rather to practice philosophy, that is, the seeking of truth, as rhetoric" (23). In this formulation, Couture rejects the traditional reading of Plato's separation of philosophy and rhetoric, which has led to a denigration of rhetoric as *techne*. This rejection is significant because neo-Sophists like Jasper Neel, who is a focus of Couture's critique, have essentially accepted the traditional Platonic separation of philosophy from rhetoric; however, they argue that because there is no possibility of absolute or transcendent truth, which Plato located in an Ideal that could be attained only through philosophy, rhetoric provides the means to attaining the only truth we can attain: contingent or relative truth. Couture challenges this reading of Plato.

According to Neel, Plato's insistence that truth arises from memory of the past "places a stranglehold on the 'endless possibility' ([Neel] 73) that writing affords." As Couture puts it, "It is the separation of writing and self, Neel argues, that allows systematic control over one's soul, to get a '*fixed*' idea" ([Neel] 75) about it. She acknowledges that "detachment from writing may indeed create the dialectic of self and other that puts one on the journey toward knowledge ... But knowledge has no meaning for us without the personal memory of what shapes it, the consciousness of having experienced what we ourselves know *as* someone" (24). For Couture, rhetoric is the process of making personal experience public and finding shared meaning in it: "It is through disclosing the private in language, then, that we come to understand our personal history, our memory, as having a larger meaning shared by others" (25). Within this framework, "writing is a means by which we get in touch with our personal history, the substantial experience that grounds our belief. That contact can be expressed publicly, but it must be experienced privately; it is what we experience deep within us that connects us to others in public" (25). Thus, writing does not change experience nor does writing replace experience as the locus of meaning; rather, writing is a means of making sense of our experience by serving as *the vehicle for sharing experience*—a vehicle for expression that moves toward intersubjective understanding.

Significantly, as Couture defines it, writing is inherently dialectical in that it enables—indeed, *requires*—the writer to move between what Couture calls the personal and the public. In this sense, writing is an act by which subjective experience can lead to intersubjective truth. The kind of reflection that Couture believes is essential for the truth-seeking she advocates is thus facilitated through writing. Indeed, writing itself is a form of reflection—and in this regard Couture's conception of writing converges with that of Elbow, for whom writing is a kind of psychological journey into and back out of the self; it also converges with the critical approaches inspired by Freire, which employ writing as a vehicle for a critical awareness of our lived reality. Here is Couture's own description of how this process works:

Through inclusive reflection upon our lived experience of the world, attending to particulars as they have some general meaning that includes our own sense and that of others; through reasoning receptively by which we let go of the idea that conclusions from direct observation can be separated from subjective belief and thus acknowledge that reasoning is motivated human action; and through regenerating concepts, that is, animating and elaborating what appears to exist for ourselves and others, willfully committing to ideas as they have implications for our very being—through practicing all of these conscious activities, we have within our power the potential to speak and write truth. (184)

Note that for Couture, meaning-making and truth-seeking are not only social but necessarily collaborative, very much akin to traditional dialectic but with a crucial difference: Couture rejects the Cartesian self that exists apart from reality and "thrives through contest with and resistance to its context (32); in its place she posits a self that "develops and achieves agency through *accepting* rather than *resisting* its worldly environment" (33). She argues for a conception of the self "as integral with all we conceive as reality, a way to accept a deepening relation to and acceptance of our environment as a mark of both personal growth and our progress toward knowledge that enfolds all experience" (62). In this regard, Couture steps toward nonduality by moving away from the Cartesian self that she believes is defined agonistically in contemporary theory. The "narcissistic rhetoric" that she sees emerging from contemporary theory, which "places the speaking subject in contest with others, ... enjoins us to present ourselves to others as unified wholes" (45). In contemporary theory, this "unified whole" is "embodied in discourse in order to render a social environment meaningful and achieve an identity within it" (42). Couture rejects this self as the locus of truth and meaning and instead advocates a phenomenological rhetoric that "limits truth neither to ourselves nor to the world we perceive to be outside ourselves, but rather finds it in the dynamic of our engagement with this world" (62). As a result, "the writer's practice of reflection ... must lead to true acknowledgement that others' interests are as valid as his or her own; the writer's reasoned receptivity to diverse ideas must be truly authentic, invested in our common human function as material and spiritual beings" (5). Here Couture implies a nondualistic relationship between self and world that encompasses the "material and spiritual." I emphasize the material here, for in this formulation, language—and therefore writing—does not separate us from the physical but expresses our physicalness, our materiality, our oneness with the world. The act of writing begins with and enacts this embrace of oneness. As Sartwell puts it, "Even writing, after all, makes use of the physical; it is the physical act of a physical body using physical bodies (yes, even a computer)" (122); he goes on to suggest that we should "stop thinking of language as something that distinguishes us from or in the order of nature and start thinking of it as a craft by which we sense our connection to the earth" (123).

As Couture moves through her phenomenological analysis of meaning-making and toward her vision of a rhetoric based on what she calls "profession," she begins to sketch out a nondualistic framework within which the writer is inherently *of* rather than *in* or apart from the world, a self defined by interaction with and reflection on the world rather than a purely intellectual being:

> Unlike Derrida's "Profession of Faith," which is entirely interior and dedicated to confirming a holy and stable ideal, rhetorical reflection is a willful, purposeful exterior expression, a 'professing' through which one declares and affirms openly a knowing relationship to the world through engaging in persistent attention, openly construing all that is perceived about the world to be part of what it means, and personally investing oneself in interpreting the truth of one's particular experience. (109)

This is not Dogen's radical nonduality, in which the self dissolves into everything, but Couture's analysis rests on a similar conception of oneness as characterizing human existence. Couture conceives of the self as inextricably linked to other selves, a dialectical entity that is not autonomous in the Cartesian sense but exists only in relation to other selves and the world and seeks truth as a function of a self-reflection that is both collaborative and inherently part of the phenomenal world.

In a similar way, Paulo Freire rests his understanding of literacy and pedagogy on a complex ontology that is consistent with Dogen's ideas about being and oneness. In a famous passage in *Pedagogy of the Oppressed*, Freire writes, "Education as the practice of freedom … denies that man [sic] is abstract, isolated, independent and unattached to the world; it also denies that the world exists as a reality apart from people" (81). For Freire, "consciousness and world are simultaneous: consciousness neither precedes the world nor follows it" (81). Often, this assertion is interpreted to underscore the crucial idea that reality is not static but a function of human interaction with the world; this dialectical relationship between humans and reality provides the grounds for agency. But it is a mistake, I think, to understand Freire to be offering a relativistic view of reality (and truth) as an exclusive function of language and therefore up for grabs. Rather, Freire assumes a reality of which humans are part but which is not entirely a function of human interaction: "I cannot exist without a not-I. In turn, the not-I depends upon that existence. The world which brings consciousness into existence becomes the world of that consciousness" (82). In other words, the world itself is integral to consciousness; we cannot have one without the other.[8]

Like Couture, Freire seeks a critical reflection that enables students to perceive the world unrestricted by received ways of knowing (82). Through reflection we can see a world that was there but invisible to us because our perception was distorted by received ways of knowing: "That which had existed objectively but had not been perceived in its deeper implications (if indeed it was perceived at all) begins to 'stand out'" (83). This reflection leads to a kind of knowing that is, ironically, akin to what Kasulis describes as Dogen's "prereflective experience." It is an effort to know the world as we could not know it before, to access what Dogen understood as "the preconceptualized experience out of which we develop our idea of the world" (361). However, although we can know that a world exists independent of our perception of it, we can only know that world *through* our perception of it. As Freire puts it, "Although the dialectical relations of women and men with the world exist independently of how these relations are perceived (or whether or not they are perceived at all), it is also true that the form of action they adopt is to a large extent a function of how they perceive themselves in the world" (83). That is, humans can act only in terms of how they perceive themselves in the world. So even as the world exists independent of human perception, human perception shapes our experience of the world and we only know the world through that interaction. This dynamic, too, is a function of nonduality. As Kasulis states, "Dogen would deny that the world is something 'antecedently real,'" because for Dogen the world does not exist apart from us. To put this in more quotidian terms, we are inextricably part of the world we perceive as separate from us. From this perspective, Freire's problem-posing pedagogy is not only an enactment of our agency, as it is usually understood, but also an expression of our being, which is a function of our inherent interconnectedness. Like Couture's, his pedagogy is ontological and fundamentally nondualistic.

To some extent, Couture's project remains a theoretical one and takes up questions that may seem more appropriate for philosophers than for teachers of writing. This is a common complaint about much of the theorizing that characterizes Composition Studies and other fields that are directly tied to systemic education.[9] But to reject theory as somehow separate from practice is to deny that our practice is always theory-driven; it is also to leave unchallenged the Cartesian view of writing that currently dominates practice (consciously or not on the part of writing teachers), for it deflects attention from the fundamental beliefs about writing and knowing that form the basis for that view of writing and for mainstream writing instruction. Ultimately, as a theorist/practitioner, Couture seeks not only to "push rhetorical theory ... toward defining communicative practice as intersubjective truth-seeking," but also—and importantly—to define a rhetorical practice in which writers "maintain knowing relationships between themselves and others"; such a "practical intersubjective rhetoric," Couture asserts, *"inscribes a way of living together,* enabling speakers and listeners to reach a mutual truth, even within the context of irreconcilable differences" (185; emphasis added). This is, in concrete terms, a practice of writing as a way of being. She uses her own experience as a university administrator to describe such a practice (see 207–14), and from her description emerges a picture of a way of being as a writer that differs dramatically from the way of being we foster among students through mainstream writing instruction. Ultimately, Couture defines writing as a practice that "bolsters our sense of worth and sustains our lives in this world, both as individuals and as members of the common family of humankind" (214).

Reading such a proclamation, you might find yourself alternating between nodding in approval and suppressing a cynical smirk. I do. For as I write these words in 2010, the public discourse about political issues, including such important matters as our ongoing destruction of our earth, which was highlighted by the disastrous explosion in 2010 of a deep oil well run by BP in the Gulf of Mexico,[10] continues to be increasingly characterized by the most odious kind of smears on the integrity of the participants that we witnessed during the 2008 U.S. presidential campaign. The often overt racism, sexism, xenophobia, and outright hatred that oozes from the discourse of political advertisements, blogs, and radio and television talk shows make Couture's phrase "irreconcilable differences" sound almost as euphemistic as the George W. Bush administration's description of torture as "enhanced coercive interrogation techniques" (Henley 3). And that's to say nothing of the brutal ongoing conflicts in Iraq and Afghanistan, where beheadings occur almost casually and are justified on the basis of twisted reasoning that defines some human beings as lesser than dogs because of their religious or political beliefs. The superficial mainstream American press coverage of these events ignores similarly horrendous happenings elsewhere, such as in Darfur or Somalia, where humans beings display the same viciousness toward each other and engage in unspeakable cruelty justified by religious fervor and ideological fundamentalism—or, worse, base economic opportunism. In such a "context of irreconcilable differences" how can we reasonably hope for a rhetorical practice defined by the kind of altruism that Couture advocates?

At the same time, as I sit at my desk writing these words, millions of American children, adolescents, and adults are learning to write in ways that teach them something fundamental about what it means to *be* in the world. They learn to enact a sense of self as separate and intellectual, and they learn to use language to define that self in opposition to other selves—notwithstanding the sugary writing assignments that many of them will be given that ask them to proclaim themselves members of one community or another. In engaging in a practice of writing that is integral to the consumerist culture they are being prepared for, defined by a Cartesian worldview, they will learn to "resist one another ... and refuse to view communication as a process that requires change not only in the perspectives of others but also within ourselves," as Couture puts it (214). As a result, Couture maintains, "we will come no closer to the truth nor acquire any greater knowledge than what we can already claim to know" (214).

I do not know what "the truth" is, but I think Couture is right that contemporary rhetorical theory and mainstream writing instruction do not lead us toward it.

This is no way to *be* in the world. We should not teach writing in ways that reinforce an often horrifying status quo. Even if we disagree with Sartwell that we should reject the teleological impulse and accept that human life is not defined by a purpose, surely we do not want to live together in deadly conflict that is understood to be somehow fundamental to human existence and thus inevitable. Surely we can hope for a more just and peaceful world and try to live accordingly. Surely we can teach writing as if such a world is possible. Surely we can write as a way of being in such a world.

ENDNOTES

1. An obvious example in American letters is Emerson's essay "The Over Soul."
2. I am using the terms *Zen* and *Buddhism* to refer to philosophical belief systems and not to suggest religion or religious practice, although, as Kasulis points out, these distinctions are problematic and reflect Western beliefs about philosophy and spirituality (see Kasulis 354–55).
3. It is important to note here that for Dogen, this kind of analysis went far beyond philosophical inquiry. As Abe points out, this radical nonduality, which emerged from Dogen's study of Zen teachings, ultimately manifested itself in his own religious practice and the conduct of his life: "The *mujo* (impermanence) of all things was not, in Dogen, the nature of the world viewed with a philosophical eye but the pain and suffering of all sentient beings and the universe felt by a religious mind" (64). In other words, what might seem to be abstract philosophical inquiry not only grew out of Dogen's direct experience of the world but also profoundly shaped how he lived his life and experienced himself in the world.
4. Derrida never explicitly defines *differance*, a key concept in his lexicon, but Neel explains it as "the infinite disappearance of either an origin of or a final resting place for meaning" (157).
5. In a sense, the digitization of literacy has brought into relief this Western tendency to associate the word with being. One dramatic example is the recent emergence of lulzing, a term used to refer to taking glee at someone else's expense as a result of online harassment or baiting. See Schwartz, "The Trolls Among Us." Online users who participate in these activities are obsessive about anonymity (indeed, some analysts argue that anonymity enables these behaviors

because it frees the participant from individual responsibility for his or her words/actions). In effect, they create themselves exclusively through language: I speak (write); therefore, I am. Their very online beings are exclusively linguistic (unless you want to account for the electrons that constitute their existence online). They are an extreme expression of the Cartesian self that is conceived, enacted, and reified in mainstream writing. I pursue this analysis of digital literacy later in this chapter.

6. Sartwell's analysis has antecedents in Sophistic rhetoric. As Bizzell and Herzberg note in *The Rhetorical Tradition*, "Gorgias argues that language, in the sense of reasonable discourse, here called *logos*, 'arises from external things impinging upon us, that is, from perceptible things.' We are moved to speak by our sensory experiences. But this makes language, as it were, caused by reality. Language is logically posterior to reality and hence incapable of encompassing and communicating it" (24). Neo-sophistic theorists, in exploring this complex interaction among language (*logos*), the phenomenal world, and truth, acknowledge the crucial role of our experience of the phenomenal world. Jarratt, for example, writes that for Gorgias, "'being' becomes recognizable through logos, but the opinions created by *logos* rely in part on the phenomenal" (54–55); she goes on, "The point is that being itself cannot be communicated, but rather *logos* is what we communicate 'to our neighbors'" (55).

7. In this quotation Couture is using the term *dif-ference* to refer to the "the continuous dynamic that is being as we actually experience our conscious existence" (106); it is part of "an attempt not to characterize the difference between beings and Being, but rather the 'dif-ference,' [philosopher John D.] Caputo's translation of Heidegger's *Austrang*, which is the differing that makes this difference possible. The distinction between finite beings and infinite Being must be expressed as a 'dif-ference,' instead of as a 'difference,' lest we lose sight of how the continuance that belongs to infinite Being is effected in ourselves who participate in it, although limitedly, as living beings" (107).

8. Freire's formulation of the self and consciousness owes much to phenomenology, about which I say much more in Chapter 4.

9. Indeed, Henry Giroux makes the provocative argument that the kind of reform necessary for overcoming what he sees as the most oppressive aspects of systemic education requires that teachers become intellectuals, in essence embracing theory as an integral part of their practice. See "Teachers as Transformative Intellectuals."

10. In April 2010, an explosion at an oil rig approximately forty miles off the coast of Louisiana called the Deepwater Horizon drilling rig, owned by a company called Transocean and leased by BP, one of the world's largest energy companies, killed eleven workers and initiated an oil spill that lasted through the summer. In late July, after several failed attempts to cap the destroyed wellhead, BP crews successfully stopped the flow of oil, which was estimated to have been between 35,000 and 60,000 gallons per day over the two months during which the oil flowed unimpeded into the Gulf of Mexico. As of August 2010, BP crews were still working to "kill" the well permanently, while some evidence that oil continued to escape from the sea floor fueled controversy about whether BP's efforts to cap the well were completely successful.

4

WRITING AS A WAY OF BEING

Focus long enough on the text and the student disappears.
—Richard Haswell

Here's what I think happens when I am writing—or at least what is happening right now as I write.

I sit at my desk in my home or my campus office or perhaps at a table in a favorite coffee shop and I type words into a file using a word-processing program on my computer. In physical terms, what I am doing is tapping a computer keyboard with my fingers while looking alternately at the screen and the keyboard. (On the rare occasions that I use a pen or pencil and paper, I sit with my right hand resting on the surface of the desk or table and use my hand to push the point of the pen across the paper lying on that same surface; my eyes are focused on the paper.) Rarely do I look at anything other than the screen (or the paper). In a sense, my writing tool (the computer or pen) becomes an extension of my hands and, to push things a bit further, my self.

That's what seems to happen physically when I write.

Psychologically (or mentally or cognitively—these terms become difficult to pin down, in part because this experience defies linguistic description, as I explained in Chapter 3), I become preoccupied with the intellectual task of writing, and my attention focuses almost exclusively on that task. I become so engrossed in my effort to use written language to create some kind of text (such as this book) that I am largely, although not entirely, unaware of my physical surroundings and what is happening around me. Those surroundings and activities partially recede, although only temporarily, from my awareness, which is consumed by the task of writing, so much so that I may seem not to hear sounds coming from upstairs in my home or from the counter in the coffee shop. Somewhere in my consciousness I remain aware of those sounds and activities, but I pay little attention to them; they become a kind of white noise, always there but, for the moment, irrelevant.[1] Of course I am aware that I am sitting at a desk or table, but that awareness is pushed to the back of my consciousness by my focus on the words I am typing onto my computer screen. In a sense, that screen becomes a kind of partial display of my consciousness as I type; significantly, however, that screen—and the text it displays—captures only a very small part of what I am thinking and experiencing, and it reflects little or nothing of my awareness of my *self* at that moment.

At *this* moment, for example, as I sit before my computer at my desk in my home, typing these words onto the screen, I am writing this sentence (which means considering words and phrases and perhaps matters of convention as I try to articulate this idea) while at the same time imagining an editor who is considering my proposal for this book; I am trying to anticipate his response to these words as well as the responses of the reviewers he will ask to evaluate my manuscript. I am also remembering (or perhaps "imagining" is the better word) the coffee shop where I often write, visualizing in my "mind's eye" the chairs and small round tables arranged haphazardly around the cramped, asymmetrical space; the counter, where a few people stand waiting for their coffee, looking over pastries and bags of coffee for sale or reading the descriptions of the day's brews on the chalkboard behind the counter; the shelves adjacent to the counter, with coffee and other items for sale; the tile floor. I can also "hear" (i.e., I am remembering) the familiar noises of the espresso machine and the voices of the baristas and customers, the hard scratch of a chair leg on the tile floor, the thump of the rest room door—noises that, when I am writing there, I vaguely hear but that remain at the rear of my attention, which, as now, stays focused on these words I am writing. I am also thinking at this moment about the "shape" of the book I am writing and whether or not some of what I expect to include in this chapter really belongs here or should be part of the next chapter or the previous one or perhaps be eliminated from the book altogether. These are rhetorical concerns that probably arise because of my years of experience as a writer and my training in rhetorical theory, but somehow they are similar in effect to my remembering the coffee shop. That is, both my memories of the coffee shop and my concerns about the structure of this text keep my attention focused on this writing; as I craft this sentence, they occupy my awareness and shape my consciousness right now.

At the same time, I am thinking of what I think about as I write, because that is what I am trying to describe in words right now. And I am wondering whether this description makes any sense—especially given what I wrote in Chapter 3 about the limited capacity of language to capture or represent our experience at any given moment. And suddenly, just now as I write this, I find myself also wondering how the description I am writing at this moment compares to the thinking captured by the think-aloud protocols that writing researchers Linda Flower and John Hayes made famous in the late 1970s and early 1980s as they explored the cognitive dimensions of writing. And at this very same instant I have just remembered an assignment I was given as a graduate student to participate in a think-aloud protocol, and I am now remembering the fellow graduate student who took notes during the session, remembering the small office we used for that session, with its tiny rectangle of a window up near the high ceiling in that old building, remembering even some of what I said then, more than twenty years ago. Simultaneously (I think) I am right now wondering to what extent Flower's think-aloud protocols resemble the "thinking" I am trying to describe right now. (And I worry about how I am defining "thinking" in this context.) As I am writing, I am beginning to develop an answer to that question (I think!), but the answer I have is still nebulous, as if it is floating in my head until I can pin it down with these words on my computer screen, which I can never quite seem to do. I am wondering how that editor and those reviewers and other potential readers might define "thinking" and what expectations they will have about my efforts to do so. And just now I noticed that the sun is shining through the small basement window that overlooks my desk.

I have just described a small part of what is happening as I write these words right now.

There is much more to it, of course—much more to what seems to be happening psychologically ("intellectually"; "mentally") as I write than I have represented here with these words you are reading. But the most important point is that I am *at this moment* thoroughly engrossed in this task of writing such that it becomes almost synonymous with my consciousness at this moment and profoundly shapes my awareness of myself *as my self*, a self existing *both separate from and part of* what is around me, both physically and metaphorically. Significantly, in this act of writing I am more intimately connected to this moment and to the physical location where it is occurring in the sense that I am intensely in the here and now while I write, and at the same time I am also connected to something larger that is not here and now—something that includes that editor and those reviewers and the professional field in which I work (which in turn encompasses both the intellectual work and the persons of Flower and Hayes, whom I mentioned a moment ago, and others in the field as well as the theories and ideas that characterize the field and the actual people who talk about those theories and ideas at conferences and write and read about them in journals and online discussions); and more: the history of this field and of writing itself and the many others who have written about writing; not to mention my own past and all the previous moments of writing that might somehow be part of this moment right now. All of this is somehow folded into this moment of writing here and now.

As I write, I *am*—but not *because* of the writing; rather, the writing intensifies my awareness of myself, my sense of being, which is prior to but, right now, coterminus with this act of writing. And if I attend to my awareness—if I become aware of that awareness, as it were; if I focus my attention on my attention during this act of writing, as I am doing right now—it is not my sense of self as a separate, thinking being that is intensified but my sense of self as existing in this moment and at the same time "inhabiting" the physical place where I am sitting as well as the scene in the coffee shop that I am imagining and trying to describe, a scene removed from me in time and space at *this* moment; thus, I am connected to this moment and those other moments I have been trying to describe and indeed to all those other selves I've mentioned and many I have not mentioned and the things around me now and those that were around me then and even you, the reader I am imagining who will, I think, at some point, really *be* a reader of this text and thus be connected to me as well in a very real way through your act of reading at some future date, which means that this moment of writing right now somehow encompasses that future moment, too.

It is in this sense that I *am* as I am writing. The *writing* does not create me, but in the *act* of writing I *am*; by writing I reaffirm and proclaim my being in the here and now. The act of writing, in this sense, is a way of being; it is an ontological act.

This sense of being that I am describing here is, I think, more than an understanding of (or belief in) a connectedness of the self to something else but rather a sense of my being as defined by this connectedness, which is made visible, in a sense, by the act of writing. What I am describing here is more than the inherently social nature of meaning-making through text that scholars like Deborah Brandt have illuminated in their attempts to challenge what Brandt has called the "strong text" theory of writing, in which meaning in a text is understood to be stable, portable, and autonomous (13). The theoretical formulations of Brandt and like-minded scholars focus on the text as a vehicle for meaning and on writing as a social process of meaning-making *through* the text, rather than on writing as an act or expression of being in the world in the here-and-now. In other words, although these scholars challenge the strong-text theory of writing as asocial, their socially minded theories remain text-based; to the extent that they illuminate the experience of writing, they do so as a way to understand how the writer produces a text or how a text "means." But such a focus on the text offers an inadequate account of what happens *as a writer writes*; furthermore, it neglects the effect of the act of writing on the writer's sense of being in the moment and over time. Whatever happens to a text *after* it is written does not affect what is happening to (or *in*) the writer *as she or he is writing that text*. Whatever happens to *this* text that I am composing right now after I have written it will not change what is happening right now *as I write it*. It is this experience that current theory fails to explain.

At this moment *I am more keenly aware of my self* than if I were just thinking about these same ideas or that scene in the coffee shop—thinking while driving my car, for instance, or while sitting on a bus or a park bench or even in that same coffee shop. In writing I am also more deeply aware of my self than if I were describing the coffee shop scene to someone orally. Many of the details of the scene, for example, are somehow more vivid, more available to my consciousness as I am writing right now than if I were simply remembering them as I sit on a park bench or saying them aloud to a listener. As I write right now, I can "see" the colors of the logos on the coffee bags, the dim light making dull yellow circles on the walls of the shop, the white apron of the barista, the glare of the afternoon light through the large windows at the front of the shop, the glint of light on the display case that contains the pastries, the people sitting in different positions on the chairs scattered about the shop. It is true that I can "see" all these things by simply trying to remember them, but writing, which happens more slowly than talking or listening or remembering, focuses my awareness more deliberately, more intensely, more fully, on these details, these things, even though they are not physically present at this moment (since at this moment I am writing in my home); until *this* act of writing, at this very second, those details have been outside my awareness. Yet at this moment, as I am writing, they are present. And *I* am present in the same moment. And so are you, whoever you are.

REPLACING WRITING WITH *WRITING*

In the late 1970s and most of the 1980s, Composition Studies became enamored of the potential of cognitive psychology to help explain what happens when we write and, more important, to provide insight into the struggles of student writers. A major purpose of this research was to understand *thinking* during the writing process in order to help writers overcome their struggles so that they could produce "effective" texts. Flower and her colleagues at Carnegie Mellon University spearheaded this effort, and their studies of experienced and inexperienced writers, using techniques adapted from cognitive psychology (including the aforementioned think-aloud protocols), led to the development of their well-known cognitive process theory of writing (Flower and Hayes). Flower's was a sustained effort to build a coherent theory of writing that might adequately explain the act of writing and provide a basis not only for further study of writers but also for developing effective writing pedagogies. It was an influential effort in part because of the widespread view that writing is a form of thinking and in part because of the widely held view in mainstream education that learning is largely a cognitive—and, significantly, an individual—process. Not incidentally, these views remain widely held in education circles today and certainly among education policymakers.

The criticisms of Flower's work and that of other "cognitivists," as Berlin labeled them ("Rhetoric and Ideology" 480), that proliferated in the 1980s and early 1990s were based not only on concerns about the apparent ideological implications of a cognitive understanding of writing and teaching (the focus of Berlin's critique), but also on the sense that a cognitive theory of writing focused too narrowly on the individual writer and did not adequately account for the many factors (social, economic, cultural, historical) that seem to play a significant role in shaping what and how a writer writes. Flower responded to these criticisms by adjusting and elaborating on her theoretical model to try to explain these factors as inherently part of any cognitive process (*The Construction of Negotiated Meaning*), but the basis of her theory was still the fundamental assumption that writing is a form of thinking. To a large extent, the field of Composition Studies seems to have lost interest in that theory as compositionists have pursued questions driven by the general view of writing as an inherently social act that is culturally mediated and context-bound; at the same time, Composition Studies was influenced by the insights of poststructuralist theory regarding the power and complexity of discourse and the contingency of meaning-making. As I explained in Chapter 2, however, these competing perspectives on writing all rest on the same Cartesian worldview and on the idea of an autonomous Cartesian self. Many compositionists (including myself) have theorized this self as multifaceted, contingent, inherently social, and constructed within discourse. In other words, the conception of self that informs contemporary theories in composition is a function of language practices that are socially situated and culturally mediated. This is indeed a social self. But for the most part this self remains an *intellectual* and linguistic entity; current theoretical perspectives in the field, therefore, reinforce the Cartesian dualities, especially the mind–body binary, on which the Cartesian conception of self is based. Writing is understood as a product of that intellectual self and the text as an artifact of that self's thought—which, in Cartesian terms, is essentially identical to the self ("I think; therefore, I am"). In the mainstream Cartesian view of writing, therefore, the text becomes the focus of attention. It is the vehicle for understanding meaning-making, even when meaning-making is assumed to be uncertain and contingent and even when the meaning of a text is assumed to be unstable. The meaning of a text may be unstable in the post-modern era, but the text, as a physical artifact of the autonomous (intellectual) self that exists separately from the world, remains paramount.

But what if we shift our theoretical gaze from the written text to the self writing—from the writer's writing to the *writer writing*? What if we conceptualize the act of writing not as the self thinking (as in a cognitive view) or communicating (as in a social view) or constructing itself (as in a poststructuralist view), but as the self *being*? What if we focus attention on the *experience* of writing rather than on the text as a product of that experience? What would such a perspective reveal about writing? How might it explain what happens when we write? How might it help explain the implications of writing? And how might it provide an alternative to a Cartesian view of writing that might better explain the effects of writing on the writer and the world of which the writer is inherently a part? These questions are the focus of this chapter.

The account of writing with which I began this chapter foreshadows what an ontology of writing might reveal. But of course my account is inherently incomplete. I cannot capture in writing what happens when I write any more than Crispin Sartwell can capture in language everything contained in a single glance, as I discussed in Chapter 3. Indeed, that's part of the point, because a theory of writing should account for the limitations of language as well as its capacities and potential. The focus of my discussion in this chapter, however, is on the ways in which an ontological account of writing can foreground aspects of the experience of writing that are minimized, dismissed, ignored, obscured, suppressed, devalued, or invisible in the mainstream Cartesian view of writing, in which the self, as an autonomous intellectual being, asserts itself through the act of writing and the product of that act—the text—is the focus of attention. An ontology of writing focuses not on what that writing self does through or with writing but rather *on the experience of the self in the act of writing*. Moreover, it focuses on what happens *now* rather than what happens later. An ontology of writing allows us to see that the experience of writing has an effect on the writer exclusive of the use of the writer's text, which is not insignificant but remains subsequent to the act of writing; an ontology of writing enables us to examine that effect instead of focusing only on the text and its impact on a reader, as mainstream writing instruction does. At the same time (and in a seeming paradox), an ontology of writing illuminates the writer's inherent connection to that reader and indeed to all other writers and readers; it illuminates how those connections affect the experience of writing and thus the writer.

In my attempt to articulate an ontological theory of writing, I explore the experience of writing *at the moment of writing* by examining some accounts of writing in addition to my own experiences while writing. In doing so, I employ a phenomenological methodology, examining the experience of writing as an empirical ground for a theory of writing. According to Dermot Moran,

> Phenomenology is best understood as a radical, anti-traditional style of philosophising, which emphasises the attempt to get at the truth of matters, to describe *phenomena*, in the broadest sense as whatever happens in the manner in which it appears, that is as it manifests itself to consciousness, to the experiencer. (4)

As Moran goes on to point out, phenomenology rejects the "representationalist account of knowledge" and assumes that "our experience properly described must acknowledge that it presents itself as the experience of engaging directly with the world" (5–6). Thus, I proceed on the basis of a fundamental assumption of phenomenology, as Couture articulates it: "all essences or truth are located in subjective experience" (64). It is to the experience of the writer writing that we must look to understand writing. On the basis of this examination of experience, I will articulate in the second part of the chapter what I see as the main components of an ontological theory of writing.

THE ONTOLOGICAL EXPERIENCE OF WRITING

In 1990, I had the opportunity to teach in a prison college-equivalency program.[2] I was assigned to teach basic writing to inmates in a medium-security prison in a rural section of central Ohio. Early in the fall semester I assigned a short essay whose primary purpose was to give the students practice in descriptive writing and develop their facility with word choice. The assignment, which I adapted from a writing class I had taken as an undergraduate and used in writing classes I taught to mainstream undergraduates, was straightforward—or so I thought. It required the students to describe a familiar place in a way that would make it vivid to someone who had never been there. I am embarrassed to say, all these years later, that I never really considered how the extreme physical limits placed on my students as inmates in that unpleasant place might be a problem for them as they tried to complete the assignment. The point, I thought, was to describe a familiar place whose very familiarity would obscure from their notice details that might stand out to a stranger visiting that place for the first time. Any familiar place would suffice for this exercise: a classroom, a street corner, a favorite diner, an office, an apartment. Even, alas, a cell or a prison yard.

When I gave the assignment at the end of class one evening, the students listened in uncharacteristic silence. These were two dozen mostly hardened men, ranging in age from 18 to 55. All but a few were Black and most hailed from one or another of Ohio's larger cities. They seemed as out of place in the middle of the rolling farmland surrounding that prison as I, a somewhat untested 32-year-old white teacher, did in their midst. I noticed their silence but didn't pay much attention to it. Only a few weeks into the semester, some of them were (understandably enough) still somewhat wary in class, and it would be a few more weeks before we began to enjoy a more relaxed atmosphere during class meetings. But the next week when I asked them to bring out their drafts of the assignment, many of them had nothing to show. That also was uncharacteristic, and this time I did take notice. It always amazed me that these men, working under hideous conditions and lacking even basic amenities that I took for granted—like a quiet space for writing—almost always had their assignments done. So I asked them why they didn't in this instance. That ended the silence, and what poured forth was their frustration, their intense hatred for that prison, and a bit of anger directed at me for asking them to write about it. As they talked, I began to realize how important that writing class was for most of them—not because they were enrolled in a college-equivalency program or because the class replaced some demeaning job they would otherwise have to do while serving their time, but because the class was a genuine escape from that depressing place, a few hours of respite from the inhumanity and degradation they experienced the rest of the week, a few moments when they were treated as students rather than inmates—treated, that is, as human beings. Writing class was a way for them to be human again. And I had asked them to write about the very same inhumane surroundings that they wished to escape.

In a sense, what I asked my students in that prison classroom to do was to experience their hated surroundings more intensely by writing about them. No wonder they resisted. They were basic writers who struggled with the basic conventions of written English, who—some of them—struggled even to write a simple sentence, yet they understood that at some level the act of writing was an intense engagement with whatever they were writing about. Completing my assignment would require them not only to struggle with the conventions of written English but to do so while focusing their attention on a place in which they struggled to maintain their dignity. Listening to them at that moment, I realized what a lousy assignment I had given them. I didn't, however, quite realize why.

As I think about that incident now, I am struck by how much those students, who were defined as remedial writers, seemed to understand intuitively about the experience of writing. As their instructor, my focus was mostly on their texts, which, given the conventions of academic writing and from the point of view the program they were enrolled in, were problematic in more ways than I could name. I attended to the act of writing as a process of creating texts, as I had been taught to do as a graduate teaching assistant—and even then only to the extent that I believed doing so would help them produce "better" texts. It didn't occur to me that the *experience* of trying to produce those texts mattered in any significant way—to them or to me. The point of writing, I believed, was to produce writing—ideally, "good" writing. The experience of producing that writing was only marginally of interest to me to the extent that it might provide insight into why these students did not produce acceptable texts (by conventional definitions). But the *experience* of writing *did* matter to those students. And it *does* matter in ways that are obscured by the mainstream Cartesian view of writing that I unconsciously embraced.

We have a few accounts that bring the experience of writing to the fore. Poet Jimmy Santiago Baca, for example, has written compellingly about his own prison experiences. As a young inmate Baca discovered the importance of language to his sense of identity. In his autobiography he tells a harrowing tale about his life in the barrios of a large southwestern American city and his descent into a criminal life, which eventually landed him in jail. His schooling left him with only a limited ability to read, but he was intrigued by the books his fellow inmates were reading. Eventually he began reading on his own, and he found his way into a Latino history that was missing from the mainstream history he was exposed to in school. His story in effect is about how his newfound literacy deepened his sense of identity as a Latino. But when he describes his efforts to *write* while incarcerated, something more than his sense of identity emerges. In the following passage, for instance, he describes the lengthy sessions during which he wrote in an old notebook while in solitary confinement:

> Whole afternoons I wrote, unconscious of passing time or whether it was day or night. Sunbursts exploded from the lead tip of my pencil, words that grafted me into awareness of Who I was; peeled back to a burning core of bleak terror, an embryo floating in the image of water, I cracked out of the shell wide-eyed and insane. Trees grew out of the palms of my hands, the threatening otherness of life dissolved, and I became one with the air and sky, the dirt and the iron and concrete. There was no longer any distinction between the other and I. Language made bridges of fire between me and everything I saw. I entered into the blade of grass, the basketball, the con's eye, and child's soul. (qtd. in Yagelski, *Literacies and Technologies* 167–68)

I say more later about the sense of connectedness that Baca describes here, the inherent oneness with the world that he experiences through writing;

this, as I read his words, is the experience of nonduality that I describe in Chapter 3. What I wish to emphasize here, however, is Baca's sense of himself as a being-in-the-world that emerges *through and during the act of writing*. You might argue, in poststructuralist terms, that in this passage he is constructing himself through his words. Perhaps. But the physical isolation of his cell and the fact that the writing he did in that cell was never intended for any audience other than himself suggest that such an explanation is insufficient to illuminate the power of that experience for Baca or to explain the nature of his experience of writing *at that moment*. As he wrote, he did not escape his physical surroundings so much as dissolve into them; he felt an intensified sense of himself being at that moment, a sense of being by which he embraced and transcended his surroundings.[3] And even if he wrote in anger as a way to resist those surroundings—his cell and his jailers—even if he wrote to rage against them or to proclaim himself free of them in spirit, it would still be his *experience of writing at that moment*, not the writing itself, that would matter most here. For at that moment the act of writing somehow intensified his sense of being-in-the-world. It did not matter whether his writing would be read or by whom, for the reading of it would be subsequent to the experience of writing of it. That experience of writing had some effect on Baca no matter what might subsequently happen to his text.

Baca goes on to describe how his struggles to write in that tiny cell led to his "birth" as a poet:

> I was born a poet one noon, gazing at weeds and creosoted grass at the base of a telephone pole outside my grilled cell window. The words I wrote then sailed me out of myself, and I was transported and metamorphosed into the images they made. From the dirty brown blades of grass came bolts of electrical light that jolted loose my old self; through the top of my head that self was released and reshaped in the clump of scrawny grass. Through language I became the grass, speaking its language and feeling its green feelings and black root sensations. Earth was my mother and I bathed in sunshine. Minuscule speckles of sunlight passed through my green skin and metabolized in my blood. (qtd. in Yagelski, *Literacies and Technologies* 169)

Again, his sense of connectedness, of oneness, emerges powerfully in this passage. Again, Baca describes an experience of writing that intensifies his sense of being in the world. I imagine his written words insufficiently convey the power of his experience. But in an important respect, the inadequacy of his words—an inevitable inadequacy, as I explained in Chapter 3—is irrelevant, for the experience of writing them and the effect of that experience on Baca are separate from the meaning we might make of them now.[4]

As I write my own words right now in the same favorite coffee shop that I described earlier in this chapter, the sun is shining on the busy street outside the shop in this little city in upstate New York. The same sounds of bustle and music that I tried to describe earlier surround me as I type these words on my computer. But what overpowers me is the strong sense of connection I am feeling at this moment to Baca and to those students in my prison class and to the nameless people who are coming in and out of this place and walking along the street or driving by in their cars, of whom I have been vaguely aware as I have been writing but who now move to front of my awareness. I am writing this text to be read by an editor and, I hope, other scholars in my field. I am writing it to you, too. And my writing— both the text and the act of writing—is shaped by the considerations that accompany my sense of my audience. But what matters right now is this writing, this act of being in my writing. What matters is my sense of connection to what is around me and beyond me, a sense deepened by this act of writing. And this feeling is as intense, right now at this moment, as the powerful sense of connectedness and well-being I felt on the mountainside that I described at the beginning of Chapter 3.

TOWARD AN ONTOLOGICAL THEORY OF WRITING

What should we make of this experience? How might we understand the experience of writing as a way of being in the world? In answering those questions, I will develop four main assertions regarding the ontological experience of writing:

1. The act of writing intensifies the writer's awareness of him or herself *at the moment of writing*.
2. This awareness-while-writing seems qualitatively different from other intense moments of self-awareness because of the role of written language.
3. The effect of the experience of writing on our sense of self is cumulative.
4. The context of an act of writing is multifaceted and plays a central role in shaping the experience of writing in the moment.

Awareness of Self in the Moment of Writing

As we write, our engagement in the act somehow affects our awareness of our selves at that moment. This seems to be true whether the writer is ostensibly writing about him or herself or about something altogether different. Baca may have been writing about himself in that cell, but he also was writing about his surroundings (the cell and the weeds and grass and sunshine he could see through his window). In my own writing experience that I described earlier, I was not writing about myself but about Baca and the idea of writing as an ontological act. Yet the experience of the self-while-writing, a self connected to something else through the act of writing, seems similar in both cases. In other words, even if I am not consciously, actively thinking of my self *as my self* as I write, the act of writing somehow brings a sense of self into focus. Paradoxically, my *self*, at least in terms of my awareness of my self *as* my self, seems to dissolve into the moment of writing—just as Baca's sense of himself "was released and reshaped in the clump of scrawny grass," just as my sense of self was defined by my sense of being part of the community of Composition Studies about which I was writing. Perhaps this experience is akin to what Crispin Sartwell describes as the "extraordinary experience of letting-go into the divine, or into the lover, or into death" (4). At the moment of writing I become the *writing* (not the noun but the participle) in some profound sense—not the text but the act of trying to convey meaning through text.

Some of the think-aloud protocols conducted by writing researchers in the 1970s and 1980s capture this intense awareness-while-writing. For example, in her study of Donald Murray's writing process, Carol Berkenkotter reproduces this excerpt from a think-aloud protocol she conducted with Murray:

> Let me take another piece of paper here. Questions, ah … examples, and ah set up … situation … *frustration of writer. Cooks a five course dinner and gets response only to the table setting … or to the way the napkins are folded* or to the … *order of the forks.* All right. I can see from the material I have how that'll go. I'll weave in. Okay. *Distance in focus. Stand back. Read fast. Question writer. Then order doubles advocate. Then voice. Close in. Read aloud.* Okay, I got a number of different things I can see here that I'm getting to. I'm putting different order because that may be, try to emphasize this one. May want to put the techniques of editing and teaching first and the techniques of the writer second. So I got a one and a two to indicate that. [Italics identify words written down.] (Berkenkotter and Murray 161)

Granting that this transcript is only a partial representation of Murray's experience of writing, it seems to reveal how deeply engrossed in the task he is at that moment. Certainly the very fact that he is speaking aloud as he writes suggests that he is aware of his physical and rhetorical situation, and his words focus on textual considerations driven by his sense of the task and, implicitly, the larger rhetorical situation. In other words, his concerns with the structure of his text ("I'm putting different order") reflect an experienced writer's sense of his audience's expectations and thus reflect the way his sense of audience might shape his awareness at that moment. His spoken words also indicate how consumed by the task he is, how much his sense of being is shaped by his engagement in that task—even though, as Murray himself tells us, "I do not assume, and neither did my researcher, that what I said reflected all that was taking place. It did reflect what I was conscious of doing, and a bit more" (170). My guess is that Murray was conscious of much more than this protocol could capture. Nevertheless, Murray's protocol describes part of his awareness-while-writing, and therefore it describes part of his sense of self at that moment.

This awareness-while-writing seems to encompass something beyond or distinct from cognition or intellection. In her classic essay, "Writing as a Mode of Learning," Janet Emig tries to describe the qualities of writing that distinguish it from other forms of "languaging processes" and make it "a unique mode of learning" (123):

> Writing is originating and creating a unique verbal construct that is graphically recorded. Reading is creating or re-creating *but not* originating a verbal construct that is graphically recorded. Listening is creating or re-creating but not originating a verbal construct that is *not* graphically recorded. Talking is creating *and* originating a verbal construct that is *not* graphically recorded (except for the circuitous routing of transcribed tape). (124)

Emig's analysis focuses on how powerfully writing engages the intellect in ways that go beyond other verbal processes, including reading. For Emig, the key to understanding the distinction lies in the notion that when writing we are both creating and originating something in language and recording it graphically all at the same time.[5]

Surely these characteristics of the act of writing contribute to the intensity of engagement and awareness that occur when a writer is writing. Murray's intense focus is certainly shaped by the fact that he is creating and originating a text and recording it at the same time. But Emig's analysis, which draws on cognitive psychology, doesn't fully account for the kind of ontological awareness-of-self that Baca seems to have experienced as he was writing. Cognition is only part of our awareness-while-writing, and psychology goes only so far in helping us understand that awareness. Phenomenology offers a richer framework for understanding that awareness and the experience of the writer while writing.

As Couture notes, phenomenology "rejects a dualistic distinction between the world as it exists and the world as we interpret it," instead locating truth "in subjective experience through equating the study of being with the study of meaning" (64). To put it somewhat differently, our experience of ourselves in the world and the meaning we make of that experience are not separate; an act of meaning-making is in effect an act of being. "Furthermore, phenomenology projects human consciousness as *the* agent that gives meaning and shape not only to social ideologies or operational systems that direct and motivate human action, but also to the existence of the world itself"; human experience is thus "the only possible origin of absolute being, truth, and objectivity" (65). Significantly, phenomenology "defines knowledge as a relation between self and other resulting in meaning"; such a philosophy of meaning "implies a relationship between a mind and an other" (65). Quoting Cornelius A. van Peursen, Couture notes that meaning "always implies a relational structure, a reciprocal reference between consciousness and world" (van Peursen 30; qtd. in Couture 65–66).

This reciprocity between consciousness and world helps explain the experience of writing. As we write, we engage in a moment of intensive meaning-making related to the larger, ongoing process of making meaning of our experience of ourselves in the world. This moment of meaning-making—the act of writing—underscores, indeed, *enacts*, the deeper relationship between our consciousness and the world around us. In the act of writing, our consciousness and the world (both in terms of the subject of our writing and the situation within which we are writing) become one; thus, our experience of our self as a being-in-the-world is intensified as we make meaning through the act of writing. If language is "a symbolic medium reflecting a relationship between individuals and their environment that is developed in subjective consciousness" (66), as Couture defines it, then the act of writing, which is an act of meaning-making through written language, is an enactment—physically, intellectually, and ontologically—of that relationship. Writing is thus an expression of our being, both in general and in the moment, since "meaning through which we know of being and being through which we know of meaning are entirely a function of human subjectivity" (66). The act of writing, then, is an expression of the self (as distinct from the more common understanding of writing as self-expression), but more: it is an expression of the self, in reciprocal relationship with the world, as the locus of meaning-making. To write, in this sense, is to *be*.

As a technology for language, writing can be understood as a manifestation of phenomenologist Maurice Merleau-Ponty's idea of speech as embodied thought. Like other phenomenologists, Merleau-Ponty rejected the traditional Cartesian dualities of mind–body, self–other, subject–object; accordingly, he also rejected the idea that language represents thought, because he saw no significant distinction between mind (thought) and body (speech). His idea of speech as embodied thought reflects this nondualistic understanding of language in general and of speech—and writing as a technology for speech—in particular. As Couture points out, for Merleau-Ponty writing is not signification in the Derridean sense "but rather a function of consciousness" (81). *In The Phenomenology of Perception*, Merleau-Ponty asserts that

> thought, in the speaking subject, is not a representation, ... it does not
> expressly posit objects or relations. The orator does not think before
> speaking, nor even while speaking. His speech *is* his thought. (209;
> emphasis added)

And because thought is a function of lived experience—that is, thought is
embodied in the sense that it is inseparable from our physical experience of
ourselves in the world—speaking is an act of embodiment and thus of being
in the world. For Merleau-Ponty, the experience of hearing a speech is similar. Strikingly, his discussion of this dynamic resembles the descriptions of
writing—Baca's, Murray's, mine—that I shared earlier:

> The orator's "thought" is empty while he is speaking and, when a text is
> read to us, provided that it is read with expression, we have no thought
> marginal to the text itself, for *the words fully occupy our mind* and exact-
> ly fulfill our expectations, and we feel the necessity of the speech.
> Although we are unable to predict its course, *we are possessed by it*. The
> end of the speech or text will be the lifting of a spell. It is at this stage
> that thoughts on the speech or text will be able to rise. (209; emphasis
> added)

Although Merleau-Ponty is not specifically referring to the act of writing in
this passage, his description can be applied to writing because in his analysis
the act of writing is similar to the act of speaking in that both writer and
speaker are using language *in the moment*: in writing as in speaking, "the
words fully occupy the mind," which for Merleau-Ponty is coterminous
with the world. In writing, as in speaking, we are in and of the world fully
at that moment.

Note that for Merleau-Ponty, an act of expression is engrossing in the
moment, encompassing the whole of the speaker's (writer's) consciousness,
which is his or her being, because mind and body do not diverge. In rejecting the traditional idea of language as representation of thought and words
as representations of things, Merleau-Ponty insists that "the word or speech
must somehow cease to be a way of designating things or thoughts, and
become *the presence of that thought in the phenomenal world*" (211; emphasis added). In this sense, writing is an act of becoming more fully present in
the world at the moment of writing:

> The process of expression, when it is successful, does not merely leave
> for the reader and the writer himself a kind of reminder, it brings the
> meaning into existence as a thing at the very heart of the text, it brings
> it to life in an organism of words, establishing it in the writer or the
> reader as a new sense organ, opening a new field or a new dimension to
> our experience. (212)

Written Language Shapes Awareness of Self

As the foregoing discussion makes clear, the intensified awareness of self that we experience while writing is a function of language. In this regard, this awareness-of-self seems qualitatively different from other intense moments of self-awareness *because of the central role of written language.* The moment of "letting-go into the divine, or into the lover" that Sartwell refers to is, as he puts it, "inarticulate": It involves no language (4). I have sometimes tried to describe to friends the experience of rock climbing or ice climbing as an extreme sense of existing fully in the moment, when awareness is completely focused on the act of moving on a vertical surface of rock or ice and consciousness is wholly consumed by that act at that moment. I have heard similar descriptions of other physical activities (e.g., surfing) or the engrossing experience of engaging in activities such as woodworking, sewing, painting, or playing music. The experience of writing shares an extreme intensity of focus with such activities, but the role of language makes the experience of writing different. (Because music can be considered a form of language, the experience of playing music might be closer to the experience of writing than these other activities.) The writer at the moment of writing is experiencing him or herself *through language.* The use of language—the effort to articulate something (it doesn't really matter what) in written language—intensifies the writer's awareness at that moment. Writing, as an act of meaning-making through language, goes beyond the intensity of focus that characterizes an activity such as climbing; it is an enactment of embodied speech, in Merleau-Ponty's formulation, in which the writer expresses his or her being in the moment of writing.

Merleau-Ponty offers insight into this dynamic with his idea that the "perceiving mind is an incarnated mind" ("Unpublished Text" 3). For Merleau-Ponty, "the body is much more than an instrument or a means. It is our expression in the world, the visible form of our intentions" (5). Body and mind are coterminous, and our sense of ourselves as beings-in-the-world is inseparable from our bodily, or perceptual, experience; thus, "the subject capable of this perceptual experience … obviously will not be a self-transparent thought, absolutely present to itself without the interference of its body and its history" (6). Instead, the subject is a function of that "interference of its body and history"; in other words, our sense of self as subject, as a being-in-the-world, encompasses mind, body, and our experience of the world at that moment as well as prior to that moment. We are aware of ourselves as beings in the world as a result of this interaction among these elements. Writing, as a technology for language that requires physical activity (moving pen across paper or tapping the keys of a computer keyboard), brings this intimate connection between the physical and the intellectual, between mind and body, to the fore; through writing, thought becomes visible, the intellectual physical. The inseparability of mind and body is encoded in the act of writing itself, and writing becomes an enactment of the unity of mind and body, self and world.

Central to Merleau-Ponty's analysis of language is the inherently social nature of meaning-making. The word, as "a passive shell" (*Phenomenology of Perception* 206), acquires meaning through its use in communication with others, and indeed thought itself, in order to have meaning—to be intelligible, to become knowledge—requires expression, which in turn requires an other: "A thought limited to existing for itself, independently of the constraints of speech and communication, would no sooner appear than it would sink into the unconscious, which means that it would not exist even for itself" (206). Because the word is not a mere sign but a "vehicle of meanings, ... speech, in the speaker, does not translate ready-made thought, but *accomplishes* it" (207; emphasis added). In this sense, thought and speech, as components of the process by which we make meaning of our experience, are always social: "There is, then, a taking up of others' thought through speech, a reflection in others, an ability to think *according to others* which enriches our own thoughts" (208). In this sense, speech, as part of our efforts to make sense of our experience of ourselves as beings-in-the-world, is always an enactment of our inherent connection to all other selves, with whom we make meaning together through expression. Writing is therefore not only an expression of the self as a being-in-the-world but also an act of meaning-making that inherently involves all other selves. In this regard, *the experience of writing is an experience of our being as inherently social.* It is this characteristic of writing, a form of embodied speech, that sets the experience of the self-while-writing apart from other intense moments of awareness-of-self.

The paradox here is that the writer *cannot* articulate all of what he or she is experiencing at the moment or what he or she is writing about at that moment, which may contribute to the intensified awareness of self: that is, the self trying to articulate itself is as aware of what it cannot articulate as it is of what it *can* render into language, which will always be an approximation of the experience at that moment. To put it somewhat differently, the self is more present to itself when writing because the inability to fully "say" (write) its being points to the part of being that cannot be said (written). In this regard, the limits of language to capture our experience of our selves help illuminate our sense of being during the act of writing.

The Cumulative Effect of the Experience of Writing

The effect of the experience of writing on the writer's sense of self as a being in the world is cumulative. For one thing, unlike spoken language, writing, as a technology for language, is not learned intuitively but rather is learned *after* spoken language develops; moreover, one's facility with writing develops over time: A six-year-old cannot write in the same way that an experienced adult writer can, for example. I have seen kindergarteners engrossed in an act of writing as intensely as any adult writer can be in the moment, but the nature of the child's experience writing is necessarily different from the adult's, given the child's more limited experience with language and more limited experience of his or her self in the world. In this sense, the nature of the experience of writing evolves over time. The awareness-of-the-self-writing that Baca describes cannot be the same as that of, say, a middle school student writing or a first-year college student writing. Indeed, the regular practice of writing *as a practice* (as distinct from the kinds of writing tasks typically assigned in schools, in which the focus is on the production of a certain kind of text) seems to foster a more conscious awareness-of-the-self-writing.

For example, David Grosskopf, a high school teacher, has described his experience of coming to a heightened awareness of himself through writing—but only after he allowed himself to engage in the practice of writing self-reflexively and regularly over time. In a brief essay that is ostensibly about the importance of encouraging regular writing practice among his students, Grosskopf describes his realization that he never fully shared with his students his insight into the *experience* of writing:

> It is writing that has led me to feel most alive. This is the part that students never heard me tell because I misunderstood the secret for so long. It's not merely the production of writing—even good writing, and the satisfaction this brings—that has powered my sense of vitality; it is the act of writing itself.

I don't think Grosskopf's use of the term secret in this context is quite right: He is describing not a secret but a newly acquired insight into and perspective on writing, one that abandons the text-focused obsession with correctness and convention that characterizes school-sponsored writing, in which the experience of writing itself is devalued or ignored. In this passage Grosskopf describes the effect of his experience of writing as a regular practice on his sense of himself as a being in the world.

In the same article, Grosskopf tells the story of a summer wilderness trip he made alone in an effort to reconnect with himself: "The idea was to be myself with myself without any possibility of escape, and I would stay at least three lonely nights to do it." But it isn't until he returns from that trip and begins writing as a daily practice that he realized his goal; in the process, he also comes to understand the crucial role that writing as a practice began to play in his sense of being-in-the-world:

What does it mean to live life well? I know there is a purposefulness to
asking the question, and I know the kind of writing that actually experiences the answer as it goes down. Writing is, for a moment at least,
manufacturing this good life as it is lived. But I already knew that. What
I might also be able to tell them [his students] now, as we study Woolf
and Henry David Thoreau, is that over the summer this year, I began to
live the poetic life. Here's what I did to do it: every week, almost every
day, I made the time to write. And if you try it yourself, even if you're
a student about to leave home for the first time, or a worker jammed
down by memo wars, or a parent dealing with kids who yell all at the
same time, you too may find that you can write yourself awake.

The point here is that Grosskopf's intense experience of self-while-writing
and the effects of that experience on his sense of himself as a being in the
world do not happen simply as a result of a single act of writing or even
many separate acts of writing. Rather, his experience of self-while-writing,
his heightened sense of self as a being in the world, emerges as a result of *the
regular practice of writing*—of many individual acts of writing engaged in as
a practice over time, without the expectation that such practice should necessarily result in a written text—and, significantly, as a result of his own
reflection on his practice of writing. In short, the practice of writing,
engaged in over time, can shape our sense of self as a being-in-the-world.
This effect remains even in the absence of the kind of reflection that
Grosskopf engaged in. A writer writing within a Cartesian view of writing,
in which the self is conceived as autonomous and fundamentally intellectual, also will experience a cumulative effect of the practice of writing,
although its effect will differ from what Grosskopf experienced—in large
measure because the rhetorical and conceptual contexts (see later) will differ
and thus shape the writer's experiences in different ways. Nevertheless, writers will experience a cumulative effect on their sense of self by engaging in
acts of writing over time.

Again, Merleau-Ponty's concept of the incarnated mind provides a
framework for understanding this process. As I noted earlier, in Merleau-
Ponty's analysis the self is not "a self-transparent thought, absolutely present to itself without the interference of its body and its history"
("Unpublished Text" 6). Mind and body, in other words, do not exist apart
from each other; therefore, "[t]he perceiving subject is not this absolute
thinker; rather, it functions according to a natal pact between our body and
the world, between ourselves and our body" (6). As a result, the perceiving
subject, as a being in the world, constantly redefines itself through its ongoing interactions with the world through its body: "Given a perpetually new
natural and historical situation to control, the perceiving subject undergoes
a continued birth; at each instant it is something new" (6).

This process is more than simple learning; rather, it is a process of the self always *becoming*, very much as Freire understood "men and women as beings in the process of *becoming*—as unfinished, uncompleted beings in and with a likewise unfinished reality" (84). Similarly, for Merleau-Ponty, both self and world, which do not exist apart from one another, are always in a process of becoming:

> [T]he perceived world, in its turn, is not a pure object of thought without fissures or lacunae; it is, rather, like a universal style shared in by all perceptual beings. While the world no doubt coordinates these perceptual beings, we can never presume that its work is finished. Our world, as Malabranche said, is an "unfinished task." ("Unpublished Text" 6)

The perceiving subject, in this formulation, is always engaged in that unfinished task. Writing, as a technology for language, has the capacity both to embody that process and to intensify its effects on our sense of self.

Interestingly, Merleau-Ponty uses writing as a metaphor to illuminate this process: "Every incarnate subject is like an open notebook in which we do not yet know what will be written" (6). Both self and world continually change through this process of interaction between self and world over time. Indeed, for Merleau-Ponty, "the writer is himself [or herself] a kind of new idiom, constructing itself, inventing ways of expression, and diversifying itself according to its own meaning" (8–9). Each act of writing, then, can be part of the process by which we make meaning of our experience of our selves in the world over time. Each act of writing, no matter the task or text produced, is an act of creation of both self and world, an enactment of what Freire called "the dynamic present" (84)—that is, the creating of self and world in each moment. But that act is shaped by all previous acts of writing; the writer engaged in an act of writing (in) the "dynamic present" is shaped by previous moments of writing—that is, by her or his history, as Merleau-Ponty uses that term. In that sense, an individual act of writing is both original, in the sense that it is rooted in the dynamic present, and cumulative, in that it contains the writer's history and is informed by all previous acts of writing and acts of meaning-making.

The Role of Context in the Experience of Writing

Not all individual acts of writing are the same, and the experience of writing can vary from one act of writing to another. That's because the context of an act of writing plays a crucial role in shaping the writer's experience of writing in the moment. The writing experiences described thus far (such as Grosskopf's, Baca's, or my own) would seem to suggest that an act of writing always (or usually) fosters (or *should* foster) a sense of connectedness, a sense of being integrally part of something larger, even if that something is relatively obvious and concrete, such as the identifiable components of the rhetorical situation (e.g., a specific teacher as the intended audience for a classroom assignment). In several important respects, this is true: Even the most self-centered act of writing always implies connectedness, if only to the extent that language itself (and writing as a technology for language) is inherently social, as noted earlier. Because language is inherently social, when we write we experience ourselves as connected to others through language, even if we are not fully aware of that connection at that moment. Moreover, as we saw earlier, meaning-making is always social; an act of writing as an act of meaning-making, therefore, always implies an other and is an act of connectedness.

However, as every student and teacher knows, the experience of writing in the moment can feel alienating and isolating. This is all too often the case with writing in schools. A timed writing test, for example, can be a deeply stressful experience for a student writer, especially for students labeled as struggling or remedial in some way. Indeed, *any* kind of writing assignment can be stressful. A student's effort to write correctly (or at least according to a teacher's instructions) after having experienced "failure" as a writer—for example, in the form of a returned paper splashed with the teacher's red markings indicating errors—can lead to anxiety and even to a sense of isolation if the student is perceived (or perceives him or herself) to be "behind" or less capable than his or her classmates. Trying to complete an assignment or a report under a tight deadline also can cause anxiety and a sense of isolation (and actually can be physically isolating if the writer intentionally removes her or himself from others in order not to be disturbed while writing under deadline); this is true even for writers deemed competent or successful. These examples suggest that an individual act of writing does not necessarily lead to a sense of connectedness and certainly not always to a sense of well-being in the moment.

Listen, for example, to Murray, an accomplished and award-winning writer and teacher of writing, describing his experience of being "protocoled." In this passage, taken from Murray's response to Berkenkotter's study of his writing process, Murray describes his experience of writing on demand for the researcher. Berkenkotter had supplied Murray with an unfamiliar writing task and a deadline for producing a draft, and she recorded Murray's spoken thoughts as he tried to write in response to these demands. The session left Murray frustrated and with little more than a few sentences of writing:

> The one-hour protocol was far worse than I had expected. If I had done that first there would have been no other protocols. I have rarely felt so completely trapped and so inadequate. I have gone through other

research experiences, but in this case I felt stronger than I ever had the need to perform. That was nothing that the researcher did. It was a matter of the conditions. I had a desperate desire to please. I thought of that laboratory experiment where subjects would push a button to cause pain to other people. I would have blown up Manhattan to get out of that room. To find equivalent feelings from my past I would have to go back to combat or to public school. I have developed an enormous compassion and respect for those who have performed for Masters and Johnson. (Berkenkotter and Murray 169)

Writing teachers will recognize their own students' frustrations and anxieties in Murray's description, which indicates the extent to which the experience of writing can be affected by what Murray calls the "conditions" of writing. When these conditions are uncomfortable for the writer and the task itself is compulsory—like so much school-sponsored writing and most standardized writing test situations—the experience can be intensely unpleasant for the writer at the moment of writing. Nevertheless, these unpleasant moments of writing are still intense experiences of the self-while-writing; they are experiences of *being* in the world. They share with the more appealing experiences of Baca and Grosskopf an intensity of awareness-while-writing, although in these less pleasant instances the experience of the self in the moment seems qualitatively different from what Baca and Grosskopf have described. Why? The answer, I think, lies in the role of context in every act of writing.

We always experience ourselves as beings in the world in relation to what is around us. We *perceive* ourselves as relating in some way to what is around us, even if only in the sense of physical proximity, and we *conceive* of ourselves as existing or acting within a setting or situation, which may directly involve others, such as when we're writing an essay for a class or a letter to a friend or an entry on a blog. Moreover, we conceive of ourselves as certain kinds of selves on the basis of prior experiences and our efforts to make sense of those experiences. Those efforts are socially mediated, because meaning-making is a social process that always involves an other and the world. In short, our sense of being in the world is context-bound; context, writ large, matters.

Here I need to distinguish among three dimensions of context that are always in place in an act of writing:

1. *Rhetorical context*: the ostensible writing situation, including the intended or assumed audience, the apparent purpose of the writing, the subject matter, the form or genre of the text being produced, and the related conventions of writing, and so on.
2. *Conceptual context*: the writer's conception of the act of writing and of him or herself as writer. This dimension of context includes prior

experiences with writing, writing instruction, and literacy; beliefs and attitudes about writing and about the self as writer that are formed on the basis of those experiences; and cultural practices and values as they relate to writing, literacy, and communication in general.

3. *The medium*: the technology used by the writer. Writing itself is a technology for language, of course, but the specific tools we use for writing affect the experience of writing in concrete ways (such as the feel of a pen on paper or fingers on keyboard) as well as in less visible ways (such as the sense of immediate connection to an audience that might accompany writing a blog entry or a text message).

Context, in these three dimensions, profoundly shapes the experience of writing and the writer's sense of him or herself as a being in the world *during* an act of writing. For *at the moment of writing*, the writer is always writing within a rhetorical context of some kind, the components of which he or she may be intensely aware of at that moment. At the same time, the writer's sense of self *as a self writing* is profoundly influenced by the conceptual context. In the examples I discussed earlier, such as a student taking a timed writing test, the rhetorical context contains elements that are likely to intensify the writer's sense of self in ways that do not foster well-being. For instance, the stakes associated with the test and the time constraints may deeply affect the student's sense of competence as a writer and thus powerfully shape the student's awareness-while-writing and sense of being-in-the-world at that moment. Similarly, the conceptual context will influence the student's experience in the moment of writing. If that student has learned to write in school, he or she is likely to be engaging in that act of writing in a way that reflects the mainstream Cartesian view of writing as a straightforward conduit for already-formed thoughts; his or her sense of self-while-writing is likely to reflect the Cartesian sense of self as an autonomous thinking being struggling to convert those thoughts into written words in "correct" ways. In other words, the student's experience with mainstream writing instruction has resulted in his or her conceiving of himself or herself as a certain kind of self-while-writing. For most students, then, the conceptual context of an act of writing shapes a sense of the self writing such that the writer experiences disconnection and isolation, and the act of writing becomes an enactment of the Cartesian self. Nevertheless, it remains an experience of the self, an awareness of the self as a certain kind of being in the world, intensified through the act of writing.[6]

These three dimensions of context also explain differences in the experience of a writer at different moments or stages in an act of writing. For instance, when editing a text we may not be as likely to experience the kinds of intense revelations Baca experienced as he wrote in his prison cell or the insights that I tried to describe as I sat writing in a coffee shop. In both these cases (Baca's and mine) the writer's attention was not directed toward the conventions of written English or the nature of the writing task, which may have been more prominent in the writer's awareness at a different moment of writing, depending on the rhetorical context. So although a writer might work on the same text during different moments of writing over a period time, the specific experience of writing can differ from one moment of writing to another, even if the same text (or a different version of the same text) is involved in those moments of writing. Similarly, the medium can affect the experience of writing differently from one act of writing to another. For example, writing on a blog might heighten a sense of self as directly connected to others because of the sense of immediacy between writer and readers within that medium, whereas writing an essay exam with pen and paper may lead to an intensified sense of disconnection. (I say more about the medium for writing later.)

As these examples suggest, the rhetorical and conceptual contexts and the medium interact to shape each individual act of writing at the moment of writing. The conceptual context can profoundly shape how an individual writer understands a given rhetorical task and thus may influence what seems to occupy that writer's awareness regarding the rhetorical situation during an act of writing as well as at different points in the process of creating a text; similarly, the medium might raise the writer's awareness of a specific component of the rhetorical situation at a given moment in an act of writing, and at the same time both those dimensions of context would be influenced by the conceptual context. In short, the dynamics of context in writing are complex, multilayered, and evolving. An act of writing is always an act of being, but the experience of being-in-the-world at the moment of writing will be shaped by the context within which the writer engages in that act.

DIGITAL LITERACY AND THE EXPERIENCE OF WRITING

The foregoing discussion raises the issue of the role of technology in the experience of writing. More specifically, given the great deal of attention devoted in the past decade to what is now routinely called "digital literacy" (or sometimes "multimodal literacies"), we might ask to what extent the conception of writing I have proposed in this book applies to what some theorists have argued is a new kind of writing (e.g., Bolter). At the very least, powerful (and increasingly available) new technologies for communications are significantly influencing how and what we write. Given what I have argued about the role of the medium in an act of writing, it is reasonable to assume that these new digital technologies, as writing tools and as new media for writing, can shape the experience of writing in significant ways. Within the framework I have constructed, in which writing is defined as an ontological act, digital literacy might be explained as a function of the medium for writing—that is, it can be understood in terms of *context* as I have defined it in this chapter. But the emergence of seemingly new literacy practices for which "digital literacy" has now become shorthand, along with the increasingly central role of digital technologies in our lives, makes it necessary to say something more here about how an ontological theory of writing might help us understand writing in digital environments.

First, we should define *digital literacy*. Since the 1980s, scholars have been trying to pin down what it means to be literate in a world increasingly shaped by digital technologies. In 1995, Richard Lanham offered this definition:

> To be deeply literate in the digital world means being skilled at deciphering complex images and sounds as well as the syntactical subtleties of words. Above all, it means being at home in a shifting mix of words, images and sounds. (198, 200)

Lanham's definition seems to capture what many scholars consider to be the essential elements of digital literacy, especially the integration of image and sound with text. A few years later, in her introduction to a special issue of *Computers and Composition* devoted to digital rhetoric, Carolyn Handa echoed Lanham's emphasis:

> Since the World Wide Web began establishing itself as a major medium of communication, scholars in rhetoric, the humanities, and education have also been calling for our increased attention to a literacy extending beyond words, one including images and sounds, in other words, to a literacy accounting for more than the purely verbal. (3)

Such a literacy, Handa wrote, includes "being able to decipher images semiotically, as well as understanding how to make images integral to an argument and, ultimately, doing so with ease"; it also includes "understanding how images are rhetorical and how rhetorical elements function in digital compositions" as well as understanding the degree to which sounds are rhetorical and can be used as an integral part of digital argumentation" (2). In other words, from the point of view of a writer writing, digital literacy involves the ability to attend to images and sounds as well as text while writing. Some scholars argue that understanding and applying principles of document design is also a critical part of digital literacy (see Kress, *Before Writing* 154), which, to my mind, is similar to considerations regarding the structure of a text when it comes to the writer's attention at a given moment of writing.

Little in these definitions of digital literacy points to anything that would call into question my argument that writing is fundamentally an experience of the self as a being in the world at the moment of writing. Although the writer's attention to image or sound during writing can certainly affect the writer's experience in the moment in the sense that such considerations occupy the writer's awareness as he or she focuses on the task at hand, attention to such matters does not seem fundamentally to change the writer's awareness-of-self-writing that I have argued is at the heart of an ontological perspective on writing. In this regard, if digital literacy "demands that we draw on our knowledge of rhetoric perhaps even more than our knowledge of HTML, design issues, or graphics software," as Handa argues (2), then it might be understood as part of the rhetorical context of writing, as I have defined rhetorical context in this chapter.[7]

Handa's statement, however, points to another crucial component of digital literacy: the use of powerful new digital *tools* for writing. Those tools obviously include the computer as well as sophisticated software (not only word-processing packages but also multimedia and web-authoring programs) and related technical instruments that a writer can use to create a text. There is little question that tools can significantly affect the experience of writing. For example, compare composing a text with pen and paper to composing with word-processing software on a computer. The physical experience is obviously different but so is the intellectual experience, in part because of the inherent connection between mind and body. In this case, the slower pace of writing with pen and paper can affect the writer's awareness in the moment in ways that differ from writing with a computer.

Some theorists argue that any technology for writing must be understood as more than a tool—that, as James Porter puts it, "computers are not merely instrumental tools of writing, but rather influence the nature of composing and our rhetorical understanding of the composing situation" (384). Porter shares his own history of writing with various tools (pencils, pens, typewriters, computers) to support this position, but he emphasizes that ultimately it is not the tools themselves that shape the composing process so much as what he calls the "pedagogical context ... the training, discipline, and practice that accompanied my use of the pencil [as a young student], along with the ideology (theology, really) that framed that use and provided its *raison d'etre*" (384). Accordingly, what makes the computer a revolutionary tool for writing is "the social/rhetorical contexts it creates and the way its use impacts publishing practices," all of which "represents a significant change, of a magnitude that the pencil and typewriter (essentially print-based tools) don't achieve" (384–85).

Porter's argument, which reflects an influential perspective among scholars in the subfield of Composition Studies that we know as Computers and Composition, supports my analysis of the role of context in the writer's experience while writing. As he notes, the social and rhetorical situations within which writers write shape their uses of technology as tools for writing; what I have called the *conceptual context* encompasses what Porter refers to as the ideology that frames one's learning and use of writing tools. Moreover, he emphasizes the physicality of writing:

> The body matters, the material matters. Physicality (for example, of the body) is not secondary to form, or mind, or language (the privileged masculinist focuses of Western thought)—it is, rather, fundamental. (388)

This view is consistent with the phenomenological perspective I have laid out in this chapter and in Chapter 3 in which mind and body do not exist apart from one another. Indeed, Porter's "posthumanist, cyborgian view" focuses on "interrelationships—in a sense, at the interfaces of human experience (humans and machines, humans with each other)" (388). Although this view does not go as far as the nonduality I propose in Chapter 3, it underscores the inherently social nature of all writing and the place of technology in the social matrix within which writers write. It also underscores the role of technology in the *experience* of writing, both in the present and in the writer's past: "The technological past matters. It shapes the writer and writes the body in significant ways—etching itself on the writer's consciousness and body, influencing how the writer learns to compose and how the writer communicates in a social milieu" (389). In other words, the tools we use for writing, understood within the dimensions of context that shape all acts of writing, play a role in the writer's experience of writing, both in the moment and as part of the writer's past experiences writing; they are part of the writer's awareness-of-self-writing. In this sense, writing in a digital environment is like any other act of writing: It is an act of being-in-the-world.

If I were to replace the description of my experience in writing this book that appears in the first few pages of this chapter with a description of my experience writing an e-mail, little of substance would change. The description of writing an e-mail would retain the sense of engagement and heightened awareness-of-self that I described earlier. It would retain as well a sense of the richness of the experience of writing. And it would retain a sense of connectedness to that something more that I described earlier in this chapter. What would be different, I think, is the possibility of a greater sense of immediacy in writing an e-mail, given the speed of the medium and given that the audience for an e-mail message is likely to be much more specific and concrete—and, significantly, known to me as writer—than the audience for a text such as this book. I would expect my intended reader to read my e-mail within minutes or hours or perhaps a few days of my writing it, and I would probably expect a reply within a similar time frame, which fosters an even greater sense of immediacy. This shorter time between the act of writing an e-mail and the reading of it—as compared with the writing of this book—can make the intended reader seem much more present to the writer as he or she is writing.[8] To this extent, the capacity of writing, as a technology for language, to overcome the obstacles of time and distance—which is one of the hallmarks of writing in the analyses of Walter Ong and Marshall McLuhan—is perhaps more evident in a digital medium such as e-mail than in more conventional print media. In these ways, my experience in writing an e-mail highlights the social nature of the act and the sense of connectedness that I described earlier. In a sense, then, writing an e-mail might be said to make the ontological experience of writing more visible or tangible than the more traditional print-based experience of writing a text for future publication in a book or newspaper or magazine. But the fundamental experience of writing in terms of an intensified awareness-of-self is the same in both instances; there is nothing about the experience of writing an email message that makes that experience fundamentally different from writing a book or college paper or magazine article when it comes to the awareness-of-self-writing. The medium, which is part of the context of that act of writing an e-mail, certainly shapes the experience in discernible ways, making it different from other acts of writing in ways that can matter to the writer, but it doesn't change the ontological nature of the experience.

Other digital media may in fact bring the ontological nature of writing even more clearly into view. Consider blogging, which in less than a decade has become a significant medium for writing that has found its way into our political, professional, cultural, and personal lives more fully than many other newly developed digital technologies. Indeed, for some bloggers, blogging is almost a way of life. And the experience of blogging seems to foreground the ways in which writing can be a way of being in the world. For example, in the following excerpt from a *New York Times Magazine* article, author Emily Gould describes the role of blogging in her personal life. Early in her article, Gould describes a conflict with her boyfriend, Henry, over a post she wrote about their relationship on her blog:

> My blog post was ridiculous and petty and small—and, suddenly, incredibly important. At some point I'd grown accustomed to the idea that there was a public place where I would always be allowed to write, without supervision, about how I felt. Even having to take into account someone else's feelings about being written about felt like being stifled in some essential way.

For Gould, the blog became "a public space" where she could *be* through writing; it provided a vehicle for an experience of writing that became a regular part of her life. Her blog posts increased tensions between her and

Henry, but her description of her experience as a blogger suggests that the act of writing her blog, more than any expectation of who might read it or why and more than any sense of its potential impact on readers, became the most important aspect of maintaining her blog:

> As Henry and I fought, I kept coming back to the idea that I had a right to say whatever I wanted. I don't think I understood then that I could be right about being free to express myself but wrong about my right to make that self-expression public in a permanent way. I described my feelings in the language of empowerment: I was being creative, and Henry wanted to shut me up. His point of view was just as extreme: I wasn't generously sharing my thoughts; I was compulsively seeking gratification from strangers at the expense of the feelings of someone I actually knew and loved. I told him that *writing, especially writing about myself and my surroundings, was a fundamental part of my personality*, and that if he wanted to remain in my life, he would need to reconcile himself to being part of the world I described. (emphasis added)

Clearly, Gould's experience raises serious questions about the ethical responsibilities of the writer/blogger, especially with respect to the subject of her writing (in this case, Henry and his relationship with Gould) and his right to privacy. Indeed, the capacity of a blog to reach millions of readers instantly can complicate traditional ethical concerns. But such concerns could be part of the writer's experience of writing *any* text, regardless of medium, to the extent that the writer attended to them. What is striking in this instance is that for Gould the blog became an integral component of her daily life, and writing it became central to her way of being in the world. Although this passage from her article describes the impact of her writing on her relationship with Henry, it also conveys the importance of the regular act of writing her blog to her.

From an ontological perspective, it is necessary to ask whether her experience of writing her blog *in the moment* differs in any fundamental way from her experience writing about similar matters in another medium, say, a diary, where a writer might record similar thoughts, feelings, and events. It is quite possible that had Gould written in a private diary rather than on a public blog, her words would not have had the impact on her relationship with Henry that her blog had. But the experience of writing those words in terms of Gould's sense of self would be fundamentally the same. That experience does not seem to be changed by the medium except that the public nature of the blog seems to have mattered to Gould—that is, she seemed to want to describe her relationship with Henry to others. In this regard, her sense of her blog as a public space shaped her experience of writing, since she wrote with the expectation that "strangers" would read her blog entries. But that expectation does not seem different from similar expectations writers might have when working in print-based media. For example, at this moment I am writing with the expectation that "strangers" will read this text. If I were writing this paragraph on a blog, my experience of myself writing (and my experience of myself being in the world) would be fundamentally the same as the experience I am having right now as I write this text on a computer with the expectation that it will eventually appear in print form, although the medium might shape my attention to specific textual concerns at given moments of writing.

Digital media such as e-mail and blogs and so-called social sites such as Facebook may open up new writing spaces that provide opportunities for connecting with readers in ways that are not available in traditional print media; moreover, the specific nature of the experience of writing—and the experience of the self-while-writing—can be shaped by these new media in identifiable ways. But as an ontological act, writing is fundamentally the same in all these media. Writers writing on a blog and writers writing for print publication, like all writers, experience themselves as beings-in-the-world through writing.

TRUTH-SEEKING AND WRITING AS A WAY OF BEING

I have argued that an ontological theory of writing rests on the basic premise that when we write, we enact a sense of our selves as beings-in-the-world. When we write, we are in the world; we enact our being in specific ways shaped by the context of our writing. Such a theory emphasizes the writer writing and shifts our focus, at least temporarily, away from the writer's writing. It demands that we attend to the *experience* of writing, in the moment and over time, and it not only places value on that experience but also illuminates it in ways that are not possible within the mainstream Cartesian view of writing. In Chapters 1 and 2, I discussed the need for such a theory in order to overcome the limitations of the Cartesian view and the problems associated with that view, most importantly the autonomous sense of self and the fundamental disconnection fostered through pedagogies based on that Cartesian view. That sense of self and disconnection, I argued, are implicated in the crisis of sustainability. An ontological theory of writing offers, I submit, a necessary alternative to the mainstream Cartesian view and a step toward a writing pedagogy that is consistent with our best hopes for a just and sustainable future.

An understanding of writing as a way of being can, I believe, help us begin to realize Couture's vision for a practice of writing as truth-seeking, a practice that "bolsters our sense of worth and sustains our lives in this world, both as individuals and as members of the common family of humankind" (214). An ontological view of writing enables us to realize this vision in two respects. First, it explains the act of writing as a way of making meaning of our experience of ourselves in the world, so that we better understand the implications of writing as a practice and of our approaches to writing instruction for our ways of being in the world. Second, it places value on the experience of writing so that we can begin to take advantage of the potential impact of that experience on the writer as a being writing—and living—within complex social networks; to understand writing as a way of being is to begin to see the power of writing to reshape our ways of being in the world. In this regard, an ontological theory of writing illuminates the capacity of writing as a vehicle for truth-seeking.

As I noted in Chapter 3, Couture seeks to reclaim rhetoric "as a truth seeking practice" (63); her phenomenological rhetoric "abandons the Western sophistic tradition of arriving at truth through conquering and consensus, and grounds it instead in a conscious commitment to collaboration with others in truth seeking" (4). Within this framework, truth is located in subjective experience and is "an outcome of intersubjective understanding" (64); that is, meaning-making—and truth-seeking—are inherently social and collaborative: "We see purpose ... in participating together in *writing* the world; and it is in doing so that we move together toward writing truth" (83). For Couture,

> the goal of our conscious existence is quite simply to make meaning together. It is to continue a conscious expression of what the world means in the hope of touching, reaching, and joining with others to advance a mutual understanding; it is to participate together in writing the truth of our shared world. Through speaking and writing we make an effort to express what is beyond ourselves and to include others; it is through such expression that we create the relation that enables us to reach the truth we share. (92)

Writing is the means by which "we create a relation with others that enables us to reach the truth we share" (94). Couture rejects mainstream theoretical perspectives that assume struggle and resistance to be inevitable; instead, she proposes a phenomenological rhetoric that "functions to establish our engaged relationship with the world," a rhetoric whose "aim is to move us from alienating resistance to open collaboration" (94).

Couture's vision rests on a theoretical understanding of the dynamic of meaning-making through "intersubjective understanding" as well as on a practice of rhetorical "profession," in which the writer "attends to the world with open acceptance ... [and] reconciles the objective world with one's self assessment of it" (131). Both her theoretical understanding of this dynamic and her proposed rhetorical practice in turn rest on a kind of introspection or reflection that is based on Edmund Husserl's notion of *phenomenological reduction*, which Couture defines as "a precise method of inner reflection" (88). In this formulation, reflection on our subjective experience of the world in the context of communication with others about our shared experiences is integral to the ongoing process by which we make sense of the world and, ultimately, move toward truth. In other words, truth is available only through a special kind of ongoing reflection by which the writer is open to transformation: "Underlying every expressive act must be genuine understanding gained from reflection upon our lived experience, an open dynamic understanding that overrides, as Husserl has said, 'every judgmental drawing-in of the world as it exists for us' ('Phenomenology' 24)" (95). From this point of view, reflection, by which we make meaning of our experience of the world, and expression, by which we share that meaning and adjust it within a social context, are integral to truth-seeking. As a technology for language and a form of expression, writing thus becomes part of the process of truth-seeking. Writing as truth-seeking encompasses an active, open, sustained reflection on our experience of ourselves in the world; at the same time, it is a vehicle by which we share our reflection with others as we make meaning together of our experience of the world. These two dimensions of writing potentially make it a truly reflective practice.

Couture recognizes that writing, by itself, and the practice of rhetoric more broadly do not inevitably lead to the kind of reflection and openness to change required for genuine truth-seeking. But she believes that a conception of truth as relative, which is the current dominant theoretical view, prevents such a practice from taking hold:

> The obstacle to finding truth is not, as the relativists claim, the absence of a truth that is universally valid, but rather the unwillingness of those who seek truth to be changed by language, that is, to view truth seeking as bound up with our very being in the world, and to see the connection of our thoughts with those of others, past, present, and to come, and the development of ourselves as a result of that experience. (91)

Her vision requires "a willingness to change, a willingness to engage with others" (91). That willingness should be encoded in our writing practice, but it also seems to me that the practice of writing itself can foster this willingness if that practice is characterized by attending more closely to the experience of writing. In other words, understanding writing as a way of being in the world illuminates the act of writing so that the possibilities for the kind of reflection and openness to transformation that Couture seeks can emerge. Within an ontological framework, writing can become a practice whereby writers both develop and enact a willingness to change and an openness to truth. In this way, writing as a way of being in the world can become an expression and enactment of nonduality rather than the proclaiming of the autonomous Cartesian self that mainstream pedagogies promote.

If Couture is right (and obviously I think she is) that "truth is an outcome of introspective understanding of consciousness obtained through the interactive state of being in the world with others" (95) and that rhetoric can be a practice of "attending to and interacting with the world with openness and acceptance" (96), then an ontological perspective on writing can not only help illuminate such a rhetoric but also provide a framework for a practice of writing as a new way of being in the world. Because an ontology of writing focuses attention on the writer's experience of the self while writing, it can reveal the reflective possibilities of writing much more readily than conventional theories of writing, which focus on the process of producing texts or on the process of meaning-making through text. And as the descriptions of writing included in this chapter suggest, writing, when engaged in over time as a genuinely reflective practice (distinct from the exclusive purpose of creating a specific kind of text), can transform the writer in powerful ways. Indeed, Grosskopf's description of writing himself "awake" seems similar in important ways to Couture's "rhetorical reflection," which she defines as "persistent attention to unfolding experience, openness to diversity of perception as it contributes to total meaning, and engagement in the personal meaning of particular experience" (114). Moreover, this kind of reflection is consistent with the self-awareness that Freire's problem-posing pedagogy is intended to promote; it is consistent as well with theories of transformative learning, such as Jack Mezirow's, which posit a kind of trajectory of deepening awareness that is necessary for truly emancipatory education:

> Emancipatory education is about more than becoming aware of one's awareness. Its goal is to help learners move from a simple awareness of their experiencing (how they are perceiving, thinking, judging, feeling, acting—a reflection on process) and beyond this to an awareness of the *reasons* why they experience as they do and to [take] action based upon these insights. (197)

It is possible, I believe, to engage in writing as a practice of truth-seeking that is characterized by this kind of reflection on our experience of ourselves in the world; moreover, it is possible to engage in the practice of writing such that we foster, through our sustained attention to our experience of our selves writing in the moment, a habit of reflection characterized by the openness to change that Couture seeks. Such a practice can move us beyond the entrenched dualities of a Cartesian view of writing and toward a connected sense of self that can become the foundation for imagining and creating more just and sustainable communities.

ENDNOTES

1. Recent psychological research on "multitasking" suggests that humans can perform a limited number of complex mental operations at a given time and can focus conscious attention effectively on only one or two such operations at a time. See Rubenstein, Meyer, and Evans; see also Tugend for an overview of this research. Research in cognitive rehabilitation, which is based on work with brain-damaged patients, suggests that there are different levels of cognitive attention, including "focused attention" and "sustained attention," which seem similar in some respects to the kind of awareness-while-writing that I describe in this chapter. See Sohlberg and Mateer.

2. I describe other experiences I had in that program in *Literacy Matters*, pp. 43–54.

3. It is possible that the students in my prison class might have had a similar experience by writing about their surroundings, but it's more likely that my focus on producing a certain kind of text, which was made clear in my assignment instructions, would have shaped their experience of writing such that their experience would be the less pleasant one that they in fact had. Later in this chapter I say more about how context can shape the writer's experience in the moment.

4. I recognize that there is a difference between Baca's experience while writing and the published account of that experience. As I noted in Chapter 3, the text is not the thing itself, and Baca must necessarily craft an incomplete account of the experience. What we have access to now is a text that represents a partial reconstruction of that experience. But his account nevertheless reveals something compelling about his experience of *being* in the act of writing; moreover, the text we have access to, no matter how incomplete an account of Baca's experience that text may be, underscores the power of his experience on his sense of himself as a being in the world. In this sense, his text is a record of the *impact* on him of his experience of writing at that moment, rather than a record of the experience itself.

5. Although many scholars have noted important distinctions between using a pen or pencil to write and using a computer (e.g., see Porter), in both cases the writer is using technology to record his or her words. Emig's focus in her analysis is on what is happening cognitively as a writer writes, and although the technology can (and almost certainly does) affect cognition during composing (as Porter suggests), for our purposes here the important point is that writing involves some form of recording, in addition to creating and originating, whereas reading, speaking, and listening do not involve recording.

6. An ontology of writing might thus help illuminate the experience of "writing anxiety" as studied the 1970s. See Daly and Miller, "Empirical Development" and "Further Studies"; see also Daly.

7. I would add here that my own experience writing in hypertext (see Yagelski, "Computers, Literacy, and Being") suggests how much the writer's attention in the moment can be shaped by the characteristics of the medium. While composing in hypertext I am intensely concerned with the shape and structure of the document I am composing in ways that seem more noticeable to me than when

I write in more traditional print forms, such as this book. I am also acutely aware of the technical operations that are required to create the web-text I am composing (e.g., coding in HTML). But my experience of my self-while-writing is not fundamentally different from what I describe earlier in this chapter. That is, although at times during the writing of that hypertext my attention is focused on these technical concerns, my awareness of my self as a self writing is not different from that awareness while writing in a print form.

8. The same might be said of newer media such as text messaging, Twitter, and Facebook. However, these media are used for composing and sharing extremely brief texts and therefore do not allow for the kind of extended writing that I am generally discussing here. In media such as text messaging, the possibilities for sustained, deeply engaged writing are limited or nonexistent. As a result, the writer's experience seems more akin to a face-to-face or telephone conversation, albeit through primarily textual media.

5

1,000 WRITERS WRITING

Contingency is an invitation to participate in history.
—Michael Pollan

Instead of teaching finished writing, we should teach unfinished writing
and glory in its unfinishedness.
—Donald Murray

Imagine 1,000 writers writing. One-thousand people gathered in the same
place all writing at the same time. Imagine them writing—together—for
themselves and for each other. Quietly, intently. And imagine that when
they are finished, nothing happens to the 1,000 texts they produce. When
they are finished writing, they turn to something else, putting aside the
product of their writing, although not the effects of the experience. It is possible that not a single one of those 1,000 texts will be read by anyone other
than the writer. Yet the experience of writing them for each of those 1,000
writers was real and, in some cases, powerful.

Now imagine that you are one of those 1,000 people writing. Imagine
that the writing you have just finished doing, as distinct from the *text* you
have just produced, is as important to you, at this moment, as any other

writing you have ever done, no matter what happens to the text itself. That text may be important in any number of ways, but it also is irrelevant, at a fundamental level, to the experience of writing you have just had. As an artifact of that experience, the text, no matter what happens to it later, is now separate from that experience. Writing that text, not the text itself, is what matters right now.

In November 2004, I was one of 1,000 writers writing. Some 1,000 educators from around the United States were gathered in a hotel ballroom in Indianapolis for the opening session of the National Writing Project's annual conference. I was new to the NWP, having just completed my first year as director of a newly established NWP site in Albany, New York. But in that year, I quickly learned that almost all NWP events, whether local or national, large or small, begin with writing. All our meetings of the Capital District Writing Project (CDWP), whether they involve five or fifty people and no matter what their focus, begin with writing. And almost never is the purpose of that writing to produce a text for later use. We write—together—for other reasons. I understand that now, having engaged in such impromptu writing so many times in the years since we established our NWP site in Albany. But in November 2004, I was unprepared for the prospect of 1,000 people writing together in the same place at the same time. In fact, I was genuinely skeptical.

For many years I had been asking students in my classes and teachers in workshops I conducted to write on demand in response to some prompt designed to focus attention on an idea or problem or to solicit reaction to a question. I still do. These brief (five- or ten-minute) writing activities always serve some specific purpose in my class or workshop. Typically, as a way to spark discussion, I ask the students or teachers to share what they have just written, or I ask them to begin small-group conversations by reading each other's impromptu writing. Sometimes these writings are part of a longer assignment, and sometimes I collect them—not to grade them but to see what was on the writers' minds. Most writing teachers I know use such strategies. I learned them as a new graduate teaching assistant at the University of New Hampshire in the early 1980s and have been using them in high school and college classes and professional workshops ever since. But I had never imagined asking 1,000 people to write at the same time in the same place. More to the point, I had never imagined simply putting the text aside once the period of writing was over. I had never considered simply writing. Why write at all, I wondered, unless it is to produce a text for some purpose?

At that moment in that ballroom in 2004, sitting among 1,000 other teachers, all of whom were writing, I assumed, like most every writing teacher I know, that a writing activity should always produce a text, even if only indirectly, to be used for some purpose—to keep a record, promote learning, generate ideas for further writing, to be published. I did not think of the act of writing itself as the purpose of the writing. But that's exactly what was happening at that NWP conference: 1,000 writers were writing for its own sake, because writing as an activity matters, separate from any text that is produced. At that moment, writing was in fact a powerful act of being, an intense awareness of ourselves, 1,000 individuals writing together, in that moment. In this regard, writing is a potentially powerful vehicle for transformation, for it opens up possibilities for reflection and awareness that writing as an act of textual production does not necessarily do. I cannot speak for the other teachers in that ballroom, but my experiences with writing, as distinct from textual production, have changed not only my view of what writing is and what it can do but also my sense of myself as a being in the world. Writing in the moment, I have come to realize, has the capacity to change us.

Writing in schools should be more like this—more like those 1,000 writers writing together in that ballroom. When it is, writing's transformative power is more likely to be realized, and it ceases to be a matter of procedure, an exercise in control, or a means of sorting and norming, as writing tends to be in formal schooling.

In this chapter I outline a pedagogy based on the idea of writing as a way of being in the world, a pedagogy that focuses as much on the writer writing as on the writer's writing. Such a pedagogy, I believe, is necessary if we wish to harness the power of writing as a vehicle for truth-seeking, as I defined it in Chapter 4, and as a means of individual and collective change. I propose this pedagogy, which is really a set of suggestions for how to think about the teaching of writing, in the context of the crisis of sustainability described in Chapter 1. In my view, the purpose of teaching writing should be defined by this crisis—and by the belief that the overriding purpose of formal education is to enable us to imagine a better future and create just and sustainable communities that contribute to our individual and collective well-being. In this regard, teaching writing should not be defined exclusively by the more limited conventional goals of producing effective communicators and academically successful learners.[1] If, as I argued in Chapters 1 and 2, mainstream schooling is based on specious assumptions about who we are and about how we know and relate to the world around us, then teaching writing for the often cited purposes of helping students succeed in school as it is currently configured and to prepare them for the existing consumer-oriented culture and for workplaces defined by economic globalization is merely a way to perpetuate the status quo that has given us the crisis of sustainability in the first place. Writing instruction, like schooling in general, ultimately should be about creating a better world. Teaching writing as a way of being might enable us to bring writing instruction more clearly into line with that goal.

Ultimately, then, writing instruction should serve two main functions:

1. to help students understand and harness the power of writing not only as a technology for communication but also as a way of understanding themselves and the world around them; and
2. to foster a different way of being in the world, one informed by a sense of the inherent interconnectedness of all life.

What I offer in this chapter is a description of an approach to teaching writing intended to serve those functions.

THE TRANSFORMATIVE POWER OF WRITING

Agnes is a fifth-grade teacher in a small, rural school district near Albany. In 2009 she was struggling with an especially challenging group of students, and in the midst of that struggle she caught a glimpse of the potential impact of writing on her students. In early 2009, at a meeting of a CDWP study group called the Teacher Research Interest Group (TRIG), Agnes shared that glimpse with some of her TRIG colleagues. She described a remarkable phenomenon that she had begun to observe in her class: Writing, it appeared, was the only activity that seemed to engage and in fact calm her otherwise rambunctious students.

We began that TRIG meeting as we usually do: by writing about our recent experiences in our classrooms. When we finished writing, we shared some of those experiences, and Agnes, in pained tones, confided her growing frustration and sense of powerlessness in the face of her fifth graders' seeming indifference to her best efforts to help them learn. She felt herself inexorably becoming the kind of impatient, authoritarian teacher that she despises, and she apologized for her apparent inability to reverse the process. After describing some of her students' recent antics, she slumped back in her chair and exclaimed in exasperation, "I just don't know what to do! This is not why I became a teacher!"

All of us around the table could empathize, for every teacher knows such moments of exasperation. And we could feel it the more so because we know Agnes to be an insightful, dedicated, and deeply caring teacher who was sincerely distressed about what was happening in her classroom. So we offered words of support, and a few of us shared our own experiences, some of them similar to hers. Then, almost as an aside, Agnes referred to the one thing that seemed to be working with her students: the five-minute "free writes" with which she begins each class. Each morning, after taking care of attendance and other classroom housekeeping chores, Agnes has her students write for five uninterrupted minutes about any topic they choose. No sharing, no grading, no guidelines, no assignments. Just writing. During this writing time, it is quiet—according to Agnes, for just about the only time during the entire day. And it is intense. Most of her students seem genuinely engaged in their writing in ways that many of them will not be for the rest of the day. Sometimes, they will ask for more time when Agnes declares the writing session over. They will even remind her to "do freewriting" if she gets sidetracked by something else in the hectic start of a school day. Agnes has no doubt that her students enjoy and seem to value this freewriting, this opportunity to write for themselves.

"It's the happiest time of the day," she told us, as though she didn't quite believe it. "The rest of the day is hell!"

What struck me most about Agnes's description of this apparent transformation of her students during their freewriting sessions was her use of the adjective *happiest*: "It's the *happiest* time of day." I wonder: How often do we think in terms of happiness—or well-being—when it comes to writing in school? Or schooling in general? Those fifth graders, it seems to me, understood something about writing that we educators seem to forget, something my prison students understood (as I described in Chapter 4), something too often ignored in school-sponsored writing instruction. Is it possible that for those five minutes of writing, Agnes's students can be in a way that they are not allowed to *be* for the rest of the school day, with its endless, onerous rules and procedures and limitations—and, not coincidentally, its lack of attention to their individual interests and needs and, yes, their well-being? After our discussion of Agnes's experience at the TRIG meeting, she decided to ask her students how they felt about their freewriting time. What she learned was stunning. Many of her students admitted that what they liked about the freewriting was that during those few moments they were, almost literally, freed from typical school worries about getting it right; they liked being able to focus on their own concerns and feelings without worrying about being judged. One student told her that the freewriting "makes me more focused." Another said it relaxes him, and several told her they felt in control of themselves when they were writing.

I found these comments from these 10-year-old students utterly remarkable, for they suggest a level of insight that we do not expect from such young students. But are fifth graders any different from any other student, of *any* age? Are they different from any other *writers*? For Agnes, those five minutes of freewriting represent not only a welcome respite from the struggles of a normal school day but also a window into the potentially transformative power of writing. For her students, those five minutes of writing seem to be transformative—at least in that moment while they are writing.

Each spring semester I teach a graduate seminar in the teaching of writing in secondary schools, which is required of students enrolled in the

English track of the teacher certification program at at my university. Most of these students are recent college graduates, having earned their bachelor's degrees in May and entered our program that following summer. A few are "career-switchers" and therefore a little older than the twenty-somethings who make up the majority of students in the program. All of them are decidedly older than fifth graders. Yet they seem to have the same kind of response as Agnes's fifth graders to the open-ended writing that I invite them to do at the beginning of each class meeting.

Like Agnes, I begin each class with a few minutes of writing. Usually, I provide a prompt as a starting point for writing, but the students know that they can write about anything. The subject matter doesn't matter. For the most part, these students are earnest, academically accomplished, and diligent; many are driven. But most of them are not terribly interested in the research and theory they encounter in my course. They want teaching methods — and understandably so, because they are in the midst of their first student-teaching experience and often are frantic to learn *how* to teach. Usually, our class discussions of the required readings tend to drift to what happened that day in the classrooms where they are student-teaching, and I often struggle to keep our focus on the more theoretical matters at hand: the social nature of writing, for example, or the connections between language and identity. But the first ten minutes of each class are quiet, intense, and focused — just like Agnes's fifth-grade class. My 20-something students seem as absorbed by their writing as her fifth graders. It is the one time during our three-hour class meetings when *every* student seems genuinely engaged. And usually, the informal discussion that follows this writing time is energizing. Those students who choose to share what they have written, usually paraphrasing rather than reading verbatim, seem invested in what they have to say, and their classmates do too. It hardly matters that I never collect these pieces of writing, for the texts themselves are not important. The benefit — for the individual students and for our classroom community of aspiring teachers — lies in the act of writing together at that moment; it has little to do with the aspects of writing that are emphasized by conventional approaches to writing instruction, such as writing "quality."

Tina, a student who enrolled in this course in 2008, had taught high school English for six years in South Central Los Angeles before returning to her hometown in upstate New York to start a family. After taking a job at a high school near Albany, she enrolled in our program to earn the master's degree that New York requires for permanent certification. It was fortuitous timing, for Tina was in the midst of profound questioning of her own teaching, and she saw my course as an opportunity to rethink some of what she believed about teaching writing. For her midterm self-evaluation, for example, she described the struggle that working with adolescent writers within the mainstream education system had become for her:

I have always loved my job, but for the past four years, I have been struggling to reconcile the contradictions inherent in writing instruction. The increasing emphasis on accountability and standardization requires us to teach one way, but what we as writers know to be true of writing requires us to teach another way. As a result of these two conflicting approaches to writing instruction, I find myself in an ongoing struggle to satisfy both the administration and my conscience.

While I had hoped this course, its required reading and writing, would help me find a middle ground, a workable compromise if you will, I am more and more coming to the realization a compromise is not what my students need. What they need is a writing teacher who is brave enough to stop "teaching" writing. As writing teachers we are simply responsible for providing our students opportunities to write in safe and constructive environments, and that is the teaching. But to do that, we have to trust they can learn without our writing prescriptions; we have to trust the process itself. While I thought my struggle was an attempt to reconcile state expectations and sound pedagogy, the real struggle has been learning to trust my students.

Tina goes on to write, "The first writing assignment for this course reminded me how important it is that we write about what we need to write about." For that assignment, which was simply to write about something that mattered to them, Tina wrote about her experiences as a teacher in Los Angeles. Through that assignment and her subsequent writing, Tina came to the realization that the enormous effort she devoted to form and correctness in her classes did not serve her students well, either as writers or as human beings coming of age in a complex world. She began to understand that her embrace of our profession's collective obsession with text ultimately prevented her students from realizing the power of writing as she herself experienced it. In the excerpt just presented, she eloquently articulates the same struggle that so many college writing teachers I have met also experience: how to reconcile the increasing institutional and cultural pressures to place greater emphasis on "standards" and writing "competencies" with the nagging sense that our collective focus on maintaining these "standards" does not truly serve our students' needs. This is the dilemma that Tina, like so many high school and college teachers I know, has been confronting in her writing, and she has written herself to a realization that our obsession with the form and features of written text obscure the real value of writing.

Our conventional ways of thinking about and teaching writing are text-focused and driven by theories that (not surprisingly) emphasize the communicative aspects of language. We teach writing mostly as a tool for communication, and we emphasize the production, form, and uses of text. Within the mainstream Cartesian view of writing that I described in Chapter 2, the text is both a container of meaning and a reflection of the autonomous Cartesian self that mainstream pedagogies assume the student writer to be.

Mainstream textbooks and conventional pedagogical practices emphasize how to produce certain kinds of texts. Progressive (or critical) pedagogies challenge the dominance of academic discourse as well as oppressive pedagogical practices and uses of writing, but in the end advocates of critical pedagogies essentially call for broadening the definition of acceptable textual forms and expanding the range of purposes for which students are asked to produce texts (e.g., writing as political action or community service rather than writing exclusively in the service of academic learning); they do not call for a redefinition of writing that shifts our focus to the transformative powers of the *act*, as distinct from the *product*, of writing. Even the so-called process movement, which ostensibly emphasizes what writers *do* when they write, is ultimately about the texts writers produce. For all the attention it has received, the process movement seems to have effected little change when it comes to where we cast our collective gaze in our efforts to understand and teach writing: Our eyes remain fixed on the text, like so many test-takers admonished to keep their eyes on their own papers.

This all seems to make sense, for writing is indeed a powerful tool for communication; it is a technology that extends the communicative capabilities of language. It is also a uniquely effective vehicle for learning as learning generally is defined in conventional academic contexts—that is, knowing a specified content, grasping a concept, or performing a certain kind of cognitive operation. Students *do* need to develop the ability to communicate effectively in writing; they benefit from writing that fosters learning across disciplines. But as I explained in Chapter 2, the mainstream Cartesian view of writing reduces writing to a skill (albeit an extremely useful one) and ultimately distances the act of writing from living in all its complexity. This mainstream obsession with the text separates writing from *being*. It compartmentalizes writing and limits it to an activity in the service of learning or communicating; as a result, we treat writing *only* as a communicative or cognitive tool, seeming to forget that language is implicated in our very sense of our selves as beings in the world, even as we invoke theorists, such as Freire, whose work is founded on the inherent connection between language and being. Merleau-Ponty's definition of speech as "the presence of . . . thought in the phenomenal world" (*Phenomenology* 211) reminds us that because thought and world are coterminous, speech is an enactment of our being in the world. In this formulation, writing is also an act of being. As such it has great power to shape our very experience of our selves and the world around us—as it seemed to do for Agnes's fifth graders and my graduate students. Mainstream writing instruction ignores this aspect of writing, locating value almost exclusively in the text itself and (sometimes) in the potential impact of a text on a reader.

We need to change that.

I suspect that most readers of this book, especially those who teach composition, will be uncomfortable (at best!) with the notion that we should, in effect, displace the text from the center of writing instruction—that we should structure the teaching of writing around the idea that what is most valuable about writing is the experience of writing in the moment. Such a reaction is understandable, given the history of writing instruction in the United States, with its focus on skills and correctness and its connections to meritocracy and corporate capitalism (see Berlin, *Rhetoric and Reality*), and given the strength of the mainstream Cartesian view of writing—not to mention the inertia of our sprawling system of institutionalized education. For most of my own history as a writing teacher, I would have shared that reaction. My approach to teaching writing was long characterized by an emphasis on the quality of the texts my students produced. But as Murray often reminded his students, it is the writing itself that teaches us—if we allow it. This idea of learning *from* writing rather than learning *to* write is an important one, but I really don't think many people understand what Murray meant. It took me twenty years to figure it out. And I figured it out only by paying attention to what happened as I wrote—something Murray spent his career doing.

In an essay called "Listening to Writing," Murray describes the process by which he tried to write an article but instead found himself writing a poem. In his essay, Murray takes us through the process by which that poem emerged from his writing, in effect providing us with a kind of record of his experience as he wrote. He began, he says, with the goal of writing an article about the importance of rewriting; in other words, he was writing to try to understand his experiences with revision. But unexpectedly, he found himself exploring his subject through a poem. In the end, he tells us, he learned about the importance of listening to writing, which in turn taught him something about teaching:

> While dictating the first draft of this article I did not expect to hear my voice developing the relationship between listening to writing and listening to students. But I did hear it, and I recognized its significance. It tied together some things I have learned about writing and teaching. (65)

In his writing, Murray often encouraged teachers to allow students to write in whatever form or genre seems most appropriate for what they have to say. It is one of the ten guidelines for teaching writing that he presents in his famous essay "Teach Writing as Process Not Product": "The student is encouraged to attempt any form of writing which may help him discover and communicate what he has to say" (16). So if a poem is the best vehicle for exploring the idea or experience about which the student is writing, that's fine. And indeed, addressing complex questions about the relationship between form and purpose—and gaining insight into how purpose drives form—can be part of the learning that occurs through writing. But the more important insight here is that the form of the writing really doesn't matter, for it is the *act* of writing that teaches us, no matter the form. We don't, most of us, seem to appreciate this capacity of writing, because we are so obsessed with the *product* of writing—the text and the form of that text—which we assume to be a reflection of a student's writing skill or lack of it. This obsession obscures the insight that we can gain from writing itself; it prevents us from learning from our writing as Murray did in writing his poem. Here's what he says about that poem:

> The experience of the poem also reminded me that I must somehow, as a teacher, a husband, a son, a father, a friend, a colleague, a citizen, a professional, a busy-busy-busy man so proud of my busyness, find time to listen so that I will hear what I have to say. If I am able to be quiet within myself something may appear on the page which may become writing and, when that happens, my job is to listen to the evolving writing. ("Listening" 63)

Here Murray connects his experience as a writer to the rest of his life as a father, teacher, son, husband, and so on. As I take it, he reminds us that what we learn through the act of writing is not just lessons about the skill or practice of writing as a means of producing a text; we also (and more importantly) learn about ourselves as human beings. This is a crucial insight about the true power of writing. If we engage genuinely in the sustained practice of writing, as Murray encourages us to do, which encompasses a careful attention to what happens as we write, then ultimately we learn something about living. Writing in this way can transform us. The writer writing is a human being living. And the practice of writing can give that writer a means to change her life. Therein lies the real transformative power of writing.

As a student, I was never exposed to the wisdom in Murray's seemingly simple dictum. That's primarily because I was never asked by my teachers to pay any attention to the writing itself. Nor were my classmates. We were required only to attend to the form of the finished text. And when I look at what happens in secondary and postsecondary classrooms today, when I listen to teachers of writing at all levels of education describe what they do, I see that little has changed in the three decades since I finished college. Students today are learning what I learned—which is to say that they are not learning to pay attention as they write; they are not learning from and through the act of writing.[2]

We must change that.

The first step is to let our students write. As Tina learned, as Agnes discovered, as Murray knew, we must provide opportunities for our students to learn *from* and *while* writing. That's the foundation of a pedagogy of writing as a way of being. To focus on the writer writing in this way is not to eliminate the text; rather, it is to place real value on the act of writing, to reposition the text in writing instruction, to abandon our obsession with textual form and demonstrations of writing skill, and to redefine the purpose of writing in the terms I set at the beginning of this chapter. In this way, the text serves the purposes of writing, rather than writing having only the purpose of producing a certain kind of text.

Let me illustrate this approach by sharing the story of Chelsea's writing.

WRITING *WITH* TEXT RATHER THAN WRITING *THE* TEXT

In spring 2007, Chelsea enrolled in my seminar in teaching writing (the same course in which Tina was a student the following year). A 22-year-old who had earned her bachelor's degree in English the previous spring, Chelsea was in her second semester of the master's-level teacher certification program at SUNY-Albany. Like her classmates, she was initially taken aback by the first assignment I gave in the course: write about something that matters to you. The assignment specifies no subject matter, no genre, no length, and no style. There is only the requirement to write about something that is somehow important to you by a specific date (about a month after I give the assignment). It seems straightforward enough, but it stumps many of my students. Despite having earned degrees in English and despite their obvious facility with written English, many are uncertain about what and how to write, and as a result the assignment generates anxiety. From my point of view, this anxiety is productive because it forces the students to confront some of their assumptions about writing and eventually to consider their own reasons for writing about something that they deem significant; moreover, it often exposes the sources of their lack of confidence as writers and the lack of pleasure or joy they take in writing. Even with a group of academically accomplished English majors, I usually field the same kinds of questions that I have so often heard in my first-year college composition courses and high school English classes: What should I write about? How long should it be? Can it be in the first person? Do we have to cite sources? Such questions, as most composition teachers know, are a function of pedagogical practices that emphasize following directions and producing a certain kind of prose in a specific form. In mainstream writing instruction, most students learn that writing is often a matter of giving teachers what they want. No surprises there.

The surprises come when the students begin writing, which of course they do despite their anxieties, for the fear of missing a deadline and getting a poor grade often trumps their fear of writing. For Chelsea, the anxiety associated with the assignment seemed less intense than for many of her classmates. She seemed happy to have a break from writing the kind of literary analysis essays required in her undergraduate English courses. My assignment gave her an opportunity to shift her attention to something that did indeed matter to her, something that was much on her mind: her evolving relationship with her parents, who had recently divorced after twenty-eight years of marriage. Satisfied that the assignment truly was open-ended and that it gave her complete choice of subject, form, length, and so on, Chelsea set to work.

In our conference about her first draft, which we held about a week after I gave the assignment, Chelsea told me that initially she didn't want to write about her parents' divorce, but about how her relationship with them had changed as she grew from an adolescent to a young adult. She wanted to write a lighthearted essay. Here's the opening paragraph of her rough draft:

> I don't know if I will ever become accustomed to seeing my parents as real people. I can remember spending weekends in our attic playing magical games of make-believe and coming across dusty cardboard boxes filled with photos and yearbooks and old clothes. I still don't know if I am over the shock I felt when I realized for the first time that my parents had actually existed and had lives prior to being parents. Boxes of pictures of my mother with her high school friends, wearing big bell bottom pants and smoking cigarettes. Photo albums filled with newspaper clippings of my dad's high school track career, surrounded by photos of him sporting way-too-short cut off jeans and tall striped socks, leaning up against his yellow and brown, zebra print interior Volkswagen Bug. I can remember sitting on my attic floor in shock, not sure how to absorb the fact that my parents were once kids and both had lived lives that had not involved me, or even each other. Sure, I had heard them tell stories about when they were kids like me, but I always had assumed they were just making the stories up to make me feel better, make me feel like they understood. But to me, the word *parent* was as far as my definition of them could extend. To me, they were this combined thing that, of course, only existed because they had three lovely little children to care for.

Chelsea goes on in the draft to describe how the divorce upset her childlike sense of her parents. She didn't write about the pain or disruption of the divorce but focused on her need "to handle the fact that my parents were actually two separate people who had ceased to exist as one entity." In fact, her draft included no information about why her parents were divorcing after so many years together. Instead, she described how "the combination 'Momanddad' that I had imagined as this real existing thing, suddenly transformed into a mom and a dad who were pursuing their own lives and their own interests." She portrayed these two "new" people with rather humorous details about their transformation: "My Dad traded in his Friday nights of watching Bob Vila home improvement shows for pursuing his apparent new found love of the art of Karaoke." "My mother, who had always gone to bed at seven o'clock at night, was spending her weekends going out for dinner and dancing . . . and spent her mornings with her Billy Blanks Tae Bo videos." Chelsea ended the draft in a way that suggests that her parents' transformation has been all for the best:

> I can now look at my Mom and Dad and realize that they *are* two very different people, probably so different that they shouldn't have been together in the first place. But then of course, where would I ever have played make-believe in an attic, and how would I have ever learned that parents are people too?

This is a perfectly acceptable—and common—angle for a student to take in writing a personal narrative about an important event in her young life. Chelsea was putting the best face on what might have been a difficult situation. But I was struck by a statement in her draft that her parents were "probably so different that they shouldn't have been together in the first place." After twenty-eight years? That seemed a remarkable statement from a daughter who clearly had a good home life and strong, loving relationships with both her parents. So I asked Chelsea about that. I also asked her about some of the details she included about her parents, especially this line describing her mother after the divorce: "She smiled a lot. She woke up smiling and went to bed happy." I couldn't help but wonder about that image in view of Chelsea's earlier statement that perhaps her parents should never have married in the first place. From my point of view—as a middle-aged, middle-class white man in a twenty-seven-year-old marriage of my own and living in a society in which marriages end in divorce as often as not—this image was both intriguing and troubling, and it provoked my curiosity.

When I first give this assignment (which is essentially the same assignment I routinely gave in my first-year and advanced composition courses as well as the high school English courses I have taught), I tell the students that during the few weeks that they will be working on the assignment, they will engage in several different kinds of conversations about their writing: one-on-one conferences, small-group peer-response sessions (which I call "writing groups"), whole-class workshops, and online discussions. In all of these contexts, I emphasize, our purpose is not to suggest ways to make the students' texts "better" but to explore what seems to be happening in their drafts and inquire into the writer's ideas or argument or story. For most of my students this is a challenge. Having come of age in classrooms influenced by the process movement, they are usually familiar with workshops and peer-response activities. And they are well schooled in identifying "problems," pointing out errors, and suggesting revisions in their peers' drafts. They are less comfortable exploring issues that arise in or through a draft, and many are decidedly uncomfortable with the notion that our conversations about their drafts are really not intended to lead to "better" essays. For example, here's how Tina described her reaction to my instructions to the writing groups:

> When instructions were given for how to conduct our first writing group in this class, I thought to myself, "Don't discuss possibilities for improvement? Just respond to the ideas? How will we be able to provide constructive criticism?"

In general, the students' experiences with writing instruction have taught them that talking about writing-in-progress is a matter of offering "constructive criticism"; it is a matter, that is, of helping the writer decide how to improve his or her text. But as we proceed with our various conversations about writing-in-progress in my class, most students eventually let down their guards enough to begin exploring possibilities in their writing—not possibilities for "improvement" but possibilities for thinking differently or more carefully about important aspects of their lives that emerge in their writing. Many of them (although not all) begin to use their texts as vehicles for inquiry and as points of departure for further writing—that is, for writing further into their experiences or deeper into the questions about the world they live in that energize or worry them.

In Chelsea's case, our conference evolved into a conversation not about her parents' divorce but about her misgivings about what that divorce seemed to reveal about her parents (especially her mother), about relationships in general, and about herself. Cultural tropes in contemporary American society about relationships as well as about so-called mid-life crises did not quite square with Chelsea's experience, about which she had conflicting feelings. One way to read her draft is as her attempt to use such tropes to tell the story of her experience—in other words, to tell a familiar story that reflects certain values and beliefs about relationships in contemporary American culture and about the possibilities for reinventing oneself in middle age. The rather happy ending of her narrative in her rough draft thus becomes almost inevitable, for a common cultural trope depicts the successful reinvention of the middle-aged man or woman after a debilitating marriage and difficult divorce—a mature adult finding him or herself through hardship and triumph. It would be reasonable to see Chelsea's first draft in these terms. But I think that to do so would obscure not only the complexity of the story Chelsea was trying to tell but also—and more important—the richness of her experience of trying to write that story; it would also obscure the impact of that experience on her sense of herself as the adult child of divorced parents. I hoped her draft and her process of revision could serve as a gateway for her continued inquiry into her experience.

In the late 1990s, David Bartholomae argued for a conception of composition that focuses on revision as "an exercise in criticism" (21), asserting that we should want our students "not only to question the force of the text [they produce] but also the way the text positions them in relationship to the history of writing" (21). To that end, he proposed a "critical project" for Composition Studies in which we "accept student writing as a starting point, as the primary text for a course of instruction, and . . . work with it carefully, aware of its and the course's role in a larger cultural project" (24). To illustrate such a project, Bartholomae shares a student essay in which the writer describes her experiences as part of a church-sponsored group that traveled to St. Croix in the Virgin Islands to help clean up hurricane damage there. The essay tells a story of how these good-hearted American volunteers, through their selfless hard work, won over the residents of St. Croix, who were initially skeptical of the Americans' motives and rather less than welcoming of the visitors. The essay concludes, "We were once looked down and frowned upon, but after working hard to prove our position we were more than accepted. Our efforts proved to change our position in that particular society and we became well respected guests on the island" (qtd. in Bartholomae 25). Bartholomae argues that this student narrative is one "that ordinarily writers cannot *not* write" (27), because in telling their stories students are drawing upon a larger cultural discourse in which certain "master narratives" (14) shape the way they understand their experiences. Such master narratives, he suggests, suppress other possible narratives. In this case, the master narrative of the well-intentioned American "missionaries" helping less fortunate people excludes the vexed history of relations between the United States and its Carribean and South American neighbors, a history that would give good cause for the St. Croix residents' hostility to their American visitors.

The problem for a composition course, Bartholomae asserts, is how to approach the prospect of revising such an essay if the purpose of revision is not to improve the essay necessarily but "to enact a critical reading of the text, and where that critical reading was not merely a critique of the formal properties of the text—where a writer would have to ask about and think about, say, the history of North American relations with St. Croix" (27). Bartholomae points out that "within the terms of the process movement, the primary goal was the efficient production of text," so revision becomes a matter of making the existing text better according to the conventions of academic writing. "Within these protocols for revision, the missionary narrative [of the St. Croix essay] may become more finished, but it will remain the missionary narrative" (27). In other words, revision does not become a vehicle for inquiry into the text or the experience that is the focus of the text but a technical process of bringing the text into line with convention—to write a "good" story by conventional standards. Instead of this conventional approach to revision, Bartholomae proposes asking "questions of the discourse as a discourse" (27):

> What is its history? Whose interests are served? What does the scene of the plantation [described in the student essay] mean? What does it mean in terms of the history of St. Croix? . . . How might one *not* write a missionary narrative and yet still tell the story of a missionary trip to St. Croix?

Such an approach "would teach students to question the text by reworking it" (28). In the end, "the product would be an essay that was, in a certain sense, less skillful or less finished or less masterful than the original" (27) but one that had served as a vehicle for a deeper inquiry into the historically situated nature of the experience about which the student had written.

Bartholomae's overarching purpose in such "critical project" is to foster in students a certain kind of critical perspective on the world and to help them develop a set of intellectual skills to interrogate the texts they encounter, including their own. He wants them to be able to place texts in historical and cultural context and understand how those contexts shape texts. I find these goals admirable and worthy but, in the end, too narrow, for they focus mostly on "critical" academic skills. However, Bartholomae's proposal to use student texts as starting points for inquiry is consistent with the pedagogy I am advocating, in which the goal isn't simply to make a better text but to provoke genuine inquiry that can lead to insight into and understanding of the issues that emerge from the writing. Moreover, his suggestion that student writing is often driven by powerful cultural narratives that remain unexamined helps expose some of the limitations of mainstream pedagogies that seek only to help students produce "good" writing. He demonstrates that our obsession with the finished text results in our leaning on the master narratives that he sees in his students' essays. These narratives—and what I referred to earlier as cultural tropes—serve as ready-to-hand frameworks for producing, revising, and evaluating texts, and they close down the kind of inquiry that writing could (and, I believe, should) foster. In other words, in mainstream instruction, with its focus on producing a "good" text, writing about an important experience like a humanitarian visit to a storm-damaged island, as Bartholomae's student did, or a divorce, as Chelsea did, becomes a matter of fitting the experience into a narrative format that is consistent not only with prevailing cultural values and myths but also with technical expectations for narrative texts in general.

From this perspective, Chelsea's task as writer becomes a matter of shaping her experience so that it fits these expectations; she fits the details of her experience into a kind of cultural and technical narrative template. Revision, then, becomes a process of mapping her experience onto a prevailing cultural narrative as well as a technical process of making the text conform to the conventions of such narratives. Such a task diverges from the broader goal of allowing the act of writing itself, as distinct from the text, to become a vehicle for genuine inquiry into her experience—of her parents' divorce and of herself as a being in the world. From my point of view, approaching Chelsea's text in the conventional way honors neither the importance of her experience nor the capacity of writing to help her explore the experience. Instead, much as Bartholomae did with his student's essay, I want to approach Chelsea's text as a starting point, but also more: as a *waypoint* in her ongoing journey of inquiring into her experience, which ultimately should supercede her text as well as any subsequent texts she might produce for this assignment.

So as Chelsea and I talked about her draft in conference, I continued to ask questions about passages that suggested to me that something more was going on than the draft seemed to reveal. In response, Chelsea began to explain the circumstances surrounding her parents' divorce, and it became clear that her text contained very little of the experience about which she had been writing. Missing from the draft, for example, was any sense of how her mother's growing dissatisfaction with her life led to serious tensions in her marriage; in fact, the draft never even hints at the source of her mother's dissatisfaction. As Chelsea filled in details of the experience, it also emerged that her father's satisfaction with his married life only seemed to provoke his wife's restlessness. That dynamic was also absent from the draft. Nor did the draft convey Chelsea's smoldering anger at her mother and her sadness about her father's deep pain when he finally began to lose the wife he loved. In fact, the more Chelsea talked about the passage describing her father's "new" life, the more vexed and complicated the passages describing her "new" parents became. Some of the details she included in her draft, such as her father's shifting taste in music, actually seemed to reveal how difficult the transition to his new life was for him—and how painful it was for Chelsea to watch. That struggle is never described in her draft; indeed, she used those details to try to present a slightly humorous picture of a middle-aged man trying on a new, rather unhip persona—very different from the image of him that was emerging in our conversation. It isn't that Chelsea's draft didn't tell the whole story; it told a *different* story from the one that was emerging in our conference. Or rather, her draft reflected a struggle to tell a version of her story that tried to fit her experience into a prevailing cultural narrative—to produce a story that wasn't really "true."

In the end, Chelsea was writing many different, even conflicting stories that didn't all fit together or conform to the larger cultural narratives about midlife crises, middle age, and parent–child relationships. Nor did her different stories fit easily into the narrative format she learned in school. And here's the main point: Her experience was available to *her as writer* but not to her readers, for the text did not—and *could* not—capture and convey that experience fully. Within the context of mainstream writing instruction, all her draft could really do was meet the rigid expectations for a certain kind of personal narrative that ultimately has no clear relationship to the experience it is purportedly about—or to the experience of writing it. Thus, focusing her efforts on revising her draft so that it conforms to these narrative expectations would inevitably result in a story that is removed from her experience—both her experience of her parents' divorce and her experience of writing about that divorce.

As it became evident that Chelsea's draft did not really reflect the depth or complexity of the experience she was writing about, the question became, Now what? In mainstream writing pedagogy, we would encourage Chelsea to revise her draft in ways that would result in a written version of her story that conforms to both cultural and technical narrative expectations. As Bartholomae noted in reference to his student's "missionary narrative," we would try to help Chelsea make her existing story "better" without necessarily trying to understand it or change it or use it in some way to help us make sense of our experience of the world. The goal would be to help her create an "effective" text according to conventional standards. For example, we might suggest filling in "gaps" in the narrative by adding an anecdote about her mother's mid-life crisis or a scene that reveals Chelsea's anger with her mother. We might suggest eliminating passages that didn't seem to advance this story about her "new" parents. We might point out ways to tighten the organization of her essay. Such suggestions might have led Chelsea to tinker with the form of her text and adjust the content so that it effectively tells a certain (familiar) story to her readers. And from that point on, the focus of her attention would be on the technical aspects of producing that narrative. In other words, her attention would shift from the experience to the text, and the connection between the two would become increasingly tenuous as Chelsea worked harder to produce the expected narrative. In this scenario, *even if Chelsea's writing of her first draft was a genuine inquiry into her experience, her writing and revising now cease to be such an inquiry and become a process of textual production*, which is the real focus of most school-sponsored writing assignments.

So instead of identifying potential revisions to help Chelsea "improve" her draft, Chelsea and I talked more about the experience that was the focus of her *writing*, an experience whose richness and import were becoming more evident as we continued our discussion. She revealed some of her antipathy toward her mother and talked about her changing relationship with her father, for whom she had become a kind of caretaker as he struggled to restructure his life. We talked about the complexities of parent–child relationships and some of the difficult lessons she was learning, and I shared my own perspective on my changing relationships with my adult children. We talked as well about the challenge of maintaining a long-term marriage and how different needs and desires on the part of the partners and their children complicate that challenge. We talked, that is, about the lives we were living: our experiences and what they mean, how they intersected and diverged, what we learned—or didn't learn—through them. Together, using Chelsea's draft as a starting point as well as a reference point, we engaged in a kind of collaborative inquiry into some fundamental questions of contemporary life. And through that process, driven by Chelsea's writing (*not* the text alone but also her experience of writing it), she came, I think, to an awareness of her vexed feelings about her parents that she previously didn't seem to have or hesitated to acknowledge. At the same time, I began to think in different ways about long-term marriages and the responsibilities such relationships place on each partner in terms of my own marriage. Both of us, I believe (I hope), gained insight into ourselves and into complex aspects of human life.

I want to emphasize here that the role of Chelsea's draft in this process was shaped by the fact that it was a *draft*, a work in progress, but also by the circumstances surrounding her writing of that draft—that is, by the way I structured and managed the assignment. Chelsea knew, for example, that her essay wouldn't be graded in a conventional way as a separate piece of writing, since my grading scheme was a modified portfolio in which the students would receive a single grade for the main writing assignments in the course, including drafts, revisions, and reflections. She also knew that she would have other conversations about her draft as well as opportunities to revise it or write a different essay before the end of the semester. Because of these circumstances, Chelsea's text could become a vehicle for inquiry—her own and her classmates'. In this sense, her text was a kind of living document, part of her effort to understand the experience she was writing about (and our collective effort to understand the issues her draft raised for us). Moreover, in our many discussions about her draft, we didn't focus on examining the technical or rhetorical aspects of her text. Those issues did arise, of course, and we addressed them in terms of the options writers have as they revise and in terms of considerations about audience and purpose as part of the rhetorical context of any writing. But these concerns did not displace our collaborative inquiry into the questions Chelsea was wrestling with as she looked more deeply into her experience of her parents' divorce—nor did they displace our larger discussion of how writing can serve as a vehicle for such inquiry into self and world.

This process of collaborative inquiry continued when we discussed Chelsea's draft a few days later in a whole-class workshop. In my course, the purpose of these workshops is to provide another forum for conversation about the students' writing—not the texts exclusively but the issues that the students are exploring in their texts. During workshops, I deflect the students' attention from the technical aspects of the draft, so that we could have a conversation about the questions that might emerge from the students' individual readings of each others' drafts; as much as I could, I keep these discussions from becoming a litany of suggestions for revision. In Chelsea's case, the workshop, like our conference, developed into a rich conversation about the complicated matter of human relationships. It also became a conversation about how writing enabled us—individually and together—to delve into such matters and how that process had the potential to lead to powerful, if sometimes uncomfortable, insights about our experiences. We talked about writing as a means of reflection in the context of the challenges of living together in an uncertain world. And we talked about the experience of writing itself: how it could open up possibilities for greater awareness of ourselves as we write about matters of significance to us. We didn't talk much about the product of the writing, because no matter what revisions Chelsea might have subsequently chosen to make on her essay, her writing had already served its purpose—for her and for us. In that sense, her revisions were irrelevant.

That's not entirely true, of course, for Chelsea did revise, and she did so in a way that reflected some of what she learned about her relationship with her parents through the process of writing her essay. As a text, her revised essay focuses more noticeably on her conflicting emotions about her parents' divorce and her own struggle to reconcile her new family situation with her memories of what had seemed a happy family life. For example, here's a passage following a scene in which Chelsea's mother has just told her about the impending divorce; Chelsea tries to make sense of the changes she is beginning to see in her mother and she wrestles with her own feelings:

> She [my mother] isn't happy. She dreads turning the corner to our house and seeing the hunter green RAV4 [her father's car] parked in the driveway. She goes to bed early every night to avoid conversation. She has found an apartment. It's really beautiful with high vaulted ceilings and tall white pillars in every room. The kitchen will have to be repainted of course, but we will finally be able to have a kitchen table. Isn't that great? A kitchen table. I can live with her, or with Dad. I can choose. *Choose where to live, or choose a parent?* I am unclear about what is happening.

In this version, some of the statements from her earlier draft have a decidedly different impact, with little of the lightheartedness she claimed to strive for in the earlier draft: "The combination 'Momanddad' that I had imagined as this real existing thing, suddenly transformed into a Mom and a Dad who were pursuing their own lives and their own interests." The revised text retained a subtle sense of the fun of coming to know her parents as adults. For example, her father "had slowly transformed into this man that I did not even recognize, yet someone that I was so intrigued to know. All this time I had been convinced that the way I had known him as a parent was really his identity; I didn't realize that my Dad was actually this completely different person who was now starting all over." But her ending told a very different—and much more ambivalent—story:

> You never really expect things to change; you never expect for lives to change so much that they affect everyone around them. You never expect people, to become new people. Yet, these two people, who I had always been so sure were just "two peas in a pod," were actually very separate people who had been struggling, for the sake of the children who saw them that way, to play a make-believe fairytale of the "Momanddad." It changed. They changed. Our family changed. And you never really expect it to happen, until it happens.

As writing teachers, we can discuss the merits of Chelsea's essay as a personal narrative and examine the rhetorical or technical effectiveness of her revisions: how well her essay now tells a complicated story, the depth of thought or insight it seems to convey, its tighter structure, Chelsea's sober but engaging voice, her careful use of details to convey her ambivalence about her new relationship with her parents. We might focus, for example, on how Chelsea uses details in the passage about her mother's unhappiness to convey her own conflicted feelings about her mother's new life—as compared to the somewhat lighthearted details about her parents' separate apartments in her rough draft. That is, we can identify the ways in which her specific revisions have made this a "better" essay in conventional terms, one that conveys more effectively the complexity of Chelsea's experience and gives greater depth to the insights she realized. There is certainly something important to say about these aspects of her essay, and I don't mean to diminish the value of either the technical aspects of revision or the discussion we might have about them. These are elements of writing that students should understand and practice and, in some cases, master. But if that's as far we go, then we turn Chelsea's experience of writing about this pivotal moment in her life into a matter of textual production, and we devalue the experience she is writing about (her parents' divorce), which becomes mere "content" for her essay; we devalue as well her experience as writer and its potentially transformative nature. This isn't just a matter of splitting form from content; it is a matter of separating writing from our experience of ourselves in the world.[3]

In her reflection on this assignment, Chelsea confided that she chose to "write about something I needed to write about, for myself," and she emphasized that writing her essay was ultimately more important than her "final draft":

> It is not necessarily about the final product, but about how you get there. My final draft (which in all honesty, I am weary about calling final because I do not feel confident that it is, or ever will be, fully complete) is very different from the original. Based on the feedback from my writing group, from our meeting [i.e., our conference], and from the rest of the class, I decided to make some choices about where I wanted my piece of writing to go. Had I not been exposed to the feedback of so many different people, I probably would not have changed my draft very drastically. However, in my opinion, the changes I made feel more honest to me than the original draft did.

In admitting that she is weary of calling her latest version of her essay a "final" draft, Chelsea acknowledges the ongoing nature of her inquiry into her experience that writing this essay had become for her. Producing a text may be part of that inquiry, but the primary purpose of the inquiry is *not* to produce a text. To my mind, the primary purpose is gaining new understanding of her experience and herself—and sharing it with us. What she is demonstrating in her reflection is her growing insight into writing's capacity to help us understand our experiences. She also reveals that she learned something significant about herself through the process of writing:

> [S]omething I learned about myself as a writer, and something that became increasingly clear with every person who read my draft, is that, even in a piece of personal writing, I try not to let too much of myself show. As was discussed in the meeting [our conference], as well as in the group discussion of my draft, it was unclear exactly what my piece was about because I had been trying to cover up one subject with another. In addition to that though, I learned that even as much as I may have tried to not get "too personal," certain things can be seen by reader's eyes that could not be seen by mine. For example, I did not mean to come across as siding with my Dad, although in reality that may be the truth.

Through writing—that is, through the *experience* of writing as distinct from writing for the sole purpose of producing a certain kind of text or demonstrating technical competence in doing so—Chelsea seems to have deepened her understanding of herself as a daughter, a young woman, and a human being. In a sense, through writing, Chelsea is learning a different way of being in the world—a way of being that is characterized by a willingness to revisit her view of herself and the sense that she was making of her experience—all of which took place in the social context of the class discussions and related pedagogical activities I asked the students to participate in. This is what I take Couture to mean when she writes that rhetoric as a practice of collaborative truth-seeking must involve an openness to alternative perspectives on our experience of ourselves and the world around us—that it must include a special kind of altruism: "It is through disclosing the private in language, then, that we come to understand our personal history, our memory, as having a larger meaning shared by others" (25). In this regard, "writing is a means by which we get in touch with our personal history, the substantial experience that grounds our belief. That contact can be expressed publicly, but it must be experienced privately; it is what we experience deep within us that connects us to others in public" (25).

Note that in her reflection Chelsea acknowledges the value of the social interactions that surrounded and helped shape the writing of her essay. She refers to the role of the discussions she had with her classmates and with me in shaping not only the essay itself but also her experience of writing it. She recognizes the value of the collaborative inquiry in our class—an inquiry for which her essay served as vehicle. In the context of this collaborative inquiry, Chelsea's experience writing her essay led her to some hard truths about herself and about living and loving. This collaborative inquiry, driven by her own writing, had an effect on her as a human being, whatever else it might have taught her as a writer. That, it seems to me, is more valuable than any technical skill she may have demonstrated by producing a "good" personal narrative, the value of such skill notwithstanding.

Ultimately, then, a pedagogy of writing as a way of being involves the production of a text and the practice of specific writing skills, but those components of the pedagogy are subordinate to the larger purpose of writing to *be* in the world in a more reflective, self-aware, and, as Couture puts it, altruistic way. Such a pedagogy does not subordinate learning through writing about ourselves and the world around us to learning *how to write*, as mainstream writing instruction does. If we ignore this potentially transformative inquiry into self and world that writing can be, then we have not served our students' interests well.

Two years after she wrote her essay in my class, Chelsea wrote in an email message to me that her essay remains "one of the more meaningful writing pieces that I have kept" from her academic programs, in which "it wasn't often that we had the opportunity to discuss writing that was important to us." I am confident that "meaningful" in this context has little to do with technical or rhetorical matters, and that's as it should be.

Part of the point here is that if, as Chelsea's instructor, I had focused only on the technical quality or effectiveness of her text as a narrative, Chelsea's insights into her experience would largely be ignored. I do not want to deny the benefits of teaching writing as technique—for example, of helping Chelsea' learn to craft an effective narrative, no matter what "story" she wants to tell. Nor do I want to downplay the necessity of helping students gain competence in the rhetorical skills necessary for writing the kinds of texts they will be required to write as students, as citizens, as workers. But teaching writing *only* as technique and rhetorical skill undermines the potentially powerful experience of writing for the writer—and, ultimately, for all of us, since the writer's insights into herself and her experiences are not only shared with us but can also shape the way we live together in the sense that they become part of our shared inquiry into living together on the earth. There is surely benefit in teaching Chelsea how to be a writer of "good" narratives or arguments or reports, but I want to suggest that there is even greater benefit in giving her the opportunity to use to writing to become more deeply aware of who she is, to understand her experiences more fully, to examine the world around her more mindfully. The text she produces can be a vehicle for that, for these broader goals are not mutually exclusive to the more conventional goal of helping students develop "technical" mastery as writers. But the nature and "quality" of the text Chelsea produced are ultimately tangential to the insights she might gain by writing that text. If we value only the text, as mainstream writing instruction tends to do, then we devalue those insights and we teach students that it is the text, not the writing, that matters.

Most of our students do not seek to become writers. They write in school because we require them to. A very few will write for their own purposes outside school or the workplace. Most won't. That's true even of professionals like teachers. Chelsea may have been working toward becoming an educator who might occasionally write, but if she's like most teachers, her own writing will never become the focus of her professional work. And like just about every student you and I have ever known, she was always unlikely to become a professional writer or some other kind of professional for whom creating certain kinds of texts is the focus of her professional work. The vast majority of our students will never produce more than a few texts that truly matter in some discernible way in their lives. But they will all have to live their lives and figure out how to make their way in a complex and dangerous and wonderful world. Writing should be a way for them to live—together— more fully and joyfully and mindfully. And we should teach it as such.

TEACHING WRITING AS A WAY OF BEING TOGETHER

A pedagogy based on the idea of writing as a way of being is fundamentally social and inherently communal. The purpose of an assignment like the one

Chelsea responded to in my class is not just to provide students with an opportunity to engage in writing as an act of inquiry into their own experience of the world (and to give them practice in the rhetorical and technical aspects of writing) but also to enable them to participate in and contribute to the shared inquiry of the class, an inquiry that is ultimately about who they are as beings in the world. In this sense, the students write the world together and potentially write their way to a different way of being together in the world. A pedagogy of writing as a way of being, then, is a pedagogy of community.

Many of the pedagogical activities I describe in this chapter will be familiar to teachers of writing: peer-response exercises, one-on-one conferences, workshops, multiple drafts, and so on. These techniques are now part of the landscape of institutionalized composition instruction. But in mainstream writing pedagogies, the ultimate purpose of these activities is to help students produce "better" texts. In a pedagogy of writing as a way of being, however, these activities are an integral part of a sustained collaborative inquiry that students pursue into their experiences and the world they inhabit. In the end, such a pedagogy subordinates writing as a skill to the act of writing as a vehicle for inquiry—and to the *experience* of writing as a potentially different way of being in the world. In this sense, process-oriented pedagogical techniques such as peer response sessions become acts of community-building as well as acts of shared meaning-making, because their purpose is not limited to the improvement of students' texts. Moreover, the students' texts become artifacts of an inherently social process. Writing thus becomes a collective process of inquiry, and the experience of writing becomes a collective act of being together in the world: 1,000 writers writing, together, to change themselves and each other—and the world they share.

A wonderful paradox of writing is that it is both an individual and a social act at the same time. As Thomas Kent's paralogy reminds us, there can be no meaning-making without an other. In this sense, writing, even when done in isolation, is inherently an acknowledgment of an other—indeed, of many others; it is an enactment of the interconnectedness of humanity. Writing as a practice is a realization of Walt Whitman's famous line, "I contain multitudes."

If we write as a way of being in the world, if we allow writing to become a practice of reflection, an awareness of ourselves in the moment, and if we do so together over time, we can begin to realize change: change in how we understand who we are in relation to those around us. Educators (and I think compositionists in particular) like to say that a classroom is a community, and we often employ pedagogies founded on that idea. But a classroom is a temporary community. It disbands, its members dispersing after a few short months to pursue their individual agendas. What happens to each of them and what each of them subsequently does no longer matters to the now-defunct classroom community. In such a temporary community, writing has value only to the extent that it matters to those individuals. But writing as a practice of being *requires* attention to the writer's inherent connection to those other individuals in a classroom, who are not only members of that temporary community but also members of many larger, overlapping communities that continue to exist and change long after the class itself ends. In this regard, to write together is to reinforce a sense of connection that transcends the classroom. Chelsea's sense of herself has been shaped by her writing in my class, but that sense of self continues to evolve, in part *because of* her writing, after she leaves the class. Likewise, her sense of connection to her classmates through their shared inquiry through writing is not bound by the classroom walls or the fifteen-week semester schedule; rather, because that sense of connection was a function of their individual and collective sense of themselves as beings in the world, they potentially take a new sense of self with them, not as "learning" in the traditional sense of that term but as the ongoing impact of their experience of writing together in order to *be* in the world.

Some recent educational reform efforts have emphasized the idea of community as a basis for curriculum and pedagogy. The school programs supported by the Center for Ecoliteracy, for example, the Common Roots curriculum in Vermont, and the increasingly popular service learning components of many composition programs are all founded on a belief that formal education is inherently connected to larger communities beyond the school itself; these efforts emphasize the responsibilities that accompany membership in various communities.[4] Progressive education reform efforts in the past, such as movements inspired by Dewey, have had a similar emphasis on community. In many ways, although there are many differences among these varied reform movements, a pedagogy of writing as a way of being is consistent with such efforts. It is conceivable that the kind of approach to writing instruction that I am advocating here can be incorporated into ongoing reform efforts and even into mainstream classrooms and schools. What matters most, however, is that students, no matter what the institutional or curricular context, be allowed to write in ways that enable them to explore their sense of who they are in the world around them. And this practice must be a collective one. Students must engage in writing, together, with the understanding that they cannot do otherwise. For ultimately writing as a practice of being is about changing how we live together on the earth.

THE CHALLENGE OF TEACHING WRITING
AS A WAY OF BEING

In The *Omnivore's Dilemma*, Michael Pollan critiques our industrial model of food production and consumption and advocates eating "with a fuller consciousness" (11). Acknowledging that to do so can seem impractical in a commodified, consumer-driven culture, Pollan argues that it is nevertheless necessary for our collective well-being and the health of the earth. He essentially advocates a way of being in the world in which our inherent interconnectedness—with each other and the planet—is enacted through dietary practices characterized by greater awareness of the implications of what and how we eat. In other words, eating becomes an act whose purpose of sustaining individual life is inextricable from the larger purpose of sustaining each other and our planet; in this sense, eating becomes part of a more deliberate, conscious, responsible way of being in the world. Pollan's insights could well apply to writing instruction—and education in general.

Pollan exposes how our industrial food system shapes our relationships to each other and to the land and upsets the delicate balance among the many complex components of the ecosystems we depend on and are part of. Such a system skews our priorities so that all manner of environmental destruction (as well as harm to human health) is tolerated, because the well-being of the environment as well as its inhabitants is redefined in terms of profit; indeed, well-being as we typically understand it is almost never factored into an equation in which profit is the goal. In the end, our relationship to the land is redefined in ways that ultimately harm both us and the land and contribute to a sense of ourselves as separate from what sustains us. In Pollan's view, the solution to this problem is a more localized food system and, significantly, mindful dietary practices based on an awareness of the interconnectedness of all of its components. Thus, reducing the damage our industrial food system does to the earth and to us requires that we change how we *think* about eating. The true challenge lies not so much in changing our specific habits as in adjusting our most fundamental views about who we are and how we relate to the world around us.

The same is true when it comes to teaching writing.

If writing instruction and schooling in general are to foster a more humane, altruistic way of being in the world, we will need an education system that is more localized in the way that Pollan suggests our food system should be. We will need a kind of educational federalism that allows for the creation of more humane schools characterized by curricula and pedagogies that take into account the complexities of human learning and human life within local contexts that are understood to be inextricably part of distinct but overlapping regional and global communities.[5] In other words, we will need a network of schools and colleges that are more fully and consciously integrated into the culture and geography of their local communities yet mindful of the reality that, as physicist David Bohm once said, everything in the universe is connected to everything else. Such a system would work against the standardization and economies of scale that characterize the industrial model of schooling we now have. It might enable us to refocus our priorities on the development of the *whole* student as part of whole communities. Such a locally focused education system should be overtly about imagining and creating just and sustainable communities, not sustaining a consumerist status quo; accordingly, schooling would be defined in terms of the well-being of those communities and the individuals who comprise them. This kind of system would require a fundamental shift away from the seemingly paradoxical ideology of individualism and conformity that informs our current education system; it would require that we abandon our obsession with standardization and standardized assessment and redefine learning as something other than the individual cognitive skills, "observable" behaviors, and "measurable" outcomes that now count as learning in schools. No longer would education be solely about individual achievement, defined by a narrow set of academic skills and content; instead, learning would encompass more complex abilities, knowledge, and responsibilities driven by a more reflective awareness of self and world and understood as a function of our inherent interconnectedness. Within such an approach, variation and diversity would be valued not as abstract qualities, identities, or characteristics of individuals but as concrete manifestations of the differences among localities and communities—differences defined as much by geography and topography as by history, culture, and related social factors. Today, classrooms in isolated locales like rural Wyoming or Vermont's "Northeast Kingdom" look and function essentially like classrooms in sprawling urban centers like New York or Los Angeles, in smaller cities like Indianapolis or Tampa, or in the well-heeled suburbs of Connecticut or Seattle. Such consistency, which ultimately separates schooling from its local contexts, should be abandoned in favor of a multiplicity of educational practices and structures all connected by the broader common goal of enhancing the well being of the communities we create and maintain together.

Writing instruction within such a system would look more like the 1,000 writers writing that I described at the beginning of this chapter. In place of thousands of students writing individually but producing the same kinds of (mostly meaningless) texts in order to demonstrate that they conform to the same set of standards, rules, and conventions, thousands of student writers would be writing together in order to understand better who they are and how they might live together more mindfully, equitably, and ethically. They would be writing not only to produce various kinds of texts for many different purposes (defined individually and collectively) but, more significantly, to enact more just and humane ways of being together on the earth.

This is the future of writing instruction I envision. 1,000 writers writing. Together.

But we need not wait for a new, radically changed, localized education system to begin realizing a vision of writing instruction that is informed by the idea of writing as a way of fostering an ethical, nondualistic way of being together on the earth. We can begin realizing this vision now.

The first step is to recognize the general inutility of most mainstream writing instruction and then to discard the obsession with textuality that results in generally ineffective writing instruction in mainstream educational settings. Although that assertion will seem laughable to many (probably *most*) educators, steeped as we all are in the ideology of the mainstream Cartesian view of writing, available data suggest that mainstream writing instruction does not necessarily produce "better" student writers. Moreover, we might critically and honestly examine our own experiences to illuminate the role that texts play in our lives and the lives of other people we encounter. If we do, we will realize that although we are surrounded by and interact with texts almost constantly every day, most people actually *produce* precious few texts, if any, that ever really matter much in their lives or the lives of those around them. In other words, writing as an activity whose purpose is to produce a certain kind of text—which is to say, writing as experienced by most students—doesn't play a significant role in the lives of most people.

Take as an example my father-in-law, now 80 years old and long since retired after working for thirty-eight years as a machinist in a factory. As the secretary for the local chapter of his union for many years, he produced and handled many documents, most of which were records of union members' dues and the union chapter's spending. Like many working-class Americans, he periodically also had occasion to write personal letters as well as more formal letters—for example, to bank loan officials or his insurance company about matters related to his family's financial well-being. But mostly his interactions with texts were as a reader, not a writer. He has read the newspaper most every morning of his adult life. He reads bank statements, auto insurance policies, and the various flyers and advertisements that arrive in his daily mail. He doesn't surf the Internet to read news stories online or visit discussion forums devoted to subjects that interest him, but if he did, those texts would likely become part of his literate life in much the same way that the print texts he regularly reads are part of his literate life. Once in a great while, one of the texts he reads makes a discernible difference in his life. Recently, for example, he received Medicare statements about payments for the physical therapy he undergoes for his arthritis. But over his eighty years on earth, he has rarely actually *written* any kind of text that truly mattered to him or to others, that made some significant difference to his personal, professional, or political life, or the lives of those around him. Writing, except when defined as little more than the act of producing a specific kind of text such a letter or a report, has never figured much into his life, and it doesn't today. He has never truly experienced the power of writing *as a writer*. He has never known what it means to write himself awake, in David Grosskopf's phrase. And in that regard he is like just about everyone else I know outside academe: my other family members (including a son now attending graduate school and a wife with an accomplished record as an accountant and human resources professional), acquaintances and neighbors (including highly educated professionals in law, medicine, engineering, finance, and international business), and even the vast majority of educators with whom I have worked.[6]

For all of these people, *literacy* is an essential part of their lives, but writing is not. Very few people I have ever encountered write in ways that truly matter in their lives. And I am confident that if you examine writing in the lives of those you know, you will come to the same conclusion. This is a truth about writing in contemporary society that I do not believe we have acknowledged. For all the time, effort, and money we expend on writing instruction at all levels of schooling, the act of writing seems to play a decidedly minimal role in the lives of most of those with whom we share this earth. Moreover, it isn't clear that writing instruction, despite the apparent value we place on it as a society, actually accomplishes the often cited goals of preparing effective writers for academic work and the workplace (see, e.g., the National Commission on Writing).

Consider these facts.

Results of the writing component of the National Assessment of Educational Progress for the past few decades suggest that few of the nation's high school seniors can produce sophisticated prose in terms of depth of thought, syntax, and structure. The NAEP writing test, which is administered every four years, is one of the most in-depth and carefully designed large-scale writing assessments currently in use, and it provides perhaps the best available picture of the writing abilities of the nation's high school seniors. For this assessment, students produce three kinds of writing (narrative, informative, and persuasive), which reflect different textual forms, audiences, and purposes. Their three texts are then evaluated according to a complicated scoring system involving general and task-specific criteria; the resulting composite score places students in one of four categories: *basic, proficient, advanced,* or *below* basic.[7]

For the past three administrations of this test, results have been strikingly consistent (see Fig. 5.1). More than 75 percent of students scored at the "basic" level or better; approximately 20 percent scored below this level, a figure that has fallen slightly in the most recent administration of the test

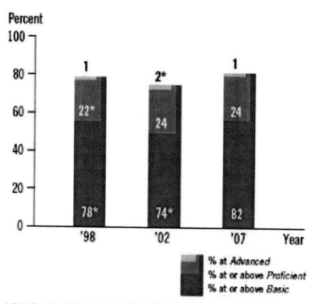

* Significantly different (p < .05) from 2007.
SOURCE: U.S. Department of Education, Institute of Education Sciences, National Center for Education Statistics, National Assessment of Educational Progress (NAEP), 1998, 2002, and 2007 Writing Assessments.

Fig. 5.1. NAEP results for twelfth grade

(from 26 percent in 2002 to 18 percent in 2006). But significantly, fewer than 25 percent of students scored at the *proficient* level or better, and *only 2 percent* or fewer have scored at the *advanced* level. If you read the NAEP description of writing that meets the standard for an *advanced* score or even a *proficient* score, you might think you are reading a description of the expectations for first-year composition or for college-level writing in general (see Fig. 5.2). In other words, the NAEP results suggest that few high school seniors seem to have developed the ability to write as they will be expected to write in college. (These results also seem to give the lie to the widely held belief that students lack "the basics" when it comes to writing: Although 20 percent or so of students do score "below basic," the overwhelming majority—some eight of ten—seem to have mastered the so-called basic skills of writing.)

The NAEP results provide a rather discouraging picture of twelfth-grade student writers, but even when we look only at college-bound seniors, the picture isn't necessarily much better. A 2010 ACT study of "college readiness" indicated that 33 percent of high school graduates failed to meet benchmarks for readiness in English composition; moreover, only 51 percent of high school juniors were found to meet the common core benchmark

Twelfth-grade students performing at the *advanced* level should be able to produce a mature and sophisticated response within the time allowed that uses analytical, evaluative, or creative thinking. Their writing should be fully developed, incorporating details and elaboration that support and extend the main idea of the piece. It should show that these students can use literary strategies—anecdotes and repetition, for example—to develop their ideas. At the same time, the writing should be well crafted, organized, and coherent, and it should incorporate techniques such as consistency in topic or theme, sequencing, and a clear introduction and conclusion. It should show that these writers can engage the audience they are expected to address through rich and compelling language, precise word choice, and variety in sentence structure. Writing by twelfth-grade students performing at the *advanced level should contain few errors in grammar, spelling, punctuation,* capitalization, and sentence structure. These writers should demonstrate a sophisticated command of these elements and may use them for stylistic effect in their work.

Twelfth-grade students performing at the *proficient* level should be able to produce an effective and fully developed response within the time allowed that uses analytical, evaluative, or creative thinking. Their writing should be organized effectively, and it should show that these students have a clear understanding of the writing task they have been assigned. It should be coherent, making use of techniques such as a consistent theme, sequencing, and a clear introduction and conclusion, and it should include details and elaboration that support and develop the main idea of the piece. The writing should show that these students are able to use precise language and variety in sentence structure to engage the audience they are expected to address. Writing by twelfth-grade students performing at the *proficient* level should contain few errors in grammar, spelling, punctuation, capitalization, and sentence structure. These writers should demonstrate a command of these elements and may use them for stylistic effect in their work.

**Fig. 5.2. Description of proficient and advanced-level writing on the NAEP.
(Source: National Assessment of Educational Progress)**

for college or career readiness in writing (ACT, *College Readiness*).[8] Data from the National Center for Education Statistics as well as other studies (e.g., Adelman, *National Crosstalk*) indicate that nearly 33 percent of entering college students either seek or are required to take remedial courses in composition and other basic academic subjects (ACT, *Crisis at the Core* 3). And this is to say nothing of the distressingly large number students who drop out of high school, those who graduate from high school but do not attend college, and those who enroll in college but do not complete their degree programs.[9]

Such data suggest that although most high school and college students develop basic competencies as writers, few seem to develop the more sophisticated writing ability that those of us in Composition Studies routinely claim to foster (or *try* to foster) in our students. Some research indicates that college students do develop as writers in a range a ways, including fluency and the complexity and maturity of their prose (e.g., Haswell; Holzman; Odell). In his excellent investigation of the development of writing ability during the college years, Richard Haswell documents the improvements in student essays he observed at the end of a first-year composition course: student essays are longer, their holistic scores are higher, and "there is a greater amount of exemplification and more material stored in the logical compartments of the top-level organization, both measures indicating an expansion of ideas. . . .The essays also improve in audience awareness, with much better introductions and more transitions between paragraphs" (316). Such changes in student writing, I suspect, would please most writing teachers, especially in the short span of a semester, and they are not trivial. But it is striking that these measures of quality are mostly matters of form as well as mastery of the conventions of academic writing. We could assume that "an expansion of ideas" is more or less equivalent to more sophisticated thinking and perhaps to in-depth learning, but that would be speculation. And Haswell himself describes "this picture of improvement during the freshman composition course . . . as highly ambivalent" (316). He notes problems that emerge in student writing as they move through their courses, including "some simplification of organization, fuzziness of word choice, and an increase in error" as well as "perhaps some regression in syntactic play" (316–17). These problems are very likely signs of development as students continue to gain a footing in academic discourse, sometimes stumbling as they do; experienced writing teachers are familiar with this seemingly uneven "progress." Haswell also points out that students' main concerns with "length, support, and explication" in their writing are likely a result of the fact that "these concerns were the writing tactics the [first-year composition] course probably emphasized"; he notes that teachers would likely see "a sign of course success" in students' expression of such concerns (317).

And that's the key point, for "success" in writing instruction is almost always defined in terms of students' ability to produce texts that exhibit a rather narrow set of textual characteristics. And we're not even sure that we really "succeed" in this way. Haswell discusses at length the well-documented "backsliding" in the quality of student writing that seems to occur in the sophomore year of college and often later, and although he offers persuasive explanations for this apparent drop in writing quality, arguing that it doesn't necessarily equate to a drop in writing competence, his proposed solutions remain squarely focused on the text.

Some longitudinal studies of college student writers complicate this picture. For example, Herrington and Curtis present complex portraits of four students during their college years who "actively use writing—including the sorts of public writing often required of them in college—for the ongoing development of their personal identities, including their sense of relation to others" (1). Their study rests on a conception of writing that encompasses psychological and emotional dimensions that are usually absent from the more conventional text-focused ways in which conceptions of writing are operationalized in college composition programs. What is striking in their report, however, is how far afield of the requirements of writing in their classes these students must travel in order to use writing in ways that genuinely matter to them as human beings. In other words, writing was for them an integral part of their complicated and sometimes difficult personal journeys, but not because the college curriculum itself encouraged such uses of writing. And it isn't clear how "good" their writing ultimately became according to conventional measures of writing quality. Similarly, Lee Ann Carroll documents the challenges students face as they write for different instructors in different disciplinary contexts across the college curriculum, offering a revealing picture of the structural obstacles to students' development as competent writers. In many ways, her study is a reminder of how much students have to learn in order to succeed as writers while in college—knowledge that often has little to do with writing itself but has mostly to do with being able to "do school."

All of which is to suggest that mainstream writing instruction does not seem to be achieving the widely accepted goals of writing instruction for *any* group of students, college-bound or not. We devote an astonishing level of attention, time, energy, and money to writing instruction, and yet so many students do not emerge from the process possessing advanced writing skills, nor do they seem to use or value writing as an important part of their lives except in terms of the gratuitous ideas that they need good writing skills to succeed in school and the workplace.

But what if we were to refocus writing instruction on the act of writing in the moment, rather than on the production of specific kinds of texts that are valued in academic settings, as mainstream writing instruction does? How might that focus shape the experience of our students? How might it have shaped the experience of someone like my father-in-law? What would he have lost if he were exposed to a pedagogy of writing as a way of being rather than being subjected to the formulaic, standardized mainstream pedagogy that emphasizes the production of a narrow range of specific kinds of texts in school? What might he have gained? What might *we* have gained?

Now imagine 1,000 students writing. Just writing. And imagine that their writing—not the texts they produce, but the act of *writing*—opens up for them the capacity of writing to understand anew their experience of themselves in the world. Together. Imagine that their acts of writing together—occur within a framework of writing instruction as a vehicle for truth-seeking. Who might those 1,000 students be in fifty years? What might the communities they have created look like? How might their experiences of writing—together—have shaped *our* experiences—together—in this world we share?

I do not know how likely it is that we could realize this vision of 1,000 writers writing. I know only that we will lose little by trying, for to perpetuate our current industrial model of writing instruction is to ensure that we will continue to produce students who fit into the consumerist status quo and contribute to the ongoing crisis of sustainability—students for whom writing is not a vehicle for truth-seeking or a practice of inquiry and awareness of self and world, but a procedure for producing sanctioned texts that matter little to them or to us.

Meanwhile, we remain mired in the crisis of sustainability that I described in Chapter 1, and mainstream writing instruction continues to promote the dualistic Cartesian worldview that is implicated in that crisis. As long as writing instruction is informed by the Cartesian view of writing, it is likely to give us—and our students—more of the same, despite the advances in our collective understanding of literacy and despite our best efforts to accommodate ourselves to bewildering technological change that is redefining literacy in our lifetime.

The greatest obstacle to changing writing instruction, then, does not ultimately lie in the enormous practical and logistical challenges that would accompany any large-scale reform effort. The greatest challenge lies in opening ourselves up to different, nondualistic ways of understanding ourselves as beings functioning within and as part of the communities and systems we create and inhabit. To change how we teach writing is ultimately a matter of changing how we think about ourselves as beings in the world.

How to begin? By writing. Together. In the end, it is as simple—and challenging—as that.

ENDNOTES

1. I have previously made versions of this argument in Yagelski, "Stasis and Change"; "English Education"; and "Computers, Literacy, and Being."
2. In their review of data on classroom writing instruction collected as part of the NAEP, Applebee and Langer report the following:

> Data over time also suggest that there has been some increase in emphasis on writing and the teaching of writing, both in English language arts classrooms

and across the curriculum, although this may have begun to decline from its high. Further, while process-oriented writing instruction has dominated teachers' reports at least since 1992, what teachers mean by this and how it is implemented in their classrooms remains unclear. The consistent emphasis that emerges in teachers' reports may mask considerable variation in actual patterns of instruction.

What is clear is that even with some increases over time, many students are not writing a great deal for any of their academic subjects, including English, and most are not writing at any length. ... Two-thirds of students in Grade 8, for example, are expected to spend an hour or less on writing for homework each week, and 40% of twelfth graders report never or hardly ever being asked to write a paper of 3 pages or more. (28)

Such data suggest that although the process movement has resulted in certain pedagogical activities, such as peer response, becoming more common in classrooms, the amount and nature of writing students are required to do has not changed significantly in the past several decades. And given the increased emphasis on standardized testing in the past decade, the traditional focus on form and correctness has become even more pronounced.

3. I recognize the potential irony of my using this text to argue for displacing the text in the teaching of writing, especially because I rest much of my argument on an analysis of the limits of the text in conveying an experience, as I demonstrated in Chapters 3 and 4. However, as I suggest later in this chapter, the text is not useless or unimportant. I am arguing that we must recognize and account for the limitations of the text and reposition the text in writing instruction so that it does not displace or devalue the experience of writing itself.

4. For information about the Center for Ecoliteracy and its "Smart by Nature program, see http://www.ecoliteracy.org/. For a discussion of the Common Roots curriculum, see Bowers, especially pp. 197–99; see also http://www.smartcommunities.ncat.org/success/Common_Roots.shtml.

5. I realize, of course, that American education has a long tradition of local control. The modern education system evolved in the late nineteenth century from a patchwork of locally developed and managed schools that might be described as "educational federalism." Technically, even today we have no national education system; instead, school districts are still managed by school boards made up of local elected officials. But in practice, our education system amounts to a standardized national system. For one thing, federal monies allocated to states for education are restricted by a variety of rules and requirements that shape local curricula and even pedagogies. The NCLB program is a good example of how the federal government uses funding for education to wield control over such matters as the use of standardized tests to evaluate student achievement and school effectiveness, curriculum reform, and professional development for teachers. Additionally, in most states curriculum standards are set and overseen not by local school boards but by state agencies, and teacher certification is managed almost exclusively by state governments. In the past two or three decades, a trend toward greater standardization has accelerated as successive presidential administrations have tried to implement their versions of education

reform. Before George W. Bush's NCLB program, President Bill Clinton championed greater "accountability" in the form of teacher testing (which he pushed as governor of Arkansas) and called for an emphasis on student achievement on standardized tests. And more recently the National Governors Association Center for Best Practices and the Council of Chief State School Officers have sponsored the Common Core State Standards Initiative, which was embraced by the administration of Barack Obama as part of its broader education reform efforts. Despite the emphasis on "state standards" in its title and its insistence that "local teachers, principals, superintendents and others will decide how the standards are to be met" ("Frequently Asked Questions"), the Common Core program is at heart an effort to establish a national core curriculum that might vary from state to state but includes a substantial core for math and English that would be embraced by all states: "Common core standards are a clear set of shared goals and expectations for what knowledge and skills will help our students succeed" ("Frequently Asked Questions"). As of winter 2011, forty states had adopted the Common Core standards and others were expected to follow suit. (Adopting the Common Core would enhance states' chances of securing federal monies under the Obama administration's "Race to the Top" education reform grants program, a significant incentive for states to adopt the Core during very tight economic times). As I note later in this paragraph, in terms of curriculum, pedagogy, scheduling, and administration, schools in the United States look and function in essentially the same way no matter their size or location. In effect, we have a national standardized education system that does not significantly reflect local cultures, politics, history, and geography in the way I am advocating.

6. New so-called social media such as Facebook seem to create new opportunities for writing that my father-in-law did not have; however, there is little evidence that, aside from a few people who use these media for social action, most people use these media to produce texts that truly matter to them or to others. It may be that these media encourage the use of writing for reflection, and in that sense, they may change somewhat the dynamic that I am describing here such that writing becomes a more important part of their ways of being in the world. But for now, the jury is still out.

7. Information about the NAEP in this and the following paragraphs is taken from Salahu-Din et al. Information about NAEP also is available at http://nationsreportcard.gov and http://nces.ed.gov/pubsearch.

8. ACT defines its College Readiness Benchmarks as "the minimum scores required on the ACT subject tests for high school students to have approximately a 75 percent chance of earning a grade of C or better, or approximately a 50 percent chance of earning a grade of B or better" in English composition and several other core subjects (ACT, *Crisis at the Core* 2).

9. According to statistics from the National Center for Education Statistics, approximately 48 percent of high school graduates did not attend college in 2006, the last date for which such data were available as of winter 2011 (*Digest of Education Statistics*, 2009; see table 203; http://nces.ed.gov/ programs/digest/d09/tables/dt09_203.asp?referrer=list), and 9 percent of high school students drop out of school before earning their diplomas or GEDs (*Digest of Education*

Statistics, 2007). The most encouraging studies of so-called "persistence rates" at four-year colleges and universities reveal that 66 percent of high school graduates who enroll as first-year students complete their bachelor's degrees within eight years; in other words, approximately 33 percent of college students drop out of college before finishing their degree programs (Adelman, *Toolbox Revisited*). Many studies show less positive numbers, with persistence rates averaging just above 50 percent. (see Advisory Committee on Student Financial Assistance). Also, it's worth noting that as of 2007, 29.6 percent of Americans between the ages of 25 and 29 had earned bachelor's degrees; that means that seven in ten Americans in this age group have not earned a bachelor's degree (*Digest of Education Statistics*: 2007; see table 8 at http:// nces.ed.gov/programs/digest/d07/tables/dt07_008.asp?referrer=report). All of which is to say that a very large number of students likely leave school (many of them before graduating from high school or college) without developing even the basic competence as writers that their peers who remain in school could be assumed to possess.

WORKS CITED

Abe, Masao. *A Study of Dogen*. Ed. Steven Heine. Albany: SUNY Press, 1992.

Abram, David. *The Spell of the Sensuous: Perception and Language in a More-Than-Human World*. New York: Pantheon, 1996.

ACT. *College Readiness: A First Look at the Common Core and College and Career Readiness*. Iowa City, IA: ACT, 2010

ACT. *Crisis at the Core: Preparing All Students for College and Work*. Iowa City, IA: ACT, 2004.

ACT *National Curriculum Survey 2009*. Iowa City, IA: ACT, 2009.

Adelman, Clifford. *National Crosstalk*. San Jose, CA: National Center for Public Policy and Higher Education, 1998.

Adelman, Clifford. *The Toolbox Revisited: Paths to Degree Completion from High School Through College*. Washington, DC: U.S. Department of Education, 2006.

Advisory Committee on Student Financial Assistance. *Reflections on College Access and Persistence: In Honor of the 40th Anniversary of the Higher Education Act*. Washington, DC: U.S. Department of Education, 2006.

Agyeman, Julian. *Sustainable Communities and the Challenges of Environmental Justice*. New York: New York University Press, 2005.

Applebee, Arthur N. *Alternative Models of Writing Development*. Albany: Center on English Learning and Achievement, 2000. <http://cela.albany.edu/ publication/article/writing.htm>. Accessed July 22, 2010.

Applebee, Arthur N. *Writing in the Secondary School: English and the Content Areas*. Urbana, IL: National Council of Teachers of English, 1981.

Applebee, Arthur N., and Judith A. Langer. *The State of Writing Instruction in America's Schools: What the Data Tell Us.* Albany: Center on English Learning and Achievement, 2006. <http://www.cela.albany.edu>. Accessed July 22, 2010.

Baca, Jimmy Santiago. *Working in the Dark: Reflections of a Poet of the Barrio.* Sante Fe, NM: Red Crane Books, 1992.

Bartholomae, David. "What is Composition and (if you know what it is) Why Do We Teach It?" In Eds. Bloom, Lynn Z., Donald A. Daiker, and Edward M. White. *Composition in the Twenty-First Century: Crisis and Change.* Carbondale: Southern Illinois University Press, 1996. 11–28.

Berkenkotter, Carol, and Donald M. Murray. "Decisions and Revisions: The Planning Strategies of a Publishing Writer, and Response of a Laboratory Rat: Or, Being Protocoled." *College Composition and Communication* 34 (May 1983): 156–72.

Berlin, James A. "Rhetoric and Ideology in the Writing Class." *College English* 50.5 (1988): 477–94.

Berlin, James A. *Rhetoric and Reality: Writing Instruction in American Colleges, 1900-1985.* Carbondale: Southern Illinois University Press, 1987.

Berlin, James A. *Rhetorics, Poetics, and Cultures: Refiguring College English Studies.* Urbana, IL: National Council of Teachers of English, 1996.

Berlin, James A. *Writing Instruction in Nineteenth-Century American Colleges.* Urbana, IL: National Council of Teachers of English, 1984.

Bizzell, Patricia. "Cognition, Convention, and Certainty: What We Need to Know About Writing." *Pre/Text* 3.3 (1982): 213–43.

Bizzell, Patricia, and Bruce Herzberg, eds. *The Rhetorical Tradition.* Boston: Bedford Books, 1990.

Bolter, Jay David. *Writing Space: The Computer, Hypertext, and the History of Writing.* Hillsdale, NJ: Erlbaum, 1991.

Bordo, Susan. *The Flight to Objectivity: Essays on Cartesianism and Culture.* Albany: SUNY Press, 1987.

Bourdieu, Pierre, and Jean-Claude Passeron. *Reproduction in Education, Society, and Culture,* 2nd ed. Thousand Oaks, CA: Sage, 1990.

Bowers, C. A. *Educating for an Ecologically Sustainable Culture: Rethinking Moral Education, Creativity, Intelligence, and Other Modern Orthodoxies.* Albany: SUNY Press, 1995.

Bowles, Samuel, and Herbert Gintis. *Schooling in Capitalist America: Educational Reform and the Contradictions of Economic Life.* New York: Basic Books, 1976.

Bowles, Samuel, and Herbert Gintis. "Schooling in Capitalist America Revisited." *Sociology of Education* 75.1 (Jan. 2002): 1–18.

Brandt, Deborah. *Literacy as Involvement: The Acts of Writers, Readers, and Texts.* Carbondale: Southern Illinois University Press, 1990.

Breuch, Lee-Ann Kastman. "Post-Process Pedagogy: A Philosophical Exercise." In *Cross-Talk in Comp Theory,* 2nd ed. Ed. Victor Villanueva. Urbana, IL: National Council of Teachers of English, 2003. 97–125.

Capra, Fritjof. *The Tao of Physics,* 3rd ed. Boston, MA: Shambala, 1991.

Carroll, Lee Ann. *Rehearsing New Roles: How College Students Develop as Writers.* Carbondale: Southern Illinois University Press, 2002.

Center for Educational Policy Research. "English." *Understanding University Success (A Project of the AAU and The Pew Charitable Trusts)*. Eugene, OR: Center for Educational Policy Research, 2003. 16–27. <http://s4s.org/understanding.php>. Accessed February 13, 2008.

Clifford, John, and Elizabeth Ervin: "The Ethics of Process." *Post-Process Theory: Beyond the Writing Process Paradigm.* Ed. Thomas Kent. Carbondale: Southern Illinois University Press, 1999. 179–97.

Connors, Robert J. "The Rise and Fall of the Modes of Discourse." *College Composition and Communication*, 32.4. (Dec. 1981): 444–55.

Connors, Robert, and Andrea A. Lunsford. "Frequency of Formal Error in Current College Writing, or Ma and Pa Kettle Do Research." *College Composition and Communication* 39.4 (1988): 395–409.

Cooper, Marilyn M. "Why Are We Talking About Discourse Communities? Or, Foundationalism Rears Its Ugle Head Once More." *Writing as Social Action.* Portsmouth, NH: Boynton/Cook, 1989. 202–20.

Couture, Barbara. *Toward a Phenomenological Rhetoric: Writing, Profession, and Altruism.* Carbondale: Southern Illinois University Press, 1998.

Cox, Stan. "Big Houses Are Not Green." *Alternet.org.* 8 Sept. 2007. <http://www.alternet.org/story/61523/>. Accessed July 15, 2009.

Cross, Gary. *An All-Consuming Century: How Commercialism Won in Modern America.* New York: Columbia University Press, 2000.

Crowley, Sharon. "Of Gorgias and Grammatology." *College Composition and Communication*, 30.3 (Oct. 1979): 279–84.

Daly, John A. "Writing Apprehension." In Ed. Mike Rose, *When a Writer Can't Write: Studies in Writer's Block and Other Composing-Process Problems.* New York: Guilford Press, 1985. 43–82.

Daly, John, and Michael D. Miller. "The Empirical Development of an Instrument to Measure Writing Apprehension." *Research in the Teaching of English* 9.3 (1975): 242–49.

Daly, John, and Michael D. Miller. "Further Studies in Writing Apprehension: SAT Scores, Success Expectations, Willingness to Take Advanced Courses and Sex Differences." *Research in the Teaching of English* 9.3 (1975): 250–56.

Davidson, Donald. "Three Varieties of Knowledge." *A. J. Ayer Memorial Essays.* Royal Institute of Philosophy Supplement, 30. Ed. A. Phillips Griffiths. London: Cambridge University Press, 1991.

Delpit, "Hello Grandfather." *Other People's Children: Cultural Conflict in the Classroom.* New York: The New Press, 1995. 91–104.

Derrida, Jacques. *Of Grammatology.* Trans. Gayatri Spivak. Baltimore: Johns Hopkins University Press, 1976.

Digest of Education Statistics, 2007. (NCES 2008–022). National Center for Education Statistics, Institute of Education Sciences, U.S. Department of Education: Washington, DC, 2008. <http://nces.ed.gov/programs/digest/d07/index.asp>. Accessed January 22, 2011.

Digest of Education Statistics, 2009. (NCES 2010–013). National Center for Education Statistics, Institute of Education Sciences, U.S. Department of Education: Washington, DC, 2010. <http://nces.ed.gov/programs/digest/d09/>. Accessed January 22, 2011.

Dobrin, Sidney I. "Paralogic Hermeneutic Theories, Power, and the Possibility for Liberating Pedagogies." *Post-Process Theory: Beyond the Writing Process Paradigm.* Ed. Thomas Kent. Carbondale: Southern Illinois University Press, 1999. 132–48.

Dobrin, Sidney I., and Christian R. Weisser. *Natural Discourse: Toward Eco-Composition.* Albany: SUNY Press, 2002.

Downs, Douglas, and Elizabeth Wardle. "Teaching About Writing, Righting Misconceptions: (Re)Envisioning 'First Year Composition' as 'Introduction to Writing Studies.'" *College Composition and Communication* 58.4 (June 2007): 552–84.

Durst, Richard. *Collision Course: Conflict, Negotiation, and Learning in College Composition.* Urbana, IL: National Council of Teachers of English, 1999.

Eagleton, Terry. "Humanity and Other Animals." *The Guardian.* September 7, 2002. <http://books.guardian.co.uk/review/story/0,12084,786573,00.html>. Accessed March 8, 2009.

Elbow, Peter. "Pedagogy of the Bamboozled." *Embracing Contraries.* New York: Oxford University Press, 1986. 85–98.

Ellsworth, Elizabeth. "Why Doesn't This Feel Empowering? Working Through the Repressive Myths of Critical Pedagogy." *Harvard Educational Review* 59 (1989): 297–324.

Emig, Janet. "Writing as a Mode of Learning." *The Web of Meaning: Essays on Writing, Teaching, Learning, and Thinking.* Portsmouth, NH: Boynton/Cook, 1983. (Original work published 1977)

Faigley, Lester. *Fragments of Rationality: Postmodernity and the Subjects of Composition.* Pittsburgh, PA: University of Pittsburgh Press, 1992.

Faigley, Lester. "Competing Theories of Process: A Critique and a Proposal." *College English* 48.6 (1986): 527–42.

Fish, Stanley. "Save the World on Your Own Time." *Chronicle of Higher Education.* 23 Jan 2003. <http://chronicle.com/article/Save-the-World-on-Your-Own/45335>. Accessed November 15, 2008.

Flower, Linda. *The Construction of Negotiated Meaning: A Social Cognitive Theory of Writing.* Carbondale: Southern Illinois University Press, 1994.

Flower, Linda, and John R. Hayes. "A Cognitive Process Theory of Writing." *College Composition and Communication* 32.4 (Dec., 1981): 365–87.

Freire, Paulo. *Pedagogy of Hope: Reliving Pedagogy of the Oppressed.* Trans. Robert R. Barr. New York: Continuum, 1990.

Freire, Paulo. *Pedagogy of the Oppressed.* 30th anniversary ed. Trans. Myra Bergman Ramos. New York: Continuum, 2005. (Original work published in English 1970)

"Frequently Asked Questions." *Common Core State Standards Initiative.* National Governors Association and Council of Chief State School Officers, 2010. <http://www.corestandards.org/frequently-asked-questions>. Accessed July 22, 2010.

Friedman, Benjamin. *The Moral Consequences of Economic Growth.* New York: Knopf, 2005.

Fulkerson, Richard. "Of Pre- and Post-Process: Reviews and Ruminations." *Composition Studies* 29.2 (Fall 2001): 93–119.

Giroux, Henry. *Ideology, Culture, and the Process of Schooling.* Philadelphia, PA: Temple University Press, 1981.

Giroux, Henry. "Teachers as Transformative Intellectuals." *Teachers as Intellectuals: Toward a Critical Pedagogy of Learning.* Granby, MA: Bergin & Garvey, 1988. 121–28

Goodlad. John. *A Place Called School.* New York: McGraw-Hill, 1983.

Gould, Emily. "Exposed." *New York Times Magazine,* 25 May 2008: 32.

Graham, Mary, and Elena Fagotto. *How to Reduce Greenhouse Gas Emissions* Now. Policy Brief no.161. Washington, DC: Brookings Institution, 2007. <http://www.brookings.edu/papers/2007/06energy_graham.aspx>. Accessed September 12, 2008.

Graham, Steve, and Dolores Perin. *Writing Next: Effective Strategies to Improve Writing of Adolescents in Middle and High Schools.* Report to the Carnegie Foundation. Washington, DC: Alliance for Excellent Education, 2007.

Gray, John. *Straw Dogs: Thoughts on Humans and Other Animals.* New York: Farrar, Straus, & Giroux, 2002.

Greenbaum, Andrea, ed. *Insurrections: Approaches to Resistance in Composition Studies.* Albany: SUNY Press, 2001.

Grondahl, Paul. "From a Bumpy Road to a Turn on Easy Street." *Albany (NY) Times Union,* April 1, 2007: A1, A5.

Gross, Daniel. "Stop Saving Now!" *Newsweek* 153 (23 March 2009): 27.

Hairston, Maxine. "Diversity, Ideology, and the Teaching of Writing." *College Composition and Communication* 43.2 (1992): 179–93.

Handa, Carolyn. "Letter From the Guest Editor: Digital Rhetoric, Digital Literacy, Computers, and Composition." *Computers and Composition* 18.1 (2001): 1–10.

Hardin, Garrett. "The Tragedy of the Commons." *Science* 162 (1968): 1243–48.

Hardin, Joe Marshall. *Opening Spaces: Critical Pedagogy and Resistance Theory in Composition.* Albany: SUNY Press, 2001.

Harris, Joseph. "Meet the New Boss, Same as the Old Boss: Class Consciousness in Composition." *College Composition and Communication* 52.1 (Sept. 2000): 43–68.

"Harvard Announces Sweeping Middle-Income Initiative." *Harvard University Gazette Online.* 10 Dec. 2007. <http://news.harvard.edu/gazette/story/2007/12/harvard-announces-sweeping-middle-income-initiative>. Accessed February 3, 2009.

Haswell, Richard H. *Gaining Ground in College Writing: Tales of Development.* Dallas, TX: Southern Methodist University Press, 1991.

Henley, John. "A Glossary of U.S. Military Euphemisms." *The Guardian.* 13 Dec. 2007: 3. <http://www.guardian.co.uk/world/2007/dec/13/usa.humanrights>. Accessed February 3, 2009.

Herrington, Anne, and Marcia Curtis. *Persons in Process: Four Stories of Writing and Personal Development in College.* Urbana, IL: National Council of Teachers of English, 2000.

Hillocks, George. *The Testing Trap: How State Assessments Control Learning.* New York: Teachers College Press, 2002.

Holzman, Michael. "Theory, Research, and Pedagogy." *College English* 42.4 (Dec. 1980): 343–49.

Intergovernmental Panel on Climate Change. *Climate Change 2007: Impacts, Adaptation, and Vulnerability.* IPCC Fourth Assessment Report. New York: Cambridge University Press, 2007.

Intergovernmental Panel on Climate Change. *Climate Change 2007: The Physical Science Basis. Summary for Policymakers.* New York: Cambridge University Press, 2007.

Jarratt, Susan. *Rereading the Sophists: Classical Rhetoric Refigured.* Carbondale: Southern Illinois University Press, 1991.

Kasulis, T. P. "The Zen Philosopher: A Review Article on Dogen Scholarship in English." *Philosophy East and West* 28.3 (July 1978): 353–73.

Kent, Thomas. *Paralogic Rhetoric: A Theory of Communicative Interaction.* Lewisburg, PA: Bucknell University Press, 1993.

Kent, Thomas, ed. *Post-Process Theory: Beyond the Writing-Process Paradigm.* Carbondale: Southern Illinois University Press, 1999.

Kolbert, Elizabeth. *Field Notes From a Catastrophe: Man, Nature, and Climate Change.* New York: Bloomsbury, 2006.

Kress, Gunther. *Before Writing: Rethinking the Paths to Literacy.* Routledge: London, 1997.

Kress, Gunther. "Representational Resources and the Production of Subjectivity: Questions for the Theoretical Development of Critical Discourse Analysis in a Multicultural Society." *Texts and Practices: Readings in Critical Discourse Analysis.* Eds. Carmen Rosa Caldas-Coulthard and Malcolm Coulthard. New York: Routledge, 1996. 15–31.

Langer, Judith A., and Arthur N. Applebee. *How Writing Shapes Thinking: A Study of Teaching and Learning.* National Council of Teachers of English Research Report no. 22. Urbana, IL: National Council of Teachers of English, 1987.

Lanham, Richard. "Digital Literacy." *Scientific American* 273.3 (Sept. 1995): 198, 200.

Loy, David. *Nonduality: A Study in Comparative Philosophy.* Amherst, NY: Humanity Books, 1998.

Lunsford, Andrea A., and Karen J. Lunsford. "'Mistakes Are a Fact of Life': A National Comparative Study." *College Composition and Communication* 59.4 (June 2008): 781–806.

Maathai, Wangari. "Nature, Nurture and Culture." *Resurgence,* 15 Nov. 2004. Web. 5 June 2007.

Mauk, Johnathon. "Location, Location, Location: The 'Real' (E)states of Being, Writing, and Thinking in College." *College English* 65.2 (March 2003): 288–368.

McCarthy, Lucille Parkinson. "A Stranger in Strange Lands: A College Student Writing Across the Curriculum." *Research in the Teaching of English* 21.3 (October 1987): 233–65.

McCormick, Kathleen. "Always Already Theorists: Literary Theory and Theorizing in the Undergraduate Curriculum." *Pedagogy is Politics: Literary Theory and Critical Teaching.* Ed. Maria-Regina Kecht. Urbana: University of Illinois Press, 1992. 111–31.

McKibben, Bill. *Deep Economy: The Wealth of Communities and the Durable Future.* New York: Henry Holt, 2007.

McLuhan, Marshall. 1962. *The Gutenberg Galaxy.* Reprinted in *Essential McLuhan,* edited by Eric McLuhan and Frank Zingrone. New York: Basic Books, 1995.

McNeil, Linda M. *Contradictions of Control: School Structure and School Knowledge.* New York: Routledge, 1986.

Merleau-Ponty, Maurice. *The Phenomenology of Perception.* Trans. Colin Smith. New York: Routledge, 2002. (Original work published 1945; translated into English 1962)

Merleau-Ponty, Maurice. "An Unpublished Text by Maurice Merleau-Ponty: A Prospectus of His Work." Trans. Arleen B. Dallery. *The Primacy of Perception: And Other Essays on Phenomenological Psychology, the Philosophy of Art, History and Politics.* Trans. William Cobb. Evanston, IL: Northwestern University Press, 1964.

Mezirow, Jack. *Transformative Dimensions of Adult Learning.* San Francisco, CA: Jossey-Bass, 1991.

Miller, Matt. "Race to the Top: A Sprint When We Need a Marathon." *Washington Post,* 3 June 2010. <http://www.washingtonpost.com/wp-dyn/content/article/2010/06/02/AR2010060202266.html>. Accessed July 20, 2010.

Miller, Richard. "The Arts of Complicity: Pragmatism and the Culture of Schooling." *College English* 61.1 (Sept. 1998): 10–28.

Miller, Susan. "Technologies of Self?-Formation." *Journal of Advanced Composition* 17.3 (Fall 1997): 497–500.

Morales, Jack. "What Have You Done For Me Lately? Critical Writing Studies in the Post-Freirean World." Paper written for ETAP 697, Fall 2007. 12 November 2007.

Moran, Dermot. *Introduction to Phenomenology.* New York: Routledge, 2000.

Murray, Donald M. "Listening to Writing." *Learning by Teaching.* Portsmouth, NH: Boynton/Cook, 1982. 53–65. (Original work published 1980)

Murray, Donald M.. "Teach Writing as Process Not Product." *Learning by Teaching.* Portsmouth, NH: Boynton/Cook, 1982. 14–17. (Original work published 1972)

National Commission on Writing. *The Neglected 'R': The Need for a Writing Revolution.* New York: The College Entrance Examination Board, 2003.

National Council of Teachers of English (NCTE). *Task Force.* "The Impact of the SAT and ACT Timed Writing Tests." April 2005. <http://www. ncte.org>. Accessed July 20, 2010.

National Intelligence Council 2020 Project. *Mapping the Global Future.* Washington, DC: GPO. 2004. < http://www.dni.gov/nic/NIC_global-trend2020.html >. Accessed July 28, 2010.

Neel, Jasper. *Plato, Derrida, and Writing.* Carbondale: Southern Illinois University Press, 1988.

Noah, Timothy. "The United States of Income Inequality." *Slate,* 3 Sept. 2010. <http://www.slate.com/id/2266025/entry/2266026>. Accessed Jan. 11, 2011.

North, Stephen M. "Revisiting 'The Idea of a Writing Center.'" *Writing Center Journal* 15 (Fall 1994): 7–19.

North, Stephen M. "Rhetoric, Responsibility, and the 'Language of the Left.'" *Composition and Resistance.* Ed. C. Mark Hurlbert and Michael Blitz. Portsmouth, NH: Boynton/Cook, 1991. 127–36.

Odell, Lee. "Redefining Maturity in Writing." In Eds. Aviva Freedman, Ian Pringle, and Janice Yalden, *Learning to Write: First Language/Second Language.* London: Longman, 1983. 96–113.

Ohmann, Richard. "Afterword." *The Relevance of English: Teaching That Matters in Students' Lives.* Eds. Robert P. Yagelski and Scott A. Leonard. Urbana, IL: National Council of Teachers of English, 2002. 413–19.

Ohmann, Richard. *English in America: A Radical View of the Profession*. New York: Oxford University Press, 1976.

Olson, Carl. *Zen and the Art of Postmodern Philosophy: Two Paths of Liberation From the Representational Mode of Thinking*. Albany: SUNY Press, 2000.

Olson, Gary A. "Toward a Post-Process Composition: Abandoning the Rhetoric of Assertion." *Post-Process Theory: Beyond the Writing Process Paradigm*. Ed. Thomas Kent. Carbondale: Southern Illinois University Press, 1999. 7–15.

Olson, Lynn. "State Test Programs Mushroom as NCLB Mandate Kicks In." *Education Week* 25.13 (30 Nov. 2005): 10–12.

Ong, Walter J. *Orality and Literacy: The Technologizing of the Word*. New York: Routledge, 1982.

O'Reilley, Mary Rose. *The Peaceable Classroom*. Portsmouth, NH: Heinemann, 1993.

Orr, David. *Ecological Literacy: Education and the Transition to a Postmodern World*. Albany: SUNY Press, 1992.

Owens, Derek. *Composition and Sustainability: Teaching for a Threatened Generation*. Urbana, IL: National Council of Teachers of English, 2001.

Petraglia, Joseph. "Is There Life after Process? The Role of Social Scientism in a Changing Discipline." *Post-Process Theory: Beyond the Writing Process Paradigm*. Ed. Thomas Kent. Carbondale: Southern Illinois University Press, 1999. 49–64.

Pollan, Michael. *The Omnivore's Dilemma*. New York: Penguin, 2006.

Porter, James E. "Why Technology Matters to Writing: A Cyberwriter's Tale." *Computers and Composition* 20 (2002): 375–94.

Pryor, J. H. et al. "The American Freshman: Forty-Year Trends, 1966–2006." Los Angeles: UCLA Higher Education Research Institute, 2007.

"Race to the Top Fund." *U.S. Department of Education*, 25 June 2010. <http://www2.ed.gov/programs/racetothetop/index.html>. Accessed July 14, 2010.

Raupach, M.R., G. Marland, P. Ciais, C. Le Quéré, J.G. Canadell, G. Klepper & C.B. Field. "Global and Regional Drivers of Accelerating CO_2 Emissions." *Proceedings of the National Academy of Sciences* 104.24 (2007): 10288-93. <http://www.pnas.org/content/104/24/10288>. Accessed June 9, 2008.

Rector, Robert, and Rea S. Hederman, Jr. "Two Americas: One Rich, One Poor? Understanding Income Inequality in the United States." Backgrounder no. 1791. The Heritage Foundation. April 24, 2004. <http://www.heritage.org/Research/Taxes/bg1791.cfm>. Accessed March 15, 2009.

"Report of the UAlbany Task Force on Undergraduate Writing." State University of New York at Albany. June 1 2007. <http://www.albany.edu/ir/UAlb_Writing_Task_Force_Final_Report_2007.pdf>. Accessed July 28, 2010.

Revkin, Andrew C. "Poor Nations to Bear Brunt as World Warms." *New York Times*, April 1, 2007, p. 1.

Romano, Carlin. "The Triumph of Smugism." *The Chronicle Review* 54.19 (18 Jan. 2008): B5.

Ronald, Kate, and Hepzibah Roskelly. "Untested Feasibility: Imagining the Pragmatic Possibility of Paulo Freire." *College English* 63.5 (May 2001): 612–32.

Rubenstein, Joshua S., David E. Meyer, and Jeffrey E. Evans. "Executive Control of Cognitive Processes in Task Switching." *Journal of Experimental Psychology: Human Perception and Performance* 27.4 (2001): 763–97.

Salahu-Din, D., H. Persky, and J. Miller. *The Nation's Report Card: Writing 2007* (NCES 2008–468). Washington, DC: National Center for Education Statistics, Institute of Education Sciences, U.S. Department of Education, 2008.

Sartwell, Crispin. *End of Story: Toward an Annihilation of Language and History.* Albany: SUNY Press, 2000.

Sawhill, Isabel, and John E. Morton. *Economic Mobility: Is the American Dream Alive and Well?* Economic Mobility Project. Washington, DC: Pew Charitable Trusts, 2008. <http://www.economicmobility.org/assets/pdfs/EMP_American_Dream.pdf>

Schwartz, Matthias. "The Trolls Among Us." *New York Times Magazine*, 3 Aug. 2008: 24.

Sextus Empiricus. *Against the Schoolmasters.* Athenaeum Reading Room. N.d. <http://evans-experientialism.freewebspace.com/sextus_empiricus.htm>. Accessed July 22, 2010.

Sledd, James. "On Buying in and Selling out: A Note for Bosses Old and New." *College Composition and Communication* 53.1 (Sept. 2001): 146–49.

Sohlberg, McKay Moore, and Catherine A. Mateer. *Introduction to Cognitive Rehabilitation: Theory and Practice.* New York: Guilford Press, 1989.

Sommers, Nancy. "Across the Drafts." *College Composition and Communication* 58.2 (Dec. 2006): 248–57.

Tanahashi, Kazuaki, ed. *Moon in a Dewdrop: Writings of Zen Master Dogen.* New York: North Point Press, 1985.

Tassoni, John Paul, and William H. Thelin, eds. *Blundering for a Change: Errors and Expectations in Critical Pedagogy.* Portsmouth, NH: Heinemann, 2000.

Teixeira, Ruy. "Public Opinion Snapshot: The Public Believes Global Warming is Happening and Is Ready for Action." Center for American Progress. 14 June 2010. <http://www.americanprogress.org/issues/2010/06/public_and_warming.html>. Accessed July 27, 2010.

Tugend, Alina. "Multitasking Can Make You Lose ... Um ... Focus." *New York Times.* 24 October 2008. <http://www.nytimes.com/2008/10/25/business/yourmoney/25shortcuts.html>. Accessed July 22, 2010.

U.S. Department of Education. *A Test of Leadership: Charting the Future of U.S. Higher Education.* Washington, DC: 2006.

Walvoord, Barbara, and Lucille McCarthy. *Thinking and Writing in College: A Naturalistic Study of Students in Four Disciplines.* Urbana, IL: National Council of Teachers of English, 1990.

"The Wealth Divide: Growing Gap in the U.S. Between the Rich and the Rest. An Interview with Edward Wolff." *The Multinational Monitor* 24.5 (May 2003). <http://multinationalmonitor.org/mm2003/03may/may03interviewswolff.htm>. Accessed July 22, 2010.

Weisser, Christian R., and Sidney I. Dobrin, eds. *Eco-Composition: Theoretical and Pedagogical Approaches.* Albany: SUNY Press, 2001.

Yagelski, Robert P. "Computers, Literacy, and Being: Teaching With Technology for a Sustainable Future." *Kairos* 6.2 (Fall 2001). <http://english.ttu.edu/kairos/6.2/features/yagelski>. Accessed July 22, 2010.

Yagelski, Robert P. "English Education."*English Studies: An Introduction to the Discipline(s).* Ed. Bruce McComiskey. Urbana, IL: National Council of Teachers of English, 2006. 275–319.

Yagelski, Robert P. *Literacies and Technologies: A Reader for Contemporary Writers.* New York: Longman, 2001.

Yagelski, Robert P. *Literacy Matters: Writing and Reading the Social Self.* New York: Teachers College Press, 1999.

Yagelski, Robert P. "Literature and Literacy: Rethinking English as a School Subject." *English Journal* 83 (March 1994): 30-36.

Yagelski, Robert P. "'Radical to Many in the Educational Community': The Process Movement After the Hurricanes." *College English* 68 (May 2006): 531–44.

Yagelski, Robert P. "Stasis and Change: English Education and the Crisis of Sustainability." *English Education.* 37 (July 2005): 262–71.

ABOUT THE AUTHOR

Robert P. Yagelski is Associate Professor of English Education in the Department of Educational Theory and Practice and an affiliated faculty member of the Department of English at the State University of New York at Albany. He teaches in the doctoral program in curriculum and instruction, masters programs in education, and the graduate program in secondary teacher certification and works with students in the doctoral program in English. He has taught courses in writing, composition theory and pedagogy, critical pedagogy, qualitative research methods, and the history of rhetoric.

As director of the Capital District Writing Project, a site of the National Writing Project, Yagelski works extensively with K-12 teachers to help improve writing instruction at all levels of schooling. He has served as a member of the Board of Directors of the Teacher Education Accreditation Council (TEAC) and the Executive Committee of the Conference on English Education. Previously, he directed the Writing Center at SUNY-Albany, co-directed the English Education program at Purdue University, and chaired the English Department at Vermont Academy, an independent high school.

Yagelski's articles about writing instruction have appeared in *College Composition and Communication, Research in the Teaching of English,*

English Education, the *Journal of Teaching Writing*, and *College English*, among others. He is the author of *Literacy Matters: Writing and Reading the Social Self* (Teachers College Press, 2000) and has written several textbooks, including *Reading Our World*, 2nd edition (Wadsworth/Cengage, 2009) and *The Informed Argument*, 8th edition (with Robert K. Miller, Wadsworth/Cengage, 2011). He is co-editor with Scott Leonard of *The Relevance of English: Teaching That Matters in Students' Lives* (NCTE, 2002) and author of *The Day the Lifting Bridge Stuck* (Bradbury Press, 1992), a children's book. He earned his Ph.D. in Rhetoric and Composition from the Ohio State University.

AUTHOR INDEX

SUBJECT INDEX

CPSIA information can be obtained
at www.ICGtesting.com
Printed in the USA
FFOW04n1127050116
19904FF